NEW YORK STATE
TRAVEL ✦ SMART®

W9-CBN-409

NEW YORK STATE
TRAVEL★SMART®

Second Edition

Deborah Williams
New York City chapters by
Julie Liebowitz

John Muir Publications
A Division of Avalon Travel Publishing

Acknowledgments

With thanks to Holly Gang, a consummate traveler and map reader, and to New York State tourism representatives, who were always enthusiastic and professional.

John Muir Publications
A Division of Avalon Travel Publishing
5855 Beaudry Street, Emeryville, CA 94608

ISSN 1525-2914
ISBN 1-56261-445-2

Editors: Ellen Cavalli, Megan Hendershott
Graphics Editor: Ann Silvia
Production: Scott Fowler
Design: Marie J.T. Vigil
Cover design: Janine Lehmann
Typesetting: Laurel Avery
Map style development: American Custom Maps—Jemez Springs, NM
Map illustration: Kathleen Sparkes—White Hart Designs, Mike Hermann—Purple Lizard Maps
Printing: Publishers Press
Front cover photos: *small*—© Esbin–Anderson/Photo Network (Brooklyn Bridge and Manhattan)
                              large—© Andre Jenny/Unicorn Stock Photos (Indian Lake, Adirondacks)
Back cover photo: © Andre Jenny/International Stock (Niagara Falls)

Julie Liebowitz wrote Chapter 1, Manhattan, and Chapter 2, New York City's Outer Boroughs. She was born on the Upper East Side and has worked for a number of women's and sports magazines.

Distributed to the book trade by
Publishers Group West
Berkeley, California

NEW YORK STATE TRAVEL·SMART: A GUIDE THAT GUIDES

Most guidebooks are basically directories, providing information but very little help in making choices—you have to guess how to make the most of your time and money. *New York State Travel·Smart* is different: By highlighting the very best of the state and offering various planning features, it acts like a personal tour guide rather than a directory.

TAKE THE STRESS OUT OF TRAVEL

Sometimes traveling causes more stress than it relieves. Sorting through information, figuring out the best routes, determining what to see and where to eat and stay, scheduling each day—all of this can make a vacation feel daunting rather than fun. Relax. We've done a lot of the legwork for you. This book will help you plan a trip that suits you—whatever your time frame, budget, and interests.

SEE THE BEST OF NEW YORK STATE

Author Deborah Williams lives on a 63-acre farm in upstate New York and has written extensively about her home state. She has picked nearly every listing in this book, and she gives you an insider's perspective on what makes each one worthwhile. So while you will find many of the big tourist attractions listed here, you'll also find lots of smaller, lesser known treasures, such as the Lucille Ball–Desi Arnaz Museum in Chautauqua County or the Women's Rights National Historical Park in the Finger Lakes region. And each sight is described so you'll know what's most—and sometimes least—interesting about it.

In selecting the restaurants and accommodations for this book, the author sought out unusual spots with local flavor. While in some areas of the state chains are unavoidable, wherever possible the author directs you to one-of-a-kind places. We also know that you want a range of options: One day you may crave steak and lobster, while the next day you would be just as happy (as would your wallet) with Buffalo wings and "beef on weck" sandwiches. Most of the restaurants and accommodations listed here are moderately priced, but the author also includes budget and splurge options, depending on the destination.

CREATE THE TRIP YOU WANT

We all have different travel styles. Some people like spontaneous weekend jaunts, while others plan longer, more leisurely trips. You may want to cover as much ground as possible, no matter how much time you have. Or maybe you prefer to focus your trip on one part of the state or on some special interest, such as history, nature, or art. We've taken these differences into account.

Though the individual chapters stand on their own, they are organized in a geographically logical sequence, so that you could conceivably fly into New York City, drive chapter by chapter to each destination in the book, and end up close to where you started. Of course, you don't have to follow that sequence, but it's there if you want a complete picture of the state.

Each destination chapter offers ways of prioritizing when time is limited: In the Perfect Day section, the author suggests what to do if you have only one day to spend in the area. Also, every Sightseeing Highlight is rated, from one to four stars: ★★★★—"must see"—sights first, followed by ★★★ sights, then ★★ sights, and finally ★—or "see if you have time"—sights. At the end of each sight listing is a time recommendation in parentheses. User-friendly maps help you locate the sights, restaurants, and lodging of your choice.

And if you're in it for the ride, so to speak, you'll want to check out the Scenic Routes described at the end of several chapters. They take you through some of the most scenic parts of the state.

In addition to these special features, the appendix has other useful travel tools:

• The Planning Map and Mileage Chart help you determine your own route and calculate travel time.

• The Special Interest Tours section shows you how to design your trip around any of six favorite interests.

• The Calendar of Events provides an at-a-glance view of when and where major events occur throughout the state.

• The Resources section tells you where to go for more information about national and state parks, individual cities and counties, local bed-and-breakfasts, and more.

HAPPY TRAVELS

With this book in hand, you have many reliable recommendations and travel tools at your fingertips. Use it to make the most of your trip. And have a great time!

WHY VISIT
NEW YORK STATE?

It could be argued that there is more to see and do in New York State than in most countries. From the awesome beauty of the Adirondacks and Niagara Falls to the majesty of the Hudson River and the cultural and commercial explosion of Manhattan, New York is certainly one of the most diverse states in the nation. From its very beginnings, when George Washington proclaimed that it would be "the seat of our Empire," New York State has been known as the Empire State. It's still possible to dine, sleep, and even worship in some of the same places the father of our country did while leading the new nation; the state is as rich in history as it is varied in landscape.

Though New York has lost its status as the nation's most populous state, the tiny island of Manhattan still makes it the artistic and economic capital of the country and, some would argue, the world. New York City inspires lists of superlatives in visitors and residents alike; its reputation as the biggest and the best in many things is well deserved. The city has long been a gateway for floods of immigrants and to this day is continually reenergized by waves of newcomers.

Psychologically, the city and the rest of the state abide in a love-hate relationship. The geographic diversity of the state creates distinct regional personalities, all worthy of exploration, yet some New Yorkers feel that the power and fame of New York City at times eclipses the glories of the rest of the state. Most non-residents of the state would probably be surprised to discover, for instance, that agriculture is the state's top industry. Orchards, vineyards, and vegetable and dairy farms dot the countryside. In fact, outside of New York City and a few other cities, New York State is predominantly rural, with open country filled with lakes, rivers, and streams, rolling hills, mountains, gorges, and waterfalls to rival any in the world. Explorers will discover that mighty Manhattan's urban sublimities are matched by natural counterparts throughout the rest of the state.

THE LAY OF THE LAND

New York has some of the most varied topography in the country—from sandy beaches and salt marshes to alpine lakes and mountain peaks—and a unique range of natural habitats and ecosystems.

If water is a region's lifeblood, then New York is indeed blessed with a great circulatory system. The Erie Canal transformed the state and the nation when it opened in 1825. Now the 524-mile New York State Canal System—which links hundreds of miles of lakes and rivers across the state—has been turned into an adventure waterway for recreational boaters.

The lakes of the Finger Lakes region were created when Ice Age glaciers retreated about one million years ago. The intense pressure of those ice masses created the long, narrow lakes lying side by side, as well as the deep gorges with rushing falls and wide, fertile valleys that extend south for many miles. These features are found nowhere else in the world. The waters are deep and blue, yielding a bountiful harvest of fish.

In the northeastern part of the state, the Adirondack Park covers 6.1 million acres of public and private land. More than 40 mountains in the Adirondacks are more than four thousand feet above sea level. The mountains were rounded off and smoothed down by the weight of glacial ice during the last Ice Age. Within the range are 2,200 glacier-formed ponds and lakes and 30,000 miles of rivers and streams.

To the south, the Catskill Mountains achieved their present form through eons of erosion. A succession of ice sheets covered the Catskills until some 15,000 years ago, leaving the region gouged and scraped, with sand and gravel heaped up and valleys turned into lakes. All of this activity produced Slide Mountain, at 4,204 feet the Catskills' highest summit. It also created a rocky wall 2,000 feet high facing miles of the Hudson River.

FLORA AND FAUNA

New York has long led the nation in the preservation of natural resources. Niagara Falls Reservation State Park was the first state park in the country, and the Adirondacks is the largest park area in the lower 48 states. Nature lovers owe much to New Yorker Theodore Roosevelt, one of the nation's earliest and most ardent conservationists, who created many national parks. His regard for the natural world undoubtedly was shaped during his summers in the wilds of the Adirondacks.

Wild turkey and deer populations have increased dramatically in much of the state, and hunters flock here during the hunting seasons. So strongly do New Yorkers believe in the preservation of the forests of the Adirondacks and the Catskills as "forever wild" that it is specified in the State Constitution.

Trees cover about 60 percent of the state, and the Adirondack Park covers much of the northern third of the state. The Adirondack Forest Preserve was established in 1885 as the 42 percent of the park that is public land, to be forever preserved as wilderness. In the southeast part of the park, oaks are predominant, while in the higher Adirondacks spruce and fir predominate. Northern hardwoods, including birch, sugar maple, basswood, ash, and yellow birch, make up the majority of trees in the rest of the state. Oaks are mingled with northern hardwoods in the Finger Lakes region and along much of the Hudson River Valley.

Common animals are the fox, raccoon, opossum, woodchuck, muskrat, deer, rabbit, and squirrel. Bears can be found in the Adirondacks and areas of the Southern Tier. A wide variety of birds, including ducks and wild turkeys, inhabit most areas of the state. At the Montezuma National Wildlife Refuge in the Finger Lakes region, as well as in other parts of the state, there are bald eagles, Canada geese, snow geese, and many kinds of ducks, including mallards, American black ducks, blue-winged and green-winged teal, American widgeon, and wood ducks as well as canvasbacks, redheads, and common and hooded mergansers. Great blue herons and loons can sometimes be seen at Montezuma and on other waterways.

HISTORY

Two major Native American groups inhabited what is now New York State when Europeans began exploration of the area. The Algonquins occupied much of the Hudson Valley, Manhattan, and Long Island, while the Iroquois controlled most of the rest of the region.

The first European sighting of New York was made in 1524 by Giovanni da Verrazano, a Florentine merchant, who described the land he found as having a "commodiousness and beauty." An early tourist mini-boom occurred in 1609, when Samuel de Champlain and Henry Hudson visited. Champlain had traveled south from Canada and named the lake that now forms the state's eastern border after himself. Henry Hudson, who was employed by the Dutch East India Company, sailed into New York harbor in 1609 on the *Half Moon* and up the river that was to become his namesake to what is now Albany. At that point he realized that, although it was a "mighty deep-throated river," it was not the Northwest Passage he had been searching for.

Because of Hudson's discoveries, the Dutch claimed the land and named it New Netherland. Peter Minuit, the first governor of the Dutch colony, bought Manhattan Island (and named it New Amsterdam) from the Algonquins in 1626 for 24 dollars' worth of tools and trinkets—surely one of the shrewdest buys in history. In 1664 Peter Stuyvesant, the peg-legged Dutch governor, surrendered beleaguered New Amsterdam and New Netherland to the British. The colony and the city were both renamed New York after the Duke of York, who later became King James II.

New York was Britain's most important outpost, and its location made it a key player in the century-long struggle between France and Britain for control of North America. Though it was still mostly wilderness at the outbreak of the Revolutionary War, nearly one-third of the war's battles were fought in New York. At the war's end, General Washington bid an emotional farewell to his soldiers at Fraunces Tavern in New York City, the new nation's first capital. Just a few years later he served in New York City as the country's first president.

Under the leadership of Governor DeWitt Clinton, the Erie Canal was built between 1817 and 1825 to link New York City with Buffalo. Its completion opened up the state to development, commerce, and settlement. Fortunes were made in trade and commerce, and a new era of industrialization began. The state quickly became the economic center of the nation. During the nineteenth century, state residents founded a religion, launched the women's rights movement, invented the camera, and founded several important colleges and universities.

Following the Civil War, European immigrants flocked to New York City and spread across the state and the nation. As the population swelled, the nation's largest city began to take on the look it has today, with its towering skyscrapers, and it soon became the pacesetter for the nation. In the twentieth century the state sent two native sons, both Roosevelts (Theodore and Franklin D.) and both former governors, to the White House, where they made their mark on world history.

CULTURES

All of the major cities in the state have long traditions of ethnic diversity. Buffalo is home to large enclaves of Polish, Irish, and Italians, as well as African Americans who came north to work in the once-flourishing steel mills. More

CENTRAL PARK, MANHATTAN

recently, Puerto Rican neighborhoods have sprung up in Buffalo and other upstate cities. Syracuse maintains a strong Irish neighborhood. The Native American presence is still felt in some areas of western and central New York, where several reservations are located; Salamanca, in Cattaraugus County, is the only city in the country on a Native American reservation.

New York City is the world's most ethnically diverse city, and immigrants from all over the globe continue to arrive daily seeking the American dream. One of the country's most enduring images is of immigrants entering the New World huddled on overcrowded ships with all their possessions in tattered cases, determined to make it in the Promised Land. Newcomers' first sight of America was the Statue of Liberty in New York's harbor. During the early nineteenth century, German and Irish immigrants began arriving. Chinese and Southern and Eastern Europeans followed in waves. Jews from Eastern Europe began arriving in the late nineteenth century, fleeing the pogroms in Russia. In the early part of this century, tens of thousands of African Americans fled the Deep South; many settled in Harlem, which later became home to Puerto Ricans as well.

Although the massive immigration period is history, immigration, legal and illegal, continues at a steady pace. Chinatown has grown dramatically in recent years. In the 1970s Russian immigrants transformed Brooklyn's Brighton Beach area. Greek residents have similarly made their mark on Astoria in Queens.

East Indians, Koreans, West Indians, Filipinos, Latinos, Eastern Europeans, and Middle Easterners are prominent among the nearly 100,000 people who settle in New York each year. All of these groups have influenced the city with their customs, languages, and cuisines. In fact, the ethnic composition of the city changes so rapidly, it's difficult to keep track of demographic effects.

The state's ethnic diversity is reflected in hundreds of annual festivals and parades, from the Pulaski Day Parade in Buffalo to the Keeper of the Western Door Pow-Wow in Salamanca; from German, Irish, Italian, and Native American festivals in the Catskills to Greek, Puerto Rican, Japanese, and Ukrainian parades in New York City.

THE ARTS

New York has a laudable reputation for supporting the arts. In the southwestern corner of the state, Chautauqua Institution—a uniquely American summer enclave of arts, theater, music, sports, and religion—has attracted visitors since its founding in 1874. Buffalo is well known for its rich architectural treasures, designed by the likes of Louis Sullivan and Frank Lloyd Wright, and for the world-famous Albright-Knox Art Gallery. Artpark, in the village of Lewiston, north of Niagara Falls, is the only state park in the country devoted to the arts. In Rochester, the George Eastman House and the International Museum of Photography and Film showcase the world's finest collection of photography. Corning's Museum of Glass is the world's largest and finest glass museum.

The Adirondack Museum in Blue Mountain Lake is rated as one of the finest regional museums in the country. In Albany, the New York State Museum is the oldest state museum in the country. Sugar Loaf Art and Craft Village is a community of more than 60 artist-owned craft shops and galleries in the Hudson Valley, the area that inspired the nineteenth-century Hudson River School artists; the magnificent landscapes they painted helped make them the driving force in American art during the decades before the Civil War.

Last but hardly least on our list is New York City, unarguably one of the world capitals of theater, art, dance, and music. The theater scene alone is legendary: back in the 1920s, George M. Cohan proclaimed, "When you are away from old Broadway you are only camping out." Many Manhattanites still believe this. Between Broadway, off-Broadway, and off-off-Broadway, there are hundreds of theaters in Manhattan. You can find just about any kind of production here, from lavish musicals to experimental productions in converted lofts. The musical and operatic life of the city plays out in such legendary houses as Carnegie Hall, Radio City Music Hall, and the Metropolitan Opera House in Lincoln Center. The greatest names in all musical genres have performed at Carnegie Hall, from Tchaikovsky and Toscanini to Gershwin and Billie Holiday. New York boasts five major ballet companies and dozens of modern dance troupes.

Some of the world's greatest museums are in New York City, including the Metropolitan Museum of Art, the Solomon R. Guggenheim Museum, the Whitney Museum of American Art, the American Museum of Natural History, and the Museum of Modern Art. Even the main branch of the New York Public Library, itself an architectural wonder, is filled with priceless collections. The museums, like everything else about the city, are on a grand scale. The city draws artists from all over the world, and hundreds of galleries showcase their work.

CUISINE

You'll find delectable meals in award-winning restaurants throughout the state. New York's many farms and vineyards supply excellent local produce and wines. The world-renowned Culinary Institute of America in Hyde Park has three restaurants where diners can sample innovative menus of great chefs-in-training. Name any country, even any region in any country, and "the City" (as modest Manhattanites generally refer to their town) will most likely have a selection of restaurants specializing in the cuisine of that area. The rule of thumb is, if it's edible, you can probably find it in New York City, where there are more restaurants per capita than anywhere else in the country. More than 17,000 dining establishments, from world-class temples of the culinary arts to corner pizza parlors, serve an astounding range of cuisines at an equally astounding range of prices.

Even Manhattan's street food is varied, from the ubiquitous hot dog and soft pretzel to such delicacies as Chinese dumplings, Jewish knishes, Middle Eastern falafel, Jamaican roti, Italian sausages, Mexican tacos, and, in the summer, good old-fashioned ice cream. Beyond the multitude of street vendors, there are more delis than in any other city, and every New Yorker has a favorite. Whatever your appetites, you will surely find copious opportunities to satisfy them here. On a humbler note, New York State gave the world Buffalo chicken wings, the potato chip, Thousand Island salad dressing, the hamburger, and, yes, the hot dog.

OUTDOOR ACTIVITIES

It would be hard to find a place with more varied opportunities for outdoor activities than New York. Hikers, climbers, and walkers have hundreds of miles of trails to wander throughout the state. Explorers who want a wilderness trip can find licensed, professional guides, who continue the tradition begun in the nineteenth century when Adirondack guides led "city sports" on canoe and hunting trips. There are more than 500 public and privately owned campgrounds, some deep in the wilderness, accessible only by boat or foot. Many hug the state's lakes and rivers as well as the Atlantic Ocean.

Beach lovers can explore some of the country's most expansive and beautiful beaches on Long Island and along the Great Lakes. There's whale watching off the tip of Long Island. Fishing enthusiasts enjoy world-class freshwater fishing. Fishing records have been set on the state's many lakes and rivers as well as on the ocean waters off Long Island. Though the state is far from the tropics, unique wrecks await scuba divers who like to explore the skeletons of sunken ships. Canoeists have miles of lakes and rivers to travel in the wilds of the Adirondacks and the Catskills. White-water rafting is popular on several rivers, especially during the high-water spring season. The fall attracts hunters to the Catskills, the Adirondacks, the Thousand Islands, the Southern Tier, the Finger Lakes, and Western New York—for white-tailed deer, pheasants, ducks, and other birds. Wild turkeys have made a comeback and there is both a spring and fall turkey season. Bears can be found in the Adirondacks and Cattaraugus areas.

In the winter, skiers can schuss down a multitude of ski hills and mountains. Ski resorts are close to all the state's metropolitan centers. Lake Placid was home to two Winter Olympics and continues as an Olympic training center. Whether your winter sport is skiing, bobsledding, luging, or skating, you'll find excellent facilities here. Snowmobiling attracts hundreds of thousands of fans, who come for the miles and miles of well-groomed trails and the snow— the Tug Hill area north of Syracuse boasts more snow than any area east of the Rockies.

The state's largest cities—New York, Buffalo, and Rochester—have Frederick Law Olmsted–designed parks that welcome joggers and walkers; a host of outdoor activities take place during all seasons in the parks. America's first golf club was established in Yonkers in 1891, and today there are more than 400 public golf courses in the state. There's even a 19-hole course overlooking the St. Lawrence River.

PLANNING YOUR TRIP

Before you set out on your trip, you'll need to do some planning. Use this chapter in conjunction with the tools in the appendix to answer some basic questions. First of all, when are you going? You may already have specific dates in mind; if not, various factors will probably influence your timing. Either way you'll want to know about local events, the weather, and other seasonal considerations. This chapter discusses all of that, while the Calendar of Events in the appendix provides a month-by-month view of major area events.

How much should you expect to spend on your trip? This chapter addresses various regional factors you'll want to consider in estimating your travel expenses. How will you get around? Check out the section on local transportation. If you decide to travel by car, the Planning Map and Mileage Chart in the appendix can help you figure out exact routes and driving times, while the Special Interest Tours section provides several focused itineraries. The chapter concludes with some reading recommendations, both fiction and nonfiction, to give you various perspectives on the area. If you want specific information about individual cities or counties, see the Resources section in the appendix.

WHEN TO GO

It's no exaggeration to say that the tourist season in New York State runs from January through December. The best time to visit depends on where you are going and which activities you wish to pursue. The high season is generally June, July, and August. During these months, prices are the highest and crowds the largest at popular destinations such as Long Island and Niagara Falls. September can be lovely in these areas, and crowds tend to be smaller. However, the summer months upstate usually offer the best weather—warm but not oppressively hot days. Of course, the winter months are the choice for winter sports enthusiasts. Skiing is usually available from late November through March in the Adirondacks, the Catskills, the Finger Lakes, and Cattaraugus County. April is usually considered mud season in the Adirondacks. May is often an ideal choice for travelers because spring is in full bloom throughout the countryside. Many attractions in upstate areas are open from May through Columbus Day.

Many people consider fall to be New York's most glorious season; the colors rival New England's. Weekend reservations are a must at many country inns during the leaf-peeping season. It's possible to follow the fall colors for a month or more from late September in the Adirondacks to late October in the New York City and Long Island areas.

Spring and fall are generally considered the best seasons to visit New York City. November and December are also quite popular visiting months because of the holiday shopping opportunities and the spectacular decorations, especially along Fifth Avenue. Summer can be quite hot and humid, and the concrete seems to intensify the temperatures.

HOW MUCH WILL IT COST?

The costs to travelers in New York State are as varied as the attractions. Upstate, budget travelers can expect to spend about $40 to $50 per night for a motel room. In the moderate range expect to pay about $60 to $70; upscale hotel rooms cost $80 and up. Bed-and-breakfasts can be as expensive as high-end hotels, depending on the accommodations and location. Campers can save the most money; there are more than 500 campgrounds in the state, with prices ranging from $10 to $25 per night. In areas of the Adirondack and Catskill parks, it's possible to camp in lean-tos for free—although even in the wilds of the Adirondacks, there's a Great Camp where one night's stay can exceed $1,000!

As a rule, prices are higher in New York City. However, even in the city special weekend and other package rates for hotels can reduce costs. A moderate city hotel room generally costs a little more than $100 per night, while luxury hotels range from $200 to $400, and a luxurious suite in a top New York City hotel can set you back $3,000 or more. At the other end of the spectrum, hostels and some bed-and-breakfasts typically charge around $50 per night for two.

Meal prices across the state also vary widely. You can expect to pay $30 to $40 for dinner for two at moderate places and $60 and up at higher-end restaurants. In New York City travelers can eat quite inexpensively at diners and ethnic eateries, where dinners average less than $25 for two. Of course, it's also possible to spend $300 or more for dinner in top city establishments. Some Long Island restaurants match or exceed Manhattan's more expensive spots.

Admission prices to parks, museums, and attractions run the gamut from free to expensive. Some attractions have free days, and others offer special discounts to seniors. Figure on an average of $5 to $8 per person. If you are a New York State resident 62 or older, you can obtain free vehicle access on any weekday (except holidays) to state parks and arboretums; free entrance to state historic sites; and fee reduction for state-operated swimming, golf, tennis, and boat rental.

Don't forget to add in New York State taxes. Sales taxes vary across the state, but they average 7 to 8.25 percent, plus bed taxes on hotel rooms in most areas of the state, including the major tourist destinations.

ORIENTATION AND TRANSPORTATION

Three major airports serve New York City: LaGuardia and John F. Kennedy in Queens and Newark in Newark, New Jersey. There are major airports in Albany, Syracuse, Rochester, and Buffalo (which serves Niagara Falls), as well as smaller airports in Ithaca, Jamestown, Saranac Lake, and White Plains.

Amtrak covers most of the state, including the cities and towns along the Hudson River and the cities along the Albany–Buffalo/Niagara Falls corridor. The Long Island Rail Road serves the entire island, from Manhattan to Montauk. Resort areas on Long Island, the Catskills, and the Hudson are geared to guests without cars, and transportation from the train or bus station to the hotel is usually not difficult to arrange.

For the rest of the state, car travel is the best way to go. The principal east-west highway is the New York State Thruway (or I-90), from the Pennsylvania border in the southwestern corner of the state to New York City. This toll highway is reputed to be the longest in the country (New York likes to be number one in everything, including tolls and taxes). Route 17 is a good (and free) alternative to the Thruway—it's a major four-lane highway that runs along the southern border of the state to New York City. Several major highways, all accessible from the Thruway, run north-south, including

U.S. 87 from Albany to the Canadian border, U.S. 81 from Binghamton to the Thousand Islands and the Canadian border, and I-390 from the Pennsylvania border to Rochester. Many areas of the state, including the Adirondacks, the Thousand Islands, Syracuse, Rochester, Buffalo, Chautauqua, and Cattaraugus, get ample snowfalls every winter. Road crews are experienced at clearing the roads, and driving is not usually a problem except in blizzard conditions.

RECOMMENDED READING

Thousands of books have been written about or set in New York State. James Fenimore Cooper, author of 32 novels, including *The Pioneers* (New American Library, 1996), *The Last of the Mohicans* (Bantam, 1982), *The Prairie* (Oxford University Press, 1992), *The Pathfinder* (Penguin, 1989), and *The Deerslayer* (Atheneum, 1990), devoted much of his writings to the frontier days in New York State. More recently, Pulitzer Prize–winning author William Kennedy set a trio of novels in the state capital: *Legs* (Penguin, 1997), *Billy Phelan's Greatest Game* (Penguin, 1997), and *Ironweed* (Penguin, 1997); he also wrote a nonfiction history of his hometown, *O Albany!* (Penguin, 1985). Prize-winning author Joyce Carol Oates is a native of Lockport in Western New York. Her novel *A Bloodsmoor Romance* is set in the state (E. P. Dutton, 1982).

The Adirondacks have inspired many works of literature. Foremost among the many books is William H. H. Murray's *Adventures in the Wilderness*, published in 1869 and no longer in print. Twentieth-century titles include William Chapman White's *Just About Everything in the Adirondacks* (Adirondack Museum, 1973) and Barbara McMartin's detailed guide *Fifty Hikes in the Adirondacks* (Backcountry Publications, 1992), which is a good choice for hikers.

For nonfiction about the state, Edmund Wilson's *Upstate: Records and Recollections* (Syracuse University Press, 1990) is a combination of family reminiscences, visits with literary figures, and sketches of local characters. An entertaining history of Niagara Falls is *Niagara: A History of the Falls*, by Pierre Berton (McClelland & Stewart, 1994). Buffalo was at its height of grandeur and greatness at the turn of the twentieth century and Lauren Belfer, a Buffalo native, captures that era brilliantly in *City of Light*, an historical novel (Dial Press, 1999).

New York City has been home to hundreds of writers who have drawn inspiration from their hometown. The city is also the publishing capital of the country. *Writing New York: A Literary Anthology* is an anthology of the city's great writers (Library of America, 1998; Philip Lopate, editor). One of the city's earliest popular writers was Washington Irving, whose satirical *A History of New York*, no longer in print, was written under the pseudonym Diedrich Knickerbocker. Under his own name he wrote the classic *The Legend of Sleepy*

Hollow (Tor Books, 1990). Walt Whitman wrote about Manhattan and the Brooklyn Bridge while living in Brooklyn, but every publisher in the city turned down *Leaves of Grass*, now considered one of the greatest works of American poetry (Bantam Classic, 1983).

New York in the 1880s is the stage for Edith Wharton's *The Age of Innocence* (Penguin, 1996) and *The House of Mirth* (Bantam Classic, 1997) and for Henry James's *Washington Square* (New American Library, 1995). The classic *Collected Stories of Louis Auchincloss* (Penguin, 1996) features stories that capture the lives of New York and Wall Street society. Irwin Shaw's family saga *Beggarman, Thief* is set primarily in New York (Delacorte Press, 1977).

The history of New York's Jewish community can be traced through novels such as *World of Our Fathers* by Irving Howe (Touchstone Books, 1994); *The Promise* by Chaim Potok (Fawcett Books, 1997); *Call It Sleep* by Henry Roth (Noonday Press, 1992); *The Assistant* by Bernard Malamud (Turtleback Books, 1991); and *Enemies, A Love Story* by Isaac Bashevis Singer (Noonday Press, 1997).

E. L. Doctorow's *Ragtime* (Modern Library, 1997), a novel about the intertwined lives of an upper-middle-class New Rochelle family, a Jewish immigrant family, and a black musician during the early twentieth century, has gained new audiences after its transformation into a musical. F. Scott Fitzgerald's *The Great Gatsby* portrays the dark side of the Jazz Age in New York and on Long Island (Scribner, 1996). Truman Capote was living in Brooklyn while he wrote *Breakfast at Tiffany's*, which depicts New York's high life in 1950s (Vintage Books, 1993). Tom Wolfe's *Bonfire of the Vanities* is a biting social satire of the city in the 1980s (Farrar Straus and Giroux, 1990).

For a behind-the-scenes look into politics and business, read *Trump: The Art of the Comeback* by Donald H. Trump (Times Books, 1997); and *The Power Broker* by Robert A. Caro (Knopf, 1974). *Gotham* (Oxford University Press, 1998) presents the history of New York City to 1898, and is the first of a two-volume work on the history of the city. Edwin G. Burrows and Mike Wallace, history professors in New York, won the Pulitzer Prize for their 20-year effort.

1
MANHATTAN

Whether you're standing in an airport in Dubuque or waiting for a bus in Atlanta, ask any New Yorker where they are from and their response will always, inevitably, be "the City." No state, no name, just "the City." As if everyone else, across the globe, knows exactly to what they're referring. And, somehow, they all do.

The 12-mile island that is Manhattan is made up of many different sections, each with its own distinctive feel. In Chinatown, the signs in all the storefronts are written in Chinese, and the dim sum is . . . well, you have to taste it to believe it. Little Italy, where the cannoli is king, is next to SoHo, known for galleries full of groundbreaking, bizarre, extraordinary art. Body piercing rules Greenwich Village; in-line skaters outnumber street vendors on the Upper East Side. But there's more—Manhattan is more than just the sum of its parts.

Everything from culture to finance to fashion runs through its streets. Wall Street runs global finance. The United Nations keeps world peace. Madison Avenue advertising agencies tell us what to buy, Seventh Avenue fashion designers tell us what to wear. Broadway and Lincoln Center define theater. The Museum of Modern Art, the Whitney, and the Museum of Natural History are home to some of the world's great art treasures. Ellis Island opened America to millions of immigrants. Every westbound train departed from Grand Central Station. The magazines and books that shape your mind are published here. This is *the* City. There is no other place quite like it.

MANHATTAN

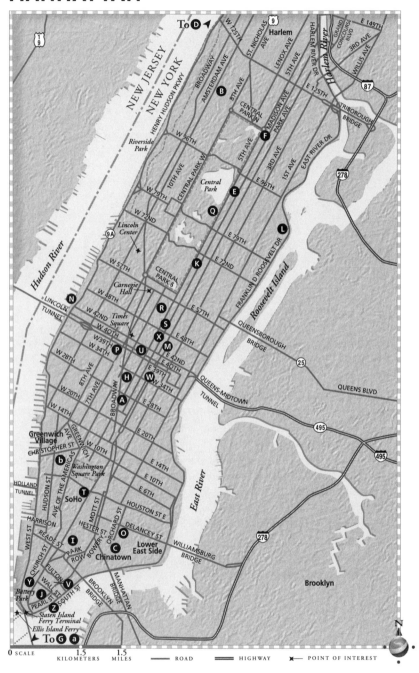

NEW JERSEY
NEW YORK

Harlem

To D

US 9

US 1 9

E 149TH

GRAND CONCOURSE BLVD

3RD AVE

WILLIS AVE

87

Harlem River

W 125TH

ST. NICHOLAS AVE

LENOX AVE

5TH AVE

HARLEM RIVER DR

TRIBOROUGH BRIDGE

E 125TH

HENRY HUDSON PKWY

BROADWAY

AMSTERDAM AVE

8TH AVE

B

CENTRAL PARK N

MADISON AVE
PARK AVE

F

278

Riverside Park

W 96TH

5TH AVE

3RD AVE

1ST AVE

EAST RIVER DR

E 96TH

10TH AVE

CENTRAL PARK W

Central Park

E

W 79TH

Q

EAST RIVER DR

W 72ND

Roosevelt Island

Lincoln Center

9A

E 79TH

L

Hudson River

W 57TH

CENTRAL PARK S

K

E 72ND

FRANKLIN D ROOSEVELT DR

Carnegie Hall

W 48TH

E 57TH

QUEENSBOROUGH BRIDGE

N

W 42ND

R

LINCOLN TUNNEL

W 40TH

Times Square

S

E 48TH

25

QUEENS BLVD

W 39TH

X

E 42ND

W 34TH

P

U

M

E 40TH

8TH AVE

7TH AVE

H

E 39TH

QUEENS-MIDTOWN TUNNEL

W 28TH

W

W 34TH

495

W 20TH

A

E 28TH

BROADWAY

W 14TH

E 20TH

495

Greenwich Village

AVE

GREENWICH AVE

W 10TH

E 14TH

CHRISTOPHER ST

b

E 10TH

Washington Square Park

E 6TH

HOLLAND TUNNEL

HUDSON ST

AVE OF THE AMERICAS

T

SoHo

MOTT ST

HESTER ST

HOUSTON ST E

East River

HARRISON

ORCHARD ST

DELANCEY ST

278

WEST ST

READE ST

I

PARK ROW

BOWERY

O

Lower East Side

WILLIAMSBURG BRIDGE

CHURCH ST

FULTON ST

C

Chinatown

Brooklyn

Y

WALL ST

V

SOUTH ST

MANHATTAN BRIDGE

J

PEARL ST

BROOKLYN BRIDGE

Battery Park

Z

Staten Island Ferry Terminal
Ellis Island Ferry

To G a

N

A PERFECT DAY IN MANHATTAN

The pulse of the city can best be felt in the early-morning hours, during the week. The streets, subways, buses, and cabs are full of people heading to work. But not just any people—these crowds make up the best and brightest, in the most influential city in the world. Start your morning with them, but when they veer off into their office skyscrapers, duck into the Plaza Hotel in Midtown for morning coffee and scones. Once the streets clear out some, stroll down Fifth Avenue, stopping at Tiffany and Cartier, or FAO Schwarz, the biggest toy store in the country, and imagine that you are one of those titans of industry buying an extravagant gift for your special someone. Then jump on the Fifth Avenue bus and ride all the way downtown, into Greenwich Village. Check out some outrageous fashions in this eclectic neighborhood. For lunch, swing west into Little Italy for some pasta, or east into Chinatown for egg rolls. Work off those calories climbing the stairs of the Statue of Liberty, across from Battery Park. Downtown Manhattan offers some of the best off-Broadway theater, and the tickets are usually far cheaper and easier to get. Check the local paper, the *Village Voice*, for show locations and times. Grab a post-theater meal at any one of a number of ethnic eateries, like

---

SIGHTS

- **A** American Museum of Natural History
- **B** Cathedral Church of St. John the Divine
- **C** Chinatown
- **D** Cloisters Museum
- **E** Cooper-Hewitt National Design Museum
- **F** El Museo del Barrio
- **G** Ellis Island National Monument
- **H** Empire State Building
- **I** Federal Hall National Monument
- **J** Fraunces Tavern Museum
- **K** Frick Collection
- **L** Gracie Mansion
- **M** Grand Central Terminal
- **N** *Intrepid* Sea-Air-Space Museum
- **O** Lower East Side Tenement Museum
- **P** Madison Square Garden
- **Q** Metropolitan Museum of Art
- **R** Museum of Modern Art
- **P** Museum of the City of New York
- **S** Museum of Television and Radio
- **T** New Museum of Contemporary Art
- **U** The New York Public Library
- **V** New York Stock Exchange
- **W** Pierpont Morgan Library
- **X** Rockefeller Center
- **S** St. Patrick's Cathedral
- **Y** St. Paul's Chapel
- **E** Solomon R. Guggenheim Museum
- **Z** South Street Seaport
- **a** Statue of Liberty
- **A** Theodore Roosevelt National Historic Site
- **B** United Nations
- **b** West Fourth Street Basketball Courts
- **C** Whitney Museum of American Art
- **Z** World Trade Center

Note: Items with the same letter are located in the same area.

Jamaican at Carib on Greenwich Street, off Perry Street. After dinner, if you have any energy left, head over to the Empire State Building for a gorgeous view of Manhattan at night.

ORIENTATION

Do not drive. Parking tickets cost $55—and there's never any parking. No parking from 7 to 8 a.m., street cleaning, alternate side of the street, commercial vehicles only, full moon on Arbor Day. The absence of a no-parking sign doesn't make it legal: if the sign has been ripped down but it's a no-parking zone, you'll get the ticket. Even longtime Manhattan residents get confused. Parking garages are even worse. The sign says $9.75 all day—if you pull in exactly at 9 a.m. and leave exactly at 5 p.m., plus the 18.75 percent parking tax, plus the tip—don't trust the sign. An hour in Midtown will cost you $20. Walk. Twenty blocks equal one mile, roughly. Most of Manhattan is a grid. East-west streets are known as crosstown streets—even-numbered streets go east, odd-numbered west. Avenues run north and south. Every road is one way except a few major crosstowners—125th, 86th, 79th, 59th, 42nd, 23rd, and 14th—that run both east and west. Fifth Avenue is the middle of the city. Everything east of Fifth is known as the East Side, and west of Fifth, well, the West Side. Above 59th Street is called the Upper East, or Upper West, Side. Smack in the center is Midtown; below 14th Street is downtown. When you run out of numbers in lower Manhattan and the streets are named, everything gets screwy. Downtown, just ask for directions. Check out a local map for more specific names of areas.

PUBLIC TRANSPORTATION

As convenient and essential as subways are to the natives, they're a little hard to figure out for visitors. You can pick up a map at a subway booth, but it might not help you any: they're hard to read. Tip: the 6 train runs up and down Third Avenue; enter the subway on Lexington or Third. The 1-9 train runs up and down Broadway; enter the subway on Broadway uptown, Eighth Avenue Midtown. If you understood that, another tip: as safe as it is during the day, do not ride the subway after 11 p.m. Why risk it?

For more diverse routes, remain above ground where you can see where you're going and take the bus. Buses run up and down avenues and across town on two-way streets (86th, 79th, 59th, 42nd . . .). Some buses take more unusual routes, so ask the driver when you step on. But ask like a New Yorker: be brief and to the point. "You go up Third?" will usually cover it. Buses are

TIMES SQUARE

also usually safe to ride at night. The bus and subway fare is $1.50, no bills or pennies allowed. MetroCards or tokens are available at subway booths. Never buy a MetroCard worth more than $10: if you lose it you're out of luck. Tip: one of the air-conditioned buses, where you can often find a seat, is a lovely way to travel, but it's time-consuming. A 15-minute trip by subway could take you an hour on the bus. For maps and other info on the subways and buses, visit www.mta.nyc.ny.us.

TAXIS

For more complex travel maneuvers, take a taxi. The stress and time you'll save will make up for the money you spend. But spend you will in a New York taxicab. No matter how far you're traveling, you will not make it out for under $5. Expect to spend at least $10 to $15. During rush hour, there are many "gypsy" cabs about. If you can't find a yellow cab, this is another way to go. Usually they are sedans with no meters. The driver will ask you how much you'd like to pay when you reach your destination. Depending on traffic, between $5 and $10 will usually cut it. Estimate what it would have cost you in a yellow cab and pay what's fair. Don't be afraid of the gypsy-cab driver. He's just another guy out there trying to make a buck. And in a rainstorm at 6 at night, you're gonna need him.

TOURS

For $22, catch a **Gray Line** double-decker bus (212/397-2620). Tickets can be purchased at most hotels or from one of two Gray Line offices, located in the Port Authority Bus Terminal and the Times Square Visitors Terminal. Gray Line offers three different tours, one of downtown Manhattan that runs about three hours, one of uptown Manhattan that runs about two hours, or one of the whole city that runs about five-and-a-half hours. These tours highlight all the top tourist attractions. If your time is tight, or if you don't relish sitting on a bus for five hours, then the downtown area of Manhattan might be worth seeing in this manner. Remember, downtown streets are not numbered but named, and the grid structure is a bit screwy, so on foot you may get confused. For a water view, the **Circle Line** cruise (212/563-3200) takes you around the island of Manhattan for three hours, at a price of $22. No reservations are necessary. The boat departs from the South Street Seaport and the docks on 42nd Street, three times during the week, five times on the weekends. Night cruises are also available.

But to really see and feel Manhattan, get off the bus, come ashore, lace up a really comfortable pair of shoes, and hit the pavement. Manhattan is a walking city. The **New York Convention and Visitors Bureau** (212/397-8200), located at 810 Seventh Avenue between 52nd and 53rd Streets, offers brochures for self-guided walking tours, as does the newly built **Times Square Visitors Terminal**. For a guided tour, call the **Municipal Art Society** (212/935-3960). The "Discover NY" tour takes you all over town, for $10, $8 seniors and students. The society also offers special-interest tours that change every month, such as "Money Matters: The Interiors of Wall Street" and "Millionaires' Mile: The Upper East Side" (each $15). Call in advance to find out what special tours are being offered the month you visit. **Big Onion Walking Tours** (212/439-1090) is run by a group of Columbia University grad students. They offer tours like "The Architectural History of TriBeCa and Irish New York," featuring such sights as St. Patrick's Cathedral, Tammany Hall, and the Five Points slum ($10). Check out their Web site at www.bigonion.com. No reservations are necessary, and private tours are available upon request.

SIGHTSEEING HIGHLIGHTS

★★★★ AMERICAN MUSEUM OF NATURAL HISTORY
Central Park West at 79th St., 212/769-5100, www.amnh.org
This must-see museum holds more than 30 million artifacts and specimens and explores the American Indian, Asian, Pacific Islander, South American, and Aztec and Mayan cultures. It is home to vast collections

of insects, invertebrates, fish, amphibians, reptiles, anthropological artifacts, and more fossil mammals and dinosaurs than any other museum in the world. It has more than 200 working scientists and welcomes millions of visitors each year. The showstopper, by far, is **Dinosaur Halls**, featuring skeletons of *Tyrannosaurus rex* and *Apatosaurus*. If you have time for nothing else, this display alone is worth the price of admission. The **Naturemax Theater** shows natural-history films on a giant IMAX screen, available also as a package with dinner in the **Garden Café**. Call in advance for special exhibits, like Shackleton's legendary 1914 Antarctic expedition or the 400-million-year-old shark.

Details: Open daily except Thanksgiving day and Christmas day, 10–5:45, Fri and Sat to 8:45. Admission $8 adults, $6 seniors and students, $4.50 children; theater $8 adults, $6 seniors, $4.50 children. Wheelchair accessible. (3 hours–full day)

★★★★ EMPIRE STATE BUILDING
34th St. at Fifth Ave., 212/736-3100

Portrayed by Hollywood as one of the world's most romantic spots, the Empire State Building soars more than one-quarter mile into the atmosphere above the heart of Manhattan. Elevators run to the outdoor observatory on the 86th floor, and another elevator takes you even higher, to the glass-enclosed observation tower on the 102nd floor. On a clear day, you can see for almost 80 miles, but the best feature is the view straight down. It's like looking at an aerial map of Manhattan. From the top of the 86th floor you can see how the streets line up, how to get around, and the distance from one side of town to the other. But be prepared to wait on line (that's "in line" for non–New Yorkers): this tourist attraction also boasts one of the longest lines in New York.

Details: Observation tower open daily 9:30–midnight (last ticket sold at 11:30 p.m.). $6 adults, $3 seniors and children. Wheelchair accessible. (Depends on line; actual time on top, under 1 hour)

★★★★ METROPOLITAN MUSEUM OF ART
1000 Fifth Ave. at 82nd St., 212/535-7710
www.metmuseum.org

Friday evening, Saturday, and Sunday, the Met hosts walking tours of the museum from the following topics: American Art; Arts of Africa, Oceania, and the Americas; Arts of Ancient Egypt; Asian Art; European Rooms; Impressionism; Islamic Art; Medieval Art; Museum

Highlights; and Old Master Paintings. This museum is massive. The walking tours are free and highly recommended. For times, consult the walking tour stanchion in the Great Hall. And that's just for starters. But if you don't have the time, this museum's showstopper is its collection of medieval art. One of the richest in the world, it encompasses the period from the fourth to the sixteenth century—roughly from the fall of Rome to the beginning of the Renaissance. Among its strengths are Early Christian and Byzantine silver; jewelry of the barbarian tribes; Romanesque and Gothic liturgical vessels; stained glass, sculpture, enamels, and ivories; and tapestries of the fourteenth and fifteenth centuries. Don't miss happy hour at the **Great Balcony Bar**. On Friday and Saturday nights from 5 to 8 have a cocktail in the middle of the museum and discuss art while listening to classical music.

Details: Open Tue–Sun 9:30–5:15, Fri and Sat until 8:45. $10 adults, $5 seniors and students, free to children under 12. Wheelchair accessible. Admission includes the Cloisters Museum in upper Manhattan (see separate listing in this section). (3 hours–full day)

★★★★ STATUE OF LIBERTY
Liberty Island, 212/269-5755, www.libertystatepark.com
Give me your tired, your poor,
Your huddled masses yearning to breathe free,
The wretched refuse of your teeming shore.
Send these, the homeless, tempest-tossed, to me;
I lift my lamp beside the golden door.
There is no greater symbol of the freedom of the United States than the Statue of Liberty, which has stood in New York Harbor since 1886. Measuring 151 feet high, this statue has welcomed millions of immigrants in its more than one-hundred-year history. Ride the ferry from Battery Park to view Lady Liberty up close and visit the **American Museum of Immigration** in the statue's base. If you have the time, and the lungs, climb the 354 steps (one way) to the crown; but be advised it can be hot and crowded.

Details: Ferry operates daily 8:30–4, weather permitting. Catch the 8:30 ferry if you wish to climb the stairs to the crown. Admission to the statue is free; ferry from Gangway S, Battery Park, $7 adults, $6 seniors, $3 children. Wheelchair accessible. (2 hours)

★★★ CHINATOWN
Bounded by Canal, Mott, Mulberry, and Bayard Sts.

Centered between Little Italy and the Lower East Side, this 40-square-block area is home to about half of New York's Chinese population. The shop signs and movie marquees are all written in Chinese, and the phone booths are built in pagoda style. Although Hong Kong banks and shops of all kinds have opened up here, for tourists this area is all about the food. Bring an empty stomach and lots of people. Each restaurant is better than the one before, and all come with a huge lazy Susan in the middle of the table for easy access to all the dishes you've ordered. Eat, eat, and then eat some more. If you're interested in more than food, visit the **Museum of Chinese in the Americas**, 70 Mulberry St., 212/619-4785. Then go and get something to eat.

Details: *Museum of Chinese in the Americas open Tue–Sat noon–5. (2 hours, or depends on size of stomach)*

★★★ CLOISTERS MUSEUM
Fort Tryon Park, Washington Heights, 212/923-3700
www.cloisters.org

This remote branch of the Metropolitan Museum of Art is worth the trek. And located in upper Manhattan, in Washington Heights, it is a trek. But it is also the only place to see the Unicorn Tapestries—and they are brilliant. Devoted to medieval art, this museum includes five French cloisters, a Romanesque chapel, and extensive gardens, plus an outstanding collection of fifteenth-century stained-glass windows. The **Herb Garden** within the Bonnefront Cloister offers the best view of the Hudson River. Truly, an unforgettable afternoon.

Details: *Open daily 9:30–5:15; Nov–Feb until 4:45. Closed Thanksgiving day, Christmas day, and New Year's Day. $10 adults, $5 seniors and students, free to children under 12. Wheelchair accessible. Admission to the Cloisters includes the Metropolitan Museum of Art. (3 hours)*

★★★ ELLIS ISLAND NATIONAL MONUMENT
Ellis Island, 212/363-3200, www.libertystatepark.com

Located close to the Statue of Liberty and reached by the same ferry that leaves Battery Park, this monument was once the main point of entry for millions of immigrants to this country. Recently completed was a $160 million restoration project and the reopening of the **Ellis Island Immigration Museum**. Inside, you can trace your ancestors' journey to the New World. More than 100 million present-day

Americans have ancestors that passed through the Ellis Island processing stations. Outside, near the ferry dock, the **American Immigrant Wall of Honor** records nearly 400,000 names, just a small percentage of those who entered here. An award-winning film about America's immigrants is shown at regular intervals.

Details: *Open daily 9–5. Admission free; ferry $7 adults, $6 seniors, $3 children. Wheelchair accessible. (3 hours)*

★★★ MUSEUM OF THE CITY OF NEW YORK
Fifth Ave. from 103rd to 104th Sts., 212/534-1672
www.mcny.org
There is only one New York City and only one museum that captures the breadth of its historic and human dimensions—the Museum of the City of New York. Situated on Manhattan's Museum Mile, it was established in 1923 to collect, preserve, and present original cultural materials related to the history of New York City.

Details: *Open Wed–Sat 10–5, Sun noon–5. $5 adults, $4 seniors and students, $10 families. (2 hours)*

★★★ MUSEUM OF MODERN ART
11 W. 53rd St., 212/708-9400, www.moma.org
From an initial gift of eight prints and one drawing, the Museum of Modern Art's world-renowned collection has grown to include more than 100,000 paintings, sculptures, drawings, prints, photographs, architectural models and drawings, and design objects. MoMA also owns some 14,000 films and 4 million film stills. Best known for Van Gogh's Starry Night, other featured artists include Picasso, Rodin, and Henry Moore. Free live jazz concerts are performed in the **Sette MoMA** restaurant on Thursday and Saturday evenings from 6 to 10 and in the **Garden Café** on Friday evenings from 5:30 to 8.

Details: *Open Sat–Tues, Thu 10:30–5:45, Fri 10:30–8:30. $9.50 adults, $6.50 seniors and students, free to children under 16. Wheelchair accessible. (3 hours)*

★★★ MUSEUM OF TELEVISION AND RADIO
25 W. 52nd St., 212/621-6800
Over 40,000 television and radio broadcasts from the 1920s to the present are stored here and available to the public. Once you've made your choice (restricted to two hours of viewing time), the show will be set up for watching at one of 100 video consoles.

Nothing beats the premiere episode of *I Love Lucy*. And learning about the history of broadcast isn't bad, either.

Details: *Open Tue–Sun noon–6, Thu noon–8. $6 adults, $4 students and seniors, $3 children. Wheelchair accessible. (2 hours)*

★★★ THE NEW YORK PUBLIC LIBRARY
Fifth Ave. and 42nd St., 212/930-0800, www.nypl.org

You can't check out a book here, but it's worth a stop if just to see the two lions that greet you at the entrance. Nicknamed "Patience" and "Fortitude" by Mayor Fiorello LaGuardia to help New Yorkers get through the Great Depression, these world-renowned marble lions have captured the affection of New Yorkers and visitors from all over the world. One even went Hollywood, making an appearance in the motion picture *The Wiz*. Inside the library you can see a 1493 letter by Christopher Columbus describing his New World discoveries, the first full folio of Shakespeare's work, and an early draft of Jefferson's Declaration of Independence. Free tours leave the information desk Monday through Saturday at 11 and 2.

Details: *Open Tue and Wed 11–7:30, Thu–Sat and Mon 10–6. Free. Wheelchair accessible. (1 hour)*

★★ CATHEDRAL CHURCH OF ST. JOHN THE DIVINE
1047 Amsterdam Ave., 212/316-7490, www.stjohndivine.com

The cornerstone of this grand Episcopal church was laid in 1892, and the structure is still under construction. Spread across 11 acres, two football fields long and 17 stories high, it is the largest church in the country and the largest Gothic church in the world. The church is built entirely of stone, including Maine granite and Indian limestone. The **Biblical Garden** contains more than one hundred plants mentioned in the Bible.

Details: *Guided tours Tue–Sat at 11 a.m.; Sun at 12:30 p.m. Open daily 7–6. Open Sun until 9. Services on Sunday and religious holidays. Admission free. Tours $2. (1 hour)*

★★ FRICK COLLECTION
One E. 70th St., 212/288-0700, www.frick.org

Nineteenth-century robber baron Henry Clay Frick built this French-style mansion to showcase his superb art collection. The beauty of this museum lies in its size and location. Right off Fifth Avenue, with a view of Central Park, the Frick remains much like a private home (if you happen to be a multimillionaire industrialist). Inside, the art on display includes works by Rembrandt, El Greco, Titian, and Turner. **Details**: *Open Tue–Sat 10–6, Sun 1–6. $7 adults, $5 seniors and students; children under 10 not permitted. (1 hour)*

★★ GRAND CENTRAL TERMINAL
42nd St. between Lexington and Vanderbilt Ave.
Almost two decades ago Jacqueline Kennedy Onassis stood up in protest against a group of businessmen who wanted to tear down Grand Central Terminal to build an office building. With influential New Yorkers behind the protest, Grand Central was deemed an historic landmark. The 10-year, $197 million project to restore and preserve this world-renowned architectural landmark has finally been accomplished, and the old giant was rededicated in October 1998. The cleaning of the famous Sky Ceiling, a grand mural representing the heavens as seen from below was completed in 1997. A fiber-optic system was installed to replace the 40-watt incandescent bulbs that formerly lit the stars. Nearly every surface in the terminal has been cleaned or restored, including the interior floors made of Tennessee marble and terrazzo and the Main Concourse walls of simulated Caen stone (imitation limestone). The massive chandeliers and details such as clocks, railings, and grillwork have been restored. This is no ordinary rail terminal. However, it is still a rail terminal. So unless you have an interest in rail travel, skip the tour. The highlight here is looking up at the ceiling, and stopping in for a steak at Michael Jordan's eponymous new restaurant before heading off into the subway on the lower level.
Details: *Open daily. (15–30 minutes)*

★★ *INTREPID* SEA-AIR-SPACE MUSEUM
Pier 86 on W. 46th St., 212/245-2533
www.intrepid-museum.com
Permanently moored on the Hudson River, the *Intrepid* is an aircraft carrier that saw service during World War II and the Vietnam War. It is filled with exhibits from its own wartime exploits—its aircraft shot down 650 enemy planes and destroyed 289 ships—and from its peacetime role retrieving Mercury and Gemini space capsules. Several dozen fighter and bomber planes are on the flight deck. Alongside the carrier are a destroyer, the USS *Edson*, and the USS *Growler*, a guided missile submarine with a nuclear cruise missile inside. This museum is for serious war and aviation buffs.

Details: Open Apr 1–Sept 30 Mon–Sat 10–5, Sun 10–6 p.m.; Oct 1–Mar 31 Wed–Sun 10–5. Closed first Mon in Jan–first Thu in Feb. $10 adults, $7.50 seniors and ages 12–17, $5 ages 6–11. (3 hours)

★★ ROCKEFELLER CENTER
Fifth Ave. to Avenue of the Americas and 48th to 51st Sts. 212/698-2950 (NBC); 212/247-4777 (Radio City)

A New York Christmas wouldn't be complete without a Rockefeller Christmas tree, the Radio City Christmas Spectacular, featuring the Rockettes (prices from $29 to $97), and a lap around the ice-skating rink. For the rest of the year, Rockefeller Center is the world's largest commercial and entertainment complex, with more than 14 buildings and numerous restaurants, shops, underground walkways, and plazas. **NBC Studio Tours** gives one-hour behind-the-scenes tours of the production area, or you can just stand outside and watch a live taping of the Today Show through its large bay window. **Radio City Music Hall**, www.radiocity.com, also hosts some of today's top performers. Call ahead for a schedule, and call early for tickets: Radio City's six thousand seats sell out quickly.

Details: NBC tours Mon–Sat 9–5:30. Tour $10 (children under 6 not permitted). (2 hours)

★★ ST. PATRICK'S CATHEDRAL
Fifth Ave. at 50th St., 212/753-2261

This Roman Catholic Gothic-style cathedral is one of the country's largest and most famous churches, with seats for 2,400. But the seats go quickly if you're looking to attend mass on a religious holiday, so arrive early.

Details: Call for mass times; open daily 6:30 a.m.–8:45 p.m.; guided tours by appointment. Free. (30 minutes)

★★ SOLOMON R. GUGGENHEIM MUSEUM
1071 Fifth Ave. at 89th St., 212/423-3600
www.guggenheim.org

The Frank Lloyd Wright spiral-shaped building is one of the city's outstanding architectural landmarks, and the museum is home to some of the finest contemporary art that has ever been on display. The best way to see the collection is to take the elevator to the top and work your way down the spiral ramp. Inside you'll find works by Kandinsky, Klee, Modigliani, and Mondrian, to name a few.

Details: Open Sun–Wed 10–6, Fri and Sat 10–8. $12 adults, $7 seniors and students, free to children under 12. Wheelchair accessible. (2 hours)

★★ SOUTH STREET SEAPORT
12 Fulton St., 212/748-8600

A tourist attraction to be sure, the South Street Seaport is located on the site of what was once the country's leading port and is now an 11-square-block historic district in lower Manhattan. Its attractions include the **Fulton Fish Market**, the nation's largest wholesale fish market, and the 1911 *Peking*, a four-masted cargo vessel open for touring. The streets are cobblestone and the restaurants offer a great view of the harbor and the Brooklyn Bridge. Back in the 1980s the Seaport was the hot spot for the after-work Wall Street yuppie crowd, but these days it's lost its trendy appeal.

Details: Ships, visitors center, and museum open Nov–Mar daily 10–5; Apr–Oct 10–6. $6 adults, $5 seniors, $4 students, $3 children. No charge for visiting the area. (2 hours)

★★ WHITNEY MUSEUM OF AMERICAN ART
945 Madison Ave. at 75th St., 212/570-3676

This museum showcases a superb collection of twentieth-century American art, with such artists represented as Georgia O'Keeffe, John Sloan, Roy Lichtenstein, and Edward Hopper. But the highlight of the Whitney is the **Andy Warhol Film Project**. In the 1980s the Whitney Museum and the Museum of Modern Art (MoMA) agreed to collaborate on the largest archival research project in the history of American avant-garde cinema. Jointly they catalogued Warhol's massive film collection, and since 1988 exhibitions of his work have been a welcome addition to the museum.

Details: Open Fri–Sun and Wed 11–6, Thu 1–8. $12.50 adults, $10.50 seniors and students, free to children under 12. (2 hours)

★★ WORLD TRADE CENTER
Church St. between Liberty and Vesey St., 212/323-2350

These twin towers are New York's tallest buildings. The elevator ride to the 107th-floor Observation Deck takes about 58 seconds. An escalator takes you up to the open rooftop level on the 110th floor. A beautiful view, not unlike the view from the Empire State Building, but without the historical significance. If the line is too long at the

Empire State Building, the World Trade Center is a good backup. But no need to see both. As cool as the view is from up high, the World Trade Center is just a building.

Details: *June–Aug open daily 9:30 a.m.–11:30 p.m.; rest of year 9:30–9:30. Observation deck admission $12.50 adults, $9.50 seniors, $10.75 children 13–17, $6.25 children 12 and under. Wheelchair accessible. (1 hour)*

★ **COOPER-HEWITT NATIONAL DESIGN MUSEUM**
Fifth Ave. and 91st St., 212/849-8300, www.si.edu/ndm
In what was once Andrew Carnegie's Fifth Avenue mansion, the Cooper-Hewitt is the nation's only museum devoted exclusively to historical and contemporary design. In 1997, two adjoining townhouses (one belonged to Carnegie's daughter) became home to the Design Resource Center, which houses most of the permanent collection. Amid the impressive collection of ceramics, wall coverings, textiles, and decorative arts is a Louis XVI music room furnished with French antiques and a set of bagpipes. On nice days in spring, doors to the garden are flung open and the public is invited to enjoy the flora. The museum is officially the Smithsonian Institution National Museum of Design.

Details: *Open Wed–Sat 10–5, Tue 10–9, Sun noon–5. $3 adults, $1.50 seniors and students, free to children under 12; free to all Tue 5 p.m.–9 p.m. (2 hours)*

★ **EL MUSEO DEL BARRIO**
Fifth Ave. at 104th St., 212/831-7272
Located across from the Museum of the City of New York, this is the city's only museum devoted to the cultures of Latin America. There's a small collection of pre-Columbian art as well as various special exhibitions of paintings, sculpture, and videos exploring the past and present of Latin America.

Details: *Open Wed–Sun 11–5, Thu until 8 during the summer. $4 adults, $2 seniors and students. (1 hour)*

★ **FEDERAL HALL NATIONAL MONUMENT**
Wall and Nassau Sts., 212/825-6888
Built in 1842 on the site of the original Federal Hall, this museum shows a short film and features a collection of exhibits relating to events that occurred on this site. Here, in April 1789, George Washington was sworn in as the country's first president; a dignified

statue of the father of our country marks the spot. A glass-encased balcony railing section shows where Washington leaned to address the crowd after his inauguration.

Details: *Open Mon–Fri 9–5. Free. (1 hour)*

★ **FRAUNCES TAVERN MUSEUM**
54 Pearl St., 212/425-1778
This is a replica of the tavern that played host to George Washington and his revolutionary friends and was home to the Department of Foreign Affairs, the War Department, and the Treasury during the country's early years. Washington made his famous emotional farewell to his Continental army officers in the tavern's Long Room, and the scene is re-created on the third floor. The museum offers changing exhibitions, such as *The Changing Image of George Washington* and *Wall Street: Changing Fortunes*. Each exhibition focuses on a unique aspect of American history. The restaurant on the first floor offers wood-burning fireplaces and more than the usual museum fare but is closed on weekends.

Details: *Open Mon–Fri 10–4:45, Sat and Sun noon–4. $2.50 adults, $1 seniors and students. (30 minutes)*

★ **GRACIE MANSION**
East End Ave. at 89th St., 212/570-4751
This mansion was once owned by shipping magnate Archibald Gracie, a prominent member of New York society who staged elegant parties that attracted Louis Philippe, later the king of France; President John Quincy Adams; Washington Irving; and Rufus King, ambassador to Britain. Gracie lost his fortune and died six years later. Since 1942 it has been home to the mayor of the City of New York. The mansion, restored in 1984 through gifts to the Gracie Mansion Conservancy, today presents the main floor to the public and is a showcase for art and antiques created by New York designers, cabinetmakers, painters, and sculptors. Several pieces belonged to the Gracie family. At the center of the faux-marble entryway floor, a painted compass recalls the ships that built the Gracie fortune.

Details: *Open for tours by reservation only Wed at 10, 11, 1, and 2. $4 adults, $3 seniors. (1 hour)*

★ **LOWER EAST SIDE TENEMENT MUSEUM**
90 Orchard St., 212/431-0233, www.tenement.org

MUSEUMS ON THE CHEAP

Museums are a must-see in Manhattan, but the price of admission can add up. If you plan on visiting more than one, purchase a City Pass, sold at the advance-sale desk at the Museum of Natural History. This pass is good for nine days and covers admission to the American Museum of Natural History, the Metropolitan Museum of Art, the Museum of Modern Art, the *Intrepid* Sea-Air-Space Museum, the Empire State Building Observatory, and the top of the World Trade Center. The pass price is $28 adults, $18.75 seniors, and $21 teens 13–18. There is no pass available for children.

This museum was once a six-story tenement building, built in 1863, that housed 11,000 people over a 70-year period. The upper floors have been re-created to show the living conditions endured by the house's tenants, including Irish, German, Russian Jewish, and Italian immigrants. The museum organizes various walking tours, each concentrating on a theme, such as tenement architecture or the lives of women.

Details: Open Tue–Fri 12–5, Sat and Sun 11–5. Museum $8 adults; $6 seniors, students, and children. Additional charge for walking tours and dramas. (1 hour)

★ **MADISON SQUARE GARDEN**
37th St. and Seventh Ave., 212/465-MSG1
For sports fans, Madison Square Garden is home to the NBA New York Knicks, the NHL New York Rangers, and the WNBA New York Liberty. New Yorkers take their teams seriously. Don't show up wearing rival game gear, and don't show up an hour before game time expecting to get a ticket. Call way, way, way in advance for tickets. Madison Square Garden also hosts concerts, championship boxing, and the occasional Grammy Awards ceremony.

Details: For ticket information, call Ticketmaster, 212/307-7171. (Hours depend on event)

★ **NEW MUSEUM OF CONTEMPORARY ART**
583 Broadway (between Houston and Prince), 212/219-1222

Located in the heart of an area filled with artists' lofts and galleries, this museum is the only one in the city devoted exclusively to art of the past two decades. The museum features solo and group exhibitions and a variety of public programs.

Details: *Open Wed and Sun noon–6, Thu, Fri, and Sat noon–8. $5 adults; $3 artists, seniors, and students; free to children under 18. (1 hour)*

★ NEW YORK STOCK EXCHANGE
20 Broad St., 212/656-5167, www.nyse.com

Have you seen the Eddie Murphy movie *Trading Places*? Or *Wall Street*? Movies that depict the chaos and mayhem of the stock-exchange floor are right on the money (pardon the pun). It's nuts down there. A large window for viewing overlooks the floor because tourists are not allowed on the floor of the exchange. Plan time to go through a metal detector. Just outside the Observation Gallery there are short videos and exhibits on the history of the exchange.

Details: *Open Mon–Fri 9:15–4. Free, but tickets are required and numbers are limited. (1 hour)*

★ PIERPONT MORGAN LIBRARY
29 E. 36th St. at Madison Ave., 212/685-0610

The private library of financier J. Pierpont Morgan is one of the country's loveliest. It is filled with rare editions, more than one thousand illustrated manuscripts, art objects, paintings, sculpture, and a glass-enclosed garden court. Some of the gems of the library collection are the three Gutenberg Bibles; a Shakespeare first folio; an autographed manuscript of Milton's *Paradise Lost*; original musical scores from Bach, Brahms, and Beethoven; and manuscripts and early editions of Rudyard Kipling, Oscar Wilde, and Gertrude Stein. Morgan's study, once described as the most beautiful room in America, is lined with Italian Renaissance paintings. The **Morgan Café**, a lovely atrium-style restaurant, serves lunch and afternoon tea.

Details: *Open Tue–Thu 10:30–5, Fri 10:30–8, Sat 10:30–6, Sun noon–6. $7 adults; $5 seniors, students, and children. (2 hours)*

★ ST. PAUL'S CHAPEL
Broadway and Fulton St., 212/602-0800

This chapel, once regularly visited by George Washington, still houses the pew where Washington sat during his inauguration service in 1789. Dedicated in 1766, the church is considered the oldest public building in continuous use in Manhattan. Classical concerts and church music are performed at noon on some Mondays and Thursdays.

Details: *Open Mon–Fri 9–3, Sun 8–4. Donation. (30 minutes)*

★ THEODORE ROOSEVELT NATIONAL HISTORIC SITE
28 E. 20th St., 212/260-1616

This is the reconstructed birthplace of Roosevelt, the only American president born in the city. The house is filled with original Roosevelt furnishings. The lower floor features an exhibition on Roosevelt's life, from his childhood struggles with illness and the tragic same-day deaths of his wife and mother to his rise to become the nation's youngest president at age 42. The room full of his hunting trophies and outdoor memorabilia captures his energetic personality.

Details: *Tours are offered every hour, on the hour. Open Wed–Sun 9–5. $2. (1 hour)*

★ UNITED NATIONS
Visitors center, First Ave. and 46th St., 212/963-7713
www.un.org

The United Nations consists of the majestic Secretariat Building, the domed General Assembly Building, the Conference Building, and the Hammarskjold Library. Various member states have donated artwork. During its mid-September to mid-December sitting, the UN General Assembly can be witnessed from the public gallery.

Details: *Open daily 9:15–4:15. Free tickets to the public gallery are issued from the information desk in the lobby on a first-come, first-served basis. Guided tours, which last about 45 minutes, are given daily about every 30 minutes, from 9:15 to 4:45. $7.50 adults, $5.50 seniors, $4.50 students, and $3.50 children grades 1–8. Children under 5 are not permitted. (1 hour)*

★ WEST FOURTH STREET BASKETBALL COURTS
W. Fourth St., west of Seventh Ave.

The Knicks may be playing at Madison Square Garden when you're in town, but only Donald Trump or Spike Lee can get you a ticket. The West Fourth Street public basketball courts are the best free sporting venue in town. From late afternoon to late evening almost any day of the week, playground legends and NBA hopefuls battle it out on the pavement court while hot-dog vendors offer snacks nearby. But be warned—unless you're a serious contender, don't even think of bringing a ball and joining in. These hoopsters may not have signed with Nike, but they sure got game.

Details: *Pick-up games are held late afternoon to late evening most days. (1 hour)*

SHOPPING

Money, money, money. That's what most people think they need when they come to Manhattan to shop. And they're right. But for your dollar, this city boasts some of the best shops in the country. Everything you've ever wanted—and some things you didn't even know you wanted—are for sale here. First, there are the department stores. Macy's, 34th St. and Sixth Ave., and Bloomingdale's, 59th St. and Third Ave., are among the best. These stores are huge. But they're just department stores. The real finds are the small boutique shops, the ones that haven't hit your local strip mall.

If you have the money and you're looking to spend it on clothes, wander up and down Madison Avenue. Brooks Brothers, Gucci, Paul Stuart, Georgio Armani, and Polo/Ralph Lauren, to name a few, are all lined up for your shopping convenience. For more eclectic clothing at cheaper prices, head down to Greenwich Village. Eighth Street, just west of Broadway, is shoe-store heaven. At any number of stores on this street you can find clogs, platforms, even vintage go-go boots, all at reasonable prices. (If you do buy the go-go boots, the Village is a great place to find cheap vintage clothing to match. Try Cheap Jacks, 841 Broadway, or Love Saves the Day, 119 Second Ave.)

For the intermediate-size wallet, Manhattan's Upper West Side is also a great place to shop. On certain weekends in the spring and summer, Amsterdam Avenue turns into one big street fair, selling everything from pottery to overalls. Other weekends, local school playgrounds turn flea market.

For avid art collectors, SoHo is the place to go. Lined with galleries, the streets of SoHo offer the most interesting contemporary art. The district is bounded by Houston Street to the north, Lafayette Street to the east, MacDougal Street/Sixth Avenue to the west (MacDougal turns into Sixth Avenue about halfway through SoHo), and Canal Street to the south.

FITNESS AND RECREATION

For native New Yorkers, Central Park, an 843-acre park in the center of Manhattan, is the country. Weekday mornings and on weekends the park, which is bounded by Central Park West, Central Park South, Fifth Avenue, and 59th through 110th Streets, is packed with joggers, in-line skaters, soft-

LET THE BUYER BEWARE

Around Midtown and Times Square you'll come across a lot of electronic stores, usually with going-out-of-business or liquidation-sale signs plastered in their front windows. Don't be drawn into this— these stores are looking to rip off tourists. If you're really in the market for a new Walkman, be wary. Never accept the first price offered. Haggle down the price, and check to see if the equipment works before you walk out of the store. The same advice holds true for the "Diamond District" on West 47th Street. If jewelry is your thing, shop at Tiffany & Co., Fifth Avenue between 56th and 57th Streets. It will cost you a bit more, but at least you'll know what you're getting.

ball players, and dog walkers. But don't be fooled. Living in a concrete jungle, this is the best thing going, but for many of those visiting from rural America, Central Park is just a park, with a few too many homeless people sleeping on the benches and one too many old newspapers flying through the grass. But in the summer . . . the Delacorte Theatre, located in the center of the park, hosts "Shakespeare in the Park," a free evening performance with some of Hollywood's leading stars. Tickets are limited to two per person and are given out on the day of the performance only, so be prepared to arrive early and stand on a long line. But it's usually worth the wait. A series called "Summer Concerts" kicks off free concerts on the Great Lawn with the New York Philharmonic. Bring blankets and wine; this is a New York City happening worth attending. The Visitors Center at 65th Street, west of the Central Park Wildlife Conservation Center, is open Tuesday through Sunday 11 to 5. Warning: Although perfectly safe during the day, don't hang out in Central Park at night. For more information, call 888/NYParks or 212/360-3456.

On the Hudson River between 17th and 23rd Streets, a 30-acre space has recently been turned into a recreation area, the Chelsea Piers Sports and Entertainment Complex, 212/336-6666. Some highlights here are a driving range, the world's largest indoor track, ice skating, a 25-yard pool, and a 10,000-foot rock-climbing wall. The most fun is a Saturday morning roller-boogie class. The complex offers a ton of different classes and lessons on all sports.

Downtown, in Greenwich Village, Washington Square Park is a favorite among New York University students and unemployed artists. Fifth Avenue ends in the park, which is bound by Waverly Place to the north, University

MANHATTAN

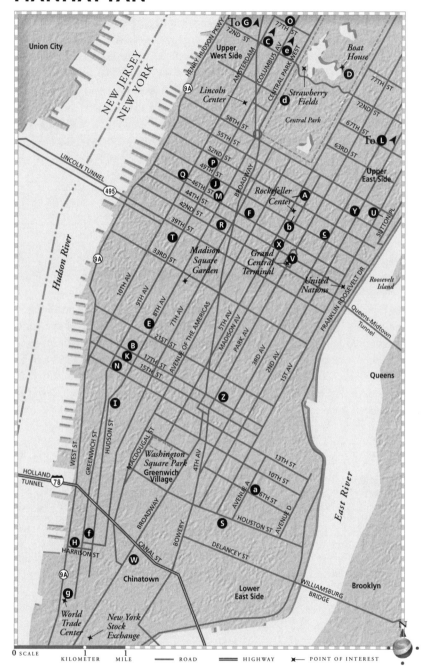

Union City

NEW JERSEY
NEW YORK

HENRY HUDSON PKWY

Hudson River

LINCOLN TUNNEL

495

9A

9A

WEST ST

GREENWICH ST

HUDSON ST

10TH AV

9TH AV

8TH AV

7TH AV

AVENUE OF THE AMERICAS

MACDOUGAL ST

BROADWAY

4TH AV

BOWERY

CANAL ST

HOLLAND
TUNNEL

78

HARRISON ST

Upper
West Side

72ND ST

AMSTERDAM

COLUMBUS AV

CENTRAL PARK WEST

To G ▲

C

O

e

Strawberry
Fields

d

Central Park

Lincoln
Center

77TH ST

72ND ST

67TH ST

63RD ST

Boat
House

D

To L ▲

Upper
East Side

58TH ST

55TH ST

52ND ST

P

49TH ST

Q

46TH ST

J

44TH ST

M

42ND ST

39TH ST

R

33RD ST

T

BROADWAY

5TH AV

MADISON AV

PARK AV

3RD AV

2ND AV

1ST AV

Rockefeller
Center

A

b

c

X

V

F

Madison
Square
Garden

Grand
Central
Terminal

United
Nations

Y

U

SUTTON PL

FRANKLIN ROOSEVELT DR

Roosevelt
Island

Queens-Midtown
Tunnel

Queens

21ST ST

17TH ST

15TH ST

E

B

K

N

I

Z

Washington
Square Park
Greenwich
Village

13TH ST

10TH ST

AVENUE A

6TH ST

AVENUE D

a

S

HOUSTON ST

DELANCEY ST

East River

f

H

g

World
Trade
Center

W

Chinatown

New York
Stock
Exchange

Lower
East Side

WILLIAMSBURG
BRIDGE

Brooklyn

N

0 SCALE

1
KILOMETER

1
MILE

ROAD   HIGHWAY   ✕ POINT OF INTEREST

Place to the east, MacDougal Street to the west, and West Fourth Street to the south. It's not uncommon to hear live music or see live performance art any day of the week at any hour. In the center of the park is a small amphitheater where many artists perform for coins in a guitar case, or just for fun. But again, as with all New York City parks, don't hang out here at night.

FOOD

Manhattan is a great place to eat. In every neighborhood, on every block, it's possible to find something to eat any time of the day or night. In certain neighborhoods, more often than not there is a diner or bodega on every corner. Street vendors sell hot dogs, pretzels, and hot nuts. There are bagel stores, sandwich shops, and coffeehouses. And there are restaurants, millions and millions of restaurants. It would be impossible to highlight all the great eateries. Most natives usually plan their meals by location. No matter where you're heading, or where you just came from, there's a great restaurant nearby.

For the Broadway area and Lincoln Center, and all points in Midtown, there are many high-priced, fancy restaurants. The **21 Club**, 21 W. 52nd St. (212/582-7200), was once a speakeasy and serves a mean cocktail along with American-style cuisine. **Café Un Deux Trois**, 123 W. 44th St., 212/354-4148, is large, loud, fun, and French. West 46th St. is known as Theater Row. Lit by gas lamps, this charming block between Eighth and Ninth Avenues is lined with restaurants on both sides. Among the most popular are **Orso**, 322

FOOD

- Ⓐ 21 Club
- Ⓑ Alley's End
- Ⓒ Barney Greengrass
- Ⓓ Boathouse Café
- Ⓔ Bright Food Shop
- Ⓕ Café Un Deux Trois
- Ⓖ Carmine's
- Ⓗ Chanterelle
- Ⓘ Cowgirl Hall of Fame
- Ⓙ Delta Grill
- Ⓚ El Cid
- Ⓛ Elaine's
- Ⓜ The Firebird
- Ⓝ Hog Pit

- Ⓞ Isabella's
- Ⓟ Island Burgers and Shakes
- Ⓠ Joe Allen
- Ⓡ John's Pizzeria
- Ⓢ Katz's Delicatessen
- Ⓣ Los Dos Rancheros Mexicanos
- Ⓤ March
- Ⓥ Michael Jordan's Steak House
- Ⓦ Montrachet
- Ⓧ Morton's of Chicago
- Ⓞ Museum Café

- Ⓝ Old Homestead
- Ⓜ Orso
- Ⓨ P.J. Clark's
- Ⓩ Pete's Tavern
- ⓐ Raga
- ⓑ Rainbow Room
- ⓒ Roettele A.G.
- ⓢ Smith and Wollensky
- ⓓ Tavern on the Green
- ⓔ The Terrace
- ⓕ TriBeCa Grill
- ⓖ Windows on the World

Note: Items with the same letter are located in the same area.

W. 46th St., 212/489-7212, and **Joe Allen**, 326 W. 46th St., 212/581-6464. **The Firebird**, 365 W. 46th St., 212/586-0244, is a beautifully decorated Russian restaurant, with ornate waiter costumes and homemade vodka. For something a little less expensive, **John's Pizzeria**, 260 W. 44th St., 212/391-7560, is a New York institution. There are John's all over the city; this particular pizzeria is in a former church, with stained-glass windows and high ceilings. And the pizza is a thin-crust coal-baked delight.

Heading east from the theater district are a trio of spectacular steak houses: **Morton's of Chicago**, 551 Fifth Ave., 212/972-3315 (also located downtown at 90 West St., 212/732-5665), **Smith and Wollensky**, 797 Third Ave., 212/753-1530, and the latest addition, **Michael Jordan's Steak House**, 23 Vanderbilt Ave., 212/271-2323, in the renovated Grand Central Station.

The Upper East Side may have more restaurants than people. One of the best is **March**, 405 E. 58th St., 212/754-6272. Located in a tony Sutton-area brownstone, the new American menu is very pricey but very worth it. Be sure to make a reservation.

Many people head down to **Windows on the World**, on the 107th floor at One World Trade Center, 212/524-7011, for an expensive meal with an incredible view of the city. For a not-so-crowded, not-so-"touristy" alternative, stay uptown. **The Terrace**, 400 W. 119th St., 212/666-9490, serves Mediterranean cuisine with the greatest of cityscapes on the side.

On the Upper West Side, **Isabella's**, 359 Columbus Ave., 212/724-2100, offers outside seating in the summer months and is a year-round local favorite. The **Museum Café**, 366 Columbus Ave. at 77th St., 212/799-0150, serves one of the best big salads in the city and is a great place to eat after spending hours inside the Museum of Natural History. The **Boathouse Café** in Central Park near 72nd St., 212/988-0576, is a great place to spend happy hour, if dinner there is out of your reach. Order the brie plate while you sip gin and tonics and gaze at the lake. For parties of six or more, **Carmine's**, 2450 Broadway, 212/362-2200, or 200 W. 44th St., 212/221-3800, is big fun. They serve Italian family-style, which means huge plates of delicious fattening food set in the center of the table and passed about until someone explodes. This place has nothing on ambiance—what it has is great food and reasonable prices.

Proceeding south on the West Side, past Midtown is Hell's Kitchen, between Ninth and Tenth Avenues from the 50s to the 40s. Renamed Clinton by Mayor Giuliani, this neighborhood has become a hot new spot for restaurants. (Be warned, though—it's hard to keep up with the restaurant scene in Manhattan, as new hot spots erupt every 6 to 12 months.) Check out the **Delta Grill**, 700 Ninth Ave., 212/956-0934, for New Orleans Cajun eats. Order the po' boy sandwich, definitely. **Island Burgers and Shakes**, 766 Ninth Ave., 212/307-

7934, could possibly be the best burger in town, with by far the best toppings. It may look like a Tijuana truck stop, but the food at **Los Dos Rancheros Mexicanos**, 507 Ninth Ave., 212/868-7780, is outstanding. These three restaurants and many you'll find in Hell's Kitchen are more reasonably priced, at least for Manhattan. You can also wander down Ninth Avenue, starting at 50th Street, and look at the menus posted in the windows. You'll rarely go wrong.

Manhattan's bodegas are a good bet to satisfy sudden hunger attacks. A bodega is a small market—nothing more than a small grocery store, really—with two or three aisles, crammed with most of what you'd find in a big grocery store, just fewer choices.

Last year's hot spot, and still loaded with tons of good restaurants, is Chelsea. **Alley's End**, 311 W. 17th St., 212/627-8899, is the most romantic spot, with a subterranean dining room, lush indoor garden, and simple French menu. **El Cid**, 322 W. 15th St., 212/929-9332, is more homespun, with a killer tapas menu. **Bright Food Shop**, 216 Eighth Ave., 212/243-4433, is a Chelsea staple. The Southwestern fusion fare is served in a glorified diner setting, but beware—it's not as cheap as it looks.

Potentially next year's trendy spot, the meatpacking district boasts **Old Homestead**, 56 Ninth Ave., 212/242-9040, the oldest steak house in New York City. Not to be missed if you're craving mama's home cooking is the **Hog Pit**, 22 Ninth Ave., 212/604-0092, where you'll find fat-laden staples like macaroni and cheese, fried chicken, and banana pudding to die for.

A couple of places worth checking out in the Village are **Chanterelle**, 2 Harrison St., 212/996-6960—very expensive, very French, and very delicious. **Montrachet**, 239 West Broadway, 212/219-2777, is very expensive, very French, and very very. (That last one means ultra hip.) The Indian fusion food at **Raga**, 433 E. Sixth St., 212/388-0957, makes this restaurant a funky stop. Try the samosas filled with goat cheese. Also downtown is **Roettele A.G.**, 126 E. Seventh St., 212/674-4140. With a Swiss-German menu and an outdoor garden, this is a must-stop for fabulous fondue. For a little homespun fun à la the Hog Pit, the **Cowgirl Hall of Fame**, 519 Hudson St., 212/633-1133, lets you enjoy excellent chicken-fried steak and margaritas while listening to Patsy Cline. It's a favorite local brunch spot.

The lowdown on some New York City favorites: **Tavern on the Green**, Central Park West at 67th St., 212/721-0068, has finally found a new chef who isn't half-bad. This dining staple, shown off in so many Hollywood movies, does have one of the best settings in the city, but the food isn't spectacular and the

MANHATTAN

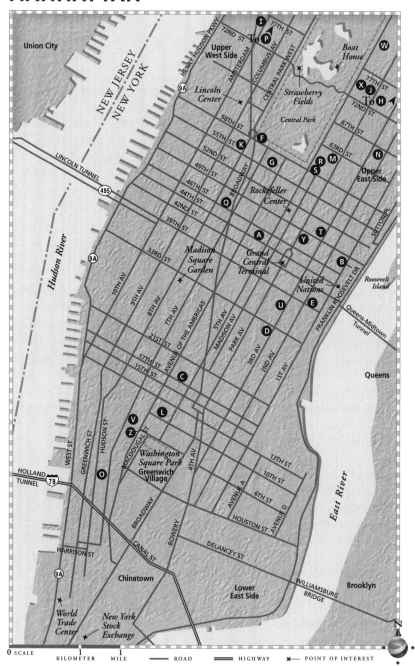

NEW JERSEY
NEW YORK

Union City

Hudson River

LINCOLN TUNNEL

495

9A

HENRY HUDSON PKWY

72ND ST

77TH ST

To

I

P

Upper
West Side

AMSTERDAM

COLUMBUS AV

CENTRAL PARK WEST

9A

Lincoln
Center

Strawberry
Fields

Boat
House

W

77TH ST

X

J

To

H

72ND ST

67TH ST

Central Park

58TH ST

55TH ST

K

52ND ST

F

63RD ST

R

M

N

49TH ST

BROADWAY

G

S

Upper
East Side

46TH ST

44TH ST

Rockefeller
Center

42ND ST

Q

39TH ST

SUTTON PL

33RD ST

A

Madison
Square
Garden

Grand
Central
Terminal

Y

T

B

9A

10TH AV

9TH AV

8TH AV

7TH AV

AVENUE OF THE AMERICAS

5TH AV

MADISON AV

PARK AV

United
Nations

FRANKLIN ROOSEVELT DR

Roosevelt
Island

U

E

Queens-Midtown
Tunnel

3RD AV

2ND AV

1ST AV

D

Queens

21ST ST

17TH ST

15TH ST

C

West St

Greenwich St

Hudson St

MACDOUGAL ST

V

L

Z

4TH AV

13TH ST

10TH ST

East River

O

Washington
Square Park
Greenwich
Village

6TH ST

HOLLAND
TUNNEL

78

BROADWAY

AVENUE A

AVENUE D

HOUSTON ST

HARRISON ST

CANAL ST

BOWERY

DELANCEY ST

9A

Chinatown

Lower
East Side

WILLIAMSBURG
BRIDGE

Brooklyn

World
Trade
Center

New York
Stock
Exchange

0 SCALE   1   1
    KILOMETER   MILE   ROAD   HIGHWAY   POINT OF INTEREST

N

prices are steep. The new chef is hoping to turn the menu around, but be cautious. Your dollar is paying for the name and the location. **Katz's Delicatessen**, E. Houston St. near Orchard St., 212/254-2246, gained fame in the movie *When Harry Met Sally*. Nowhere will you find a better pastrami on rye. **TriBeCa Grill**, 375 Greenwich St. at Franklin St., 212/941-3900, has garnered fame from its owner, Robert De Niro. Referred to by some as Miramax's cafeteria, this restaurant is as good as any if you're in the neighborhood but not worth a special trip. **Pete's Tavern**, 18th St. and Irving Place, 212/473-7676, is where O. Henry is said to have written "The Gift of the Magi." If you're a literary buff, definitely drop by for a drink. **P.J. Clark's**, 915 Third Ave., 212/759-1650, where many famous writers used to hang, was the setting for the classic hard-drinking film *The Lost Weekend*. It's a little run-down, but they serve a good burger and it is a New York institution. **Elaine's**, 1703 Second Ave., 212/534-8103, was notorious for attracting the literati and celeb crowd. You'll rarely see any celebrity under the age of 50 these days. Don't go for the food—it's nothing special—but some say it has nostalgia appeal. Don't miss **Barney Greengrass**, 541 Amsterdam Ave., 212/724-4707, for the best brunch in Manhattan. Act like a native and order a bagel with lox. If you're looking for expensive and romantic, avoid the **Rainbow Room**, 30 Rockefeller Center, 212/632-5000. This overpriced tourist attraction is about as romantic as Graceland. Head for March, Alley's End, or Firebird (listed above) instead.

P.S. Don't forget to eat in Chinatown. Anywhere, anytime, all the time. New Yorkers are fanatical about their bagels and Chinese food, and it shows.

LODGING

Manhattan hotels are expensive—there's really no getting around that. But some are more spendy than others. Beware of the too-cheap, which usually

LODGING

Ⓐ Algonquin	Ⓚ Hotel Newton	Ⓣ Plaza Fifty
Ⓑ Beekman Tower	Ⓛ Larchmont Hotel	Ⓤ Shelburne Murray Hill
Ⓒ Chelsea Inn	Ⓜ Lowell	Ⓥ Southgate Tower
Ⓓ Dumont Plaza	Ⓝ Lyden Gardens	Ⓦ Stanhope
Ⓔ Eastgate Tower	Ⓞ Mercer Hotel	Ⓧ Surrey Hotel
Ⓕ Essex House	Ⓟ New York International	Ⓨ The Waldorf-Astoria
Ⓖ Four Seasons Hotel	Youth Hostel	Ⓩ Washington Square
Ⓗ Franklin	Ⓠ Paramount	Hotel
Ⓘ Hotel Beacon	Ⓡ Pierre	
Ⓙ Hotel Carlyle	Ⓢ The Plaza	

equals seedy. For those willing to spend a buck, Manhattan is full of plush, high-style hotels. **The Plaza**, 768 Fifth Ave., between 58th St. and Central Park South, 212/759-3000, is a New York institution, with incredible views of Central Park. **Essex House**, 160 Central Park South, between Sixth and Seventh Aves., 212/247-0300, also has a great view of Central Park and two outstanding restaurants, Les Célébrités and Cafe Botanica. **The Waldorf-Astoria**, 301 Park Ave., 212/355-3000, is one of the city's most famous hotels. The **Pierre**, 795 Fifth Ave., at 61st St., 212/838-8000, was artist Salvador Dalí's favorite hotel. The **Four Seasons Hotel**, 57 E. 57th St., between Park and Madison Aves., 212/758-5700, designed by famous architect I. M. Pei, has wonderful spacious art deco rooms. The **Hotel Carlyle**, 35 E. 76th St., between Park and Madison Aves., 212/744-1600, is an elegant European-style grand hotel, with live cabaret performances in the Café Carlyle. The **Lowell**, 28 E. 63rd St., between Park and Madison Aves., 212/838-1400, gained fame as Madonna's favorite hotel. Rumor has it that the "gym suite" was built specifically for her. The **Stanhope**, 995 Fifth Ave., between 80th and 81st Sts., 212/288-5800, is located right across the street from the Metropolitan Museum.

For those looking for a hotel that's a little less expensive, **Manhattan East Suite Hotels** is a family-owned group of comfortable, moderately priced Midtown and Upper East Side suite hotels that all include fully equipped kitchens. Call 800/ME-SUITE or 212/465-3600 for reservations at any of the following hotels: **Beekman Tower**, 3 Mitchell Pl.; **Dumont Plaza**, 150 E. 34th St.; **Eastgate Tower**, 222 E. 39th St.; **Lyden Gardens**, 215 E. 64th St.; **Plaza Fifty**, 155 E. 50th St.; **Shelburne Murray Hill**, 303 Lexington Ave.; **Southgate Tower**, 371 Seventh Ave.; and **Surrey Hotel**, 20 E. 76th St. Also relatively moderately priced is the **Chelsea Inn**, 46 W. 17th St., between Fifth and Sixth Aves., 212/645-8989. The **Hotel Beacon**, 2130 Broadway, between 74th and 75th Sts., 212/787-1100, is in a great location. **Larchmont Hotel**, 27 W. 11th St., between Fifth and Sixth Aves., 212/989-9333, is a guest house in the West Village. You have to share a bathroom, but breakfast is included. **Hotel Newton**, 2528 Broadway, 212/678-6500 or 800/643-5553, offers reasonably priced rooms close to theaters. The recently renovated **Washington Square Hotel**, 103 Waverly Pl., at MacDougal St., 212/777-9515, is a favorite among visiting parents of NYU students. The rooms are a little shabby, but the location is in the heart of the hip Village.

For something with a little New York arrogance and attitude, try the fabulous **Paramount**, 235 W. 46th St., between Broadway and Eighth Ave., 212/764-5500. The rooms are small and the staff is gorgeous (tip: they hang out in the adjoining Whisky Bar after hours). The **Mercer Hotel**, 99 Prince St., at Mercer St., 212/966-6060, is a trendy boutique hotel that has recently opened a restaurant in the basement serving French food. This hotel is très chic and is consistently booked. The **Franklin**, 164 E. 87th St., between Lexington and Third Aves., 212/369-1000, is another prominent boutique hotel.

The historic **Algonquin**, as in Dorothy Parker and the Algonquin Round Table, 59 W. 44th St., between Fifth and Sixth Aves., 212/840-6800, has just undergone a $20 million renovation.

There are several bed-and-breakfast registries, including the **B&B Network of New York**, 212/645-8134 or 800/900-8134, and **New World B&B**, 212/675-5600 or 800/443-3800. But be careful—most of these accommodations, although quite charming, are not that much cheaper than a hotel stay. There is also the **New York International Youth Hostel**, 891 Amsterdam Ave., 212/932-2300.

NIGHTLIFE

The bright lights of Broadway are legendary. But so are the ticket prices and the sellouts. If you were to spend serious money on just one evening, this should be your choice. Broadway has long been known for its high standard of theater. Practically every actor in the industry has dreamed of one day making his or her Broadway debut. Purchase tickets way, way in advance for any show that has "been up" for less than a year, especially those that have won over the critics as well as the fans. Tickets are generally sold out up to one year in advance. Tickets for hot new shows will run approximately $80. For shows that have been running a while longer, or are not that popular, half-price day-of-performance tickets are sold at TKTS, on 47th Street between Broadway and Seventh Avenue and in the South Tower of the World Trade Center, between 3 p.m. and 8 p.m. for evening shows. TKTS accepts cash only, and be prepared to wait on a tremendously long line.

If you're unable to purchase Broadway tickets, more than two hundred off-Broadway and off-off Broadway houses often show equally great theater. Many popular Broadway productions actually started off-Broadway. For a listing of shows, check out the *Village Voice* newspaper or *The New York Times* theater listing.

The spectacular Lincoln Center, 63rd St. and Columbus Ave., is home to many world-renowned companies and performance venues. The New York Philharmonic plays in Avery Fisher Hall, 212/875-5030; and Alice Tully Hall, 212/875-5050, is an important place for chamber music. The New York City Ballet is based in the New York State Theatre, 212/870-5570, where the New York City Opera also performs. The Metropolitan Opera Company performs at the Metropolitan Opera House, 212/362-6000, as does the American Ballet Theatre.

For more culture, as if all that wasn't enough, Carnegie Hall, 212/247-7800, presents visiting orchestras, recitals, and chamber music. The City Center, 212/239-6200, is home to the Alvin Ailey American Dance Theatre, the Dance Theatre of Harlem, and the Merce Cunningham Dance Company.

If you're traveling during football season and want to catch your team in action, Manhattan offers a slew of sports bars. Boomer's Sports Club, 349 Amsterdam Ave., 212/362-5400, owned by former Jets quarterback and current Monday Night Football commentator Boomer Esiason, is one of the rowdier choices. Be sure to get there ahead of game time for a seat and order the wings. The Official All-Star Café, 1540 Broadway, 212/840-8326, has more than 60 television sets. At Sushi Generation, 1571 Second Ave., 212/249-2222, you can enjoy a pretty good spring roll while sitting on one of their leather couches and watching the game on their big-screen TV.

Club Macanudo, 26 E. 63rd St., 212/752-8200, could possibly be the best cigar bar in New York. Another popular cigar option is the Oak Room and Bar (at the Plaza), 768 Fifth Ave., 212/546-5330.

For a little live jazz, the Evelyn Lounge, 380 Columbus Ave., 212/724-5145, offers an intimate setting and an Upper West Side yuppie crowd to accompany the great music. Michael's Pub, 55th St. and Third Ave., is a favorite of Woody Allen, who shows up to play clarinet with the New Orleans–style jazz house band every Monday night. For music of a different sort—think Earth, Wind and Fire—Café Wha?, 115 MacDougal St., 212/245-3706, is a cabaret of fun, with one of the best house bands in the city. The Kit Kat Klub, 124 W. 43rd St., 212/819-0377, hosts the revival of the musical Cabaret (a huge Broadway hit), and then turns into the German nightclub after the last curtain call.

Bars on the Upper East Side and Upper West Side draw a mostly post-college yuppie crowd. The Village, with its downtown club scene, attracts NYU students, starving artists and musicians, and wanna-be hipsters from the suburbs. On occasion a great band will appear—check out the Village Voice or New York Magazine for a listing. Most dance clubs don't heat up until after midnight, and frankly they can be a little scary. (Too crowded, too young, too high.) Most will have a cover charge ranging from $10 to $20. It's best to go with a native New Yorker, which will up your odds for gaining entrance (not always easy) and getting served at the bar (sometimes nearly impossible).

Whatever you choose, make sure it's something that you could only experience in New York. There's plenty to go around, and it's all fabulous.

2
NEW YORK CITY'S
OUTER BOROUGHS

Brooklyn, Queens, Staten Island, and the Bronx make up the four other boroughs that total the City of New York. To be frank, Manhattan, the crown jewel, is where you want to spend your time. But the boroughs do have something to offer: space. Brooklyn, the largest of the boroughs, at more than 75 square miles, was the first to tender refuge to thousands of Manhattanites fleeing the island in search of an improved quality of life. Manhattan, although on an island, is no stranger to urban sprawl. For decades the outer boroughs have been home to many residents looking for more space, cheaper rent, and maybe a tree that Manhattan just can't grow.

The first borough, and the hardest hit by a 1980s wave of outward-bound Manhattanites, was Brooklyn. The rents in Brooklyn Heights, an area just past the Brooklyn Bridge and closest to Manhattan, reached epic proportions, as did those in the now tony Victorian-lined streets of Park Slope. But along with skyrocketing rents came a little culture, a little fine dining, and a little suburban community within a stone's throw of Wall Street.

Queens is home to Shea Stadium and the New York Mets, JFK and LaGuardia airports, and, for two weeks every summer, the U.S. Open tennis tournament. Staten Island is perhaps the most residential of the boroughs. Not much is there except houses. But it does stand out as the only borough not accessible from Manhattan by subway. To reach this borough you have to take a ferry.

Yankee Stadium is in the Bronx. Enough said.

NEW YORK CITY'S OUTER BOROUGHS

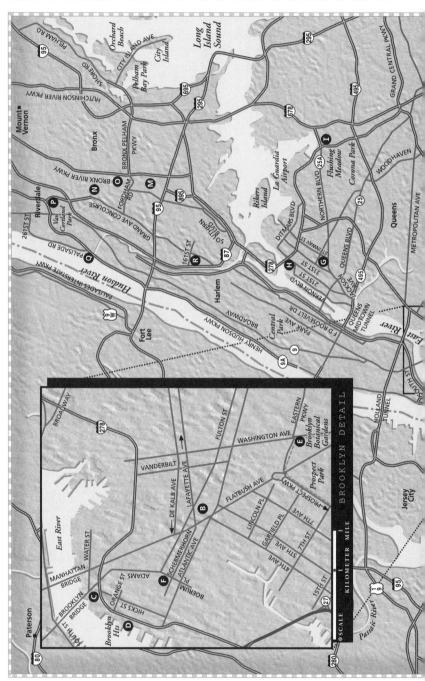

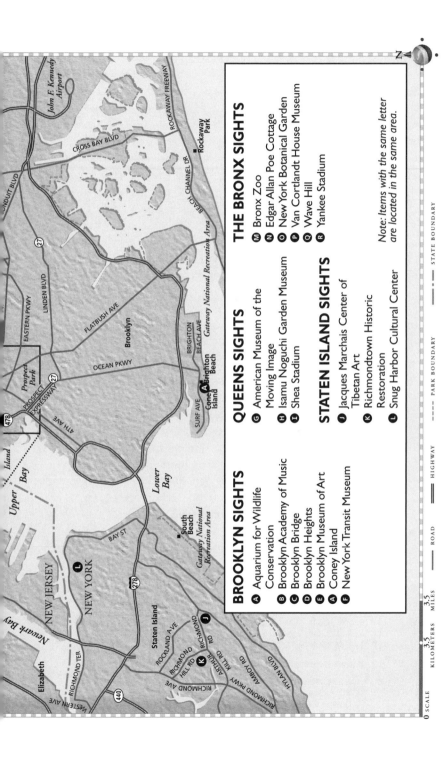

N

BROOKLYN SIGHTS

- Ⓐ Aquarium for Wildlife Conservation
- Ⓑ Brooklyn Academy of Music
- Ⓒ Brooklyn Bridge
- Ⓓ Brooklyn Heights
- Ⓔ Brooklyn Museum of Art
- Ⓐ Coney Island
- Ⓕ New York Transit Museum

QUEENS SIGHTS

- Ⓖ American Museum of the Moving Image
- Ⓗ Isamu Noguchi Garden Museum
- Ⓘ Shea Stadium

STATEN ISLAND SIGHTS

- Ⓙ Jacques Marchais Center of Tibetan Art
- Ⓚ Richmondtown Historic Restoration
- Ⓛ Snug Harbor Cultural Center

THE BRONX SIGHTS

- Ⓜ Bronx Zoo
- Ⓝ Edgar Allan Poe Cottage
- Ⓞ New York Botanical Garden
- Ⓟ Van Cortlandt House Museum
- Ⓠ Wave Hill
- Ⓡ Yankee Stadium

Note: Items with the same letter are located in the same area.

John F. Kennedy Airport

CROSS BAY BLVD

ROCKAWAY FREEWAY

Rockaway Park

BEACH CHANNEL DR

CONDUIT BLVD

27

LINDEN BLVD

EASTERN PKWY

FLATBUSH AVE

Brooklyn

OCEAN PKWY

BRIGHTON BEACH AVE

Brighton Beach

SURF AVE

Cone A
Island

PROSPECT EXPRESSWAY

27

4TH AVE

Prospect Park

478

Upper Bay

Lower Bay

Island

BAY ST

South Beach

Gateway National Recreation Area

Gateway National Recreation Area

NEW JERSEY

Ⓛ

NEW YORK

278

Staten Island

ROCKLAND AVE

RICHMOND RD

Ⓙ

RICHMOND HILL RD

Ⓚ

ARTHUR KILL RD

AMBOY RD

RICHMOND PKWY

RICHMOND AVE

HYLAN BLVD

440

WESTERN AVE

RICHMOND TER

Elizabeth

Newark Bay

0 SCALE

3.5
KILOMETERS

3.5
MILES

ROAD

HIGHWAY

- - - PARK BOUNDARY

STATE BOUNDARY

A PERFECT DAY IN THE OUTER BOROUGHS

Take the 4 subway on the East Side of Manhattan to Yankee Stadium. Watch the best team ever assembled play the game of baseball. Eat a hot dog. Go back to Manhattan.

Without tickets to a ball game or close friends in the area, there aren't many reasons to take time away from your sightseeing stops in Manhattan to see the outer boroughs. But if they're on your mind, head to Brooklyn. Start your morning off with a walk over the Brooklyn Bridge on the footpath for a great view and some strenuous exercise (one mile each way). Grab lunch in one of the restaurants on the tree-lined streets of Brooklyn Heights. (If you've been in Manhattan for a while, you might be missing trees.) Catch a show at the Brooklyn Academy of Music. Innovative musical and dance performances are the highlight of this borough. Dinner should follow at the famous Peter Luger Steakhouse, located at the foot of the Williamsburg Bridge. This is one restaurant Manhattanites will leave the island for.

SIGHTSEEING HIGHLIGHTS—BROOKLYN

★★★★ BROOKLYN BRIDGE
Access from Park Row in Manhattan and Cadman Plaza West in Brooklyn

"All modern New York, heroic New York, started with the Brooklyn Bridge," wrote Kenneth Clark. It was the first suspension bridge, and for more than 20 years the longest. The designers pioneered the use of steel-wire cable to support the suspension bridge, and the criss-crossing network gives it a spiderweb effect. The mile-long pedestrian pathway is a popular workout spot for walkers, joggers, bikers, and in-line skaters, with a steep incline and an awesome view.

Details: *The bridge is across the street from City Hall Park in Manhattan. Enter on the Manhattan side off Park Row. Enter from Brooklyn off Cadman Plaza West. To get to the bridge from the subway in Manhattan take 4, 5, or 6 line to Brooklyn Bridge/City Hall Station; the N or R line to City Hall; the 2 or 3 line to Park Place; the A, C, or E line to High Street. (30 minutes)*

★★★★ BROOKLYN HEIGHTS
Bounded by the East River, Fulton St., Atlantic Ave., and Court St.

THE BROOKLYN BRIDGE

New York Convention and Visitors Bureau

Just off the Brooklyn Bridge are the tree-lined streets of Brooklyn Heights, set on the bluffs above the East River. This 30-block area of brownstone dwellings became a National Historic Landmark in 1965. These history-filled streets are ideal for strolling. The area was a major stopping point on the Underground Railroad; at the **Plymouth Church of the Pilgrims**, on Orange and Hick Streets, Henry Ward Beecher delivered impassioned sermons against slavery before the Civil War. After the war he became the highest-paid preacher in the nation, and thousands arrived in Brooklyn in "Beecher boats" every Sunday to hear him.

The Heights have been home to some of the country's most famous literary figures, from Walt Whitman to Thomas Wolfe. Whitman lived here for 40 years and set Leaves of Grass in type himself in a print shop while he served as editor of the Brooklyn Eagle. The ferry ride to Manhattan inspired one of his best-known poems, "Crossing Brooklyn Ferry." Novelists Bernard Malamud and Joseph Heller were born here. Truman Capote lived in a basement apartment on Willow Place while writing Breakfast at Tiffany's and In Cold Blood. Hart Crane conceived his masterpiece, The Bridge, in Columbia Heights, the area in which Norman Mailer now lives. Henry Miller set parts of Tropic of Capricorn in the neighborhood, and Arthur

Miller wrote his Pulitzer Prize–winning play *Death of a Salesman* at 31 Grace Court. Thomas Wolfe wrote parts of *Of Time and the River* while living in this area.

The **Brooklyn Heights Promenade** with its breathtaking views of the Manhattan skyline has made numerous film appearances.

Details: Brooklyn Heights Promenade open daily; main entrance on west end of Court Street, other entrances on Montague Street and Atlantic Avenue. (2 hours)

★★★ AQUARIUM FOR WILDLIFE CONSERVATION
Coney Island Boardwalk, 718/265-FISH

Situated on 14 acres by the sea in Coney Island, the New York Aquarium is home to thousands of fish and a multitude of marine creatures, including beluga whales, sharks, walruses, and dolphins. Two highlights here are the Discovery Cove, an interactive exhibit in which you can walk through a salt marsh and touch sea stars, crabs, and urchins, and the Aquatheater, where you'll get splashed by Atlantic bottlenose dolphins.

Details: Open Mon–Fri 10–4; Sat, Sun, and holidays 10–6. Admission $8.75 adults, $4.50 seniors and children. (2 hours)

★★★ BROOKLYN ACADEMY OF MUSIC
30 Lafayette Ave., 718/636-4100

Referred to as BAM by its loyal patrons, the Brooklyn Academy of Music is a first-rate avant-garde experimental theater, home to the Brooklyn Philharmonic, the Brooklyn Opera Company, and various innovative music and dance programs. A shuttle bus leaves the Whitney Museum at Park Avenue and 42nd Street in Manhattan one hour before curtain time and returns after the performance, making several stops on both the east and west sides of Manhattan. The fare is $5 one way, and reservations are a must. The BAM Café serves dinner two hours before events.

Details: Ticket prices vary; call for information. (3–4 hours)

★★ BROOKLYN MUSEUM OF ART
200 Eastern Pkwy., 718/638-5000, www.brooklynart.com

This museum was the first in America to display African objects as art. Strongest in works from Central Africa, this is undoubtedly the largest and most important African art collection in the country. Also not to be missed is the world-renowned Egyptian art collection, specifically the chronological presentation ranging from 1350 B.C. and the reign of Akhenaten and his wife, Nefertiti, through the regime of Cleopatra VII. If you have time after the exhibits, take a stroll through the **Brooklyn Botanical Garden**, 718/622-4433, www.bbg.org, located next to the museum. The Garden's **Terrace Café** is open year-round.

Details: Museum open Wed–Fri 10–5, Sat and Sun 11–6, and the first Sat of every month 11–11. $4 adults, $1.50 seniors, $2 students, free to children accompanied by an adult. (2 hours)

★★ NEW YORK TRANSIT MUSEUM
Boerum Pl. and Schermerhorn St., Brooklyn Heights
718/243-3060
Transportation buffs and children of all ages enjoy this small museum that lets you travel back in time. It's filled with vintage cars, photographs, old turnstiles, and bus and subway memorabilia.

Details: Open Tue–Fri 10–4, Sat and Sun noon–5. $3 adults, $1.50 seniors and children under 17. (1 hour)

★ CONEY ISLAND
Coney Island Boardwalk, 718/265-2100
The glory days of this amusement park, when hundreds of thousands of people packed the park and the adjoining beach on the Atlantic on busy weekends, are long gone. However, if you visit the aquarium next door, a quick ride on the Cyclone, the park's 1927 roller coaster, would be worth the stop. But forget about spending a day here. Kids today are used to the size and scope of Epcot Center, Sea World, and Disneyland. To them, and to fans of amusement parks of all ages, Coney Island is old, small, and tired—not to mention dangerous once the sun goes down.

Details: Open daily Memorial Day through Labor Day noon–midnight; Easter Sunday to Memorial Day open weekends, noon–8. (15 minutes for the Cyclone, depending on the line)

SIGHTSEEING HIGHLIGHTS—QUEENS

★★ SHEA STADIUM
126th St. and Roosevelt Ave., 718/507-8499
www.mets.com

This 55,601-seat stadium is home to the New York Mets. Often overshadowed by the rival New York Yankees, the team advanced to the National League Championship Series in 1999, losing to the Atlanta Braves in one of the most thrilling series in recent memory. Ticket prices range from $10 to $25.

Details: *Game times vary, call for information. (3 hours on game days)*

★ **AMERICAN MUSEUM OF THE MOVING IMAGE**
35th Ave. and 36th St., Astoria, 718/784-0077
Opened in 1988, this museum is housed in a historic film-studio complex that once hosted Gloria Swanson, W. C. Fields, the Marx Brothers, and other early movie stars. It provides a comprehensive look at how movie images are made, marketed, and shown. Interactive stations give visitors firsthand experience of jobs such as sound editing, computer graphics design, bluescreen effects, automatic dialogue replacement, and animation. The work of cinematographers, TV directors, screenwriters, musical composers, and others is introduced through screenings of historic films and documentaries played on monitors and in mini-theaters.

Details: *Open Tue–Fri noon–5, Sat and Sun 11–6. $8.50 adults, $5.50 seniors and students, $4.50 children 5–18. (1 hour)*

★ **ISAMU NOGUCHI GARDEN MUSEUM**
3237 Vernon Blvd. at 33rd Rd., Long Island City
718/204-7088
This museum, which opened in 1985, is devoted entirely to the work of one artist, Isamu Noguchi (1904–1988). There are 12 galleries and an outdoor sculpture garden, with free films and tours offered daily at 2 p.m. On Saturday and Sunday a shuttle bus runs from Park Avenue and 70th Street in Manhattan ($5 round trip), every hour on the half-hour. No reservation necessary: first come, first served.

Details: *Open Apr–Oct Wed–Fri 10–5, Sat and Sun 11–6. Suggested donation $4 adults, $2 seniors and students. (1 hour)*

SIGHTSEEING HIGHLIGHTS— STATEN ISLAND

★★ **RICHMONDTOWN HISTORIC RESTORATION**
441 Clark Ave., 718/351-1611

This restored 100-acre village re-creates three centuries of local history. The buildings, moved from other areas of Staten Island and restored, range from a Dutch structure that doubled as a local church and schoolhouse to a general store packed with 1840s consumer goods. Guides dressed in period costumes provide insight into earlier times.

Details: *Open July and Aug Mon–Fri 10–5, Sat–Sun 1–5; rest of year Wed–Sun 1–5. $4 adults; $2.50 seniors, students, and children. (2 hours)*

★ **JACQUES MARCHAIS CENTER OF TIBETAN ART**
388 Lighthouse Ave., 718/987-3500
This large private collection of Tibetan art includes a wondrous stock of sculpted deities, ritual objects, incense burners, and other objects from the world's Buddhist cultures. The collection is housed in a stone cottage on Lighthouse Hill intended to replicate a Tibetan mountain temple.

Details: *Open Apr–Nov Wed–Sun 1–5; rest of the year by appointment Wed–Sun 1–5. $3 adults, $2.50 seniors and students, $1 children under 12. (1 hour)*

★ **SNUG HARBOR CULTURAL CENTER**
1000 Richmond Terr., 718/448-2500
Considered the city's fastest growing center of the arts, this 80-acre National Landmark District park includes more than 25 restored and converted historic buildings. The hospital, founded in 1801 as the nation's first maritime hospital and home for "decrepit and worn-out sailors," was built in the classical style of the period. Jazz, classical, chamber, and folk music concerts are held in the **Newhouse Center for the Arts**.

Details: *Grounds open daily during daylight hours. Free except for concerts, where prices vary. (2 hours)*

SIGHTSEEING HIGHLIGHTS—THE BRONX

★★★ **BRONX ZOO**
Fordham Rd. and Bronx River Pkwy., 718/367-1010
Officially called the Bronx Zoo/Wildlife Conservation Park to emphasize its role as a refuge for endangered species, this is the largest city

zoo in the nation. One of the first zoos to recognize that the animals both looked and felt better out in the open, its four thousand wild animals live in natural surroundings. The Wild Asia exhibit, with nearly 40 acres of wilderness through which elephants, antelopes, rhinoceroses, and sika deer roam, is viewable only on a narrated monorail ride. Visitors can explore the rest of the zoo by foot, aboard the safari train, or via the aerial tramway. At the Children's Zoo, kids learn about animals by acting as they do—climbing spiderwebs or crawling through prairie-dog tunnels. They can also pet and feed domestic animals.

Details: *Open Mon–Fri 10–5, Sat and Sun 10–5:30. $7.75 adults, $4 seniors and children 2–12. Free Wed. (3 hours)*

★★★ **YANKEE STADIUM**
161st St. and River Ave., 718/293-6000, www.yankees.com
This 57,545-seat stadium is home to the New York Yankees. This is the house that Ruth built (as in Babe Ruth). And wouldn't he and other Yankee legends like Roger Maris, Joe DiMaggio, Lou Gehrig, and Mickey Mantle be proud of the 1998 team—breaking the regular-season winning percentage and sweeping the San Diego Padres to win the World Series. With hardly a name changed from last year's roster, the Yanks won their twenty-fifth World Series title to close out the millennium.

Details: *Call for game days and times. Ticket prices $8–$29. (3 hours on game days)*

★★ **NEW YORK BOTANICAL GARDEN**
Zoo St. and Southern Blvd., 718/293-6000, www.nybg.org
There's a wonderful mixture of formal gardens, rock gardens, and a 40-acre virgin hemlock forest here. Within the last remaining primeval forest in the city is the Bronx River Gorge, best reached from the botanical garden's arched stone footbridge. The **Enid A. Haupt Conservatory**, a crystal palace of grand proportions, is full of flower delights, banana plants, palm trees, and cacti. This National Historic Landmark, which recently underwent a $25 million restoration, is modeled after the Palm House at the Royal Botanic Gardens in Kew, England. A 350-foot scenic pathway along the Bronx River offers a view of a waterfall.

Details: *Open Oct 15–May 14 Tue–Sun 9–4:30; May 15–Oct 14 Tue–Sun 9–5:30, Friday until dusk. $3 adults, $2 seniors and students, $1 children 2–12. (2 hours)*

★ EDGAR ALLAN POE COTTAGE
E. Kingsbridge Rd. at Grand Concourse, 718/881-8900
This 1812 house was occupied by the writer Edgar Allan Poe from 1846 to 1849. He moved here hoping that the country air would improve his wife's health. Sadly, she died of tuberculosis in that first winter, and Poe himself died three years later. He did, however, write some of his finest works here, including "Annabel Lee," "Ulalume," "The Bells," and "Eureka." The cottage contains a few of the couple's furnishings. An audiovisual presentation is shown.

Details: Open Wed–Fri 9–5, Sat 10–4, Sun 1–5. $2 adults, free to children under 12. (30 minutes)

★ VAN CORTLANDT HOUSE MUSEUM
Broadway and W. 246th St., Riverdale, 718/543-3344
This Colonial mansion in the heart of Van Cortlandt Park was the military headquarters for George Washington at various times. Built in 1748, it has been accurately restored and filled with period antiques.

Details: Open Tue–Fri 10–3, Sat and Sun 11–4. $2 adults, $1.50 seniors and students, free to children under 12. (30 minutes)

★ WAVE HILL
249th St. and Independence Ave., Riverdale, 718/549-3200
www.wavehill.org
This 28-acre Hudson River estate, where by turns Mark Twain, Theodore Roosevelt, and Arturo Toscanini lived, was given to New York by financier George Perkins in 1965. The nineteenth-century mansion now hosts chamber-music concerts, gardening and cooking workshops, botany lectures, tours of the extensive plant collection, and more. The gardens and greenhouses are extraordinary. This is a convenient stop if you are traveling up to Westchester or upstate.

Details: Open Oct 15–May 14 Tue–Sun 9–4:30; May 15–Oct 14 Tue–Sun 9–5:30, Fri until dusk. Mar 15–Nov 14 Wed–Sun $4 adults, $2 seniors and students. Free Tue all day and Sat 9–noon. Free Nov 15–Mar 14. (1 hour)

FITNESS AND RECREATION
Several parks in the outer boroughs are good for jogging and such if you happen to be there but aren't worth a special trip. Prospect Park (bounded by

NEW YORK CITY'S OUTER BOROUGHS

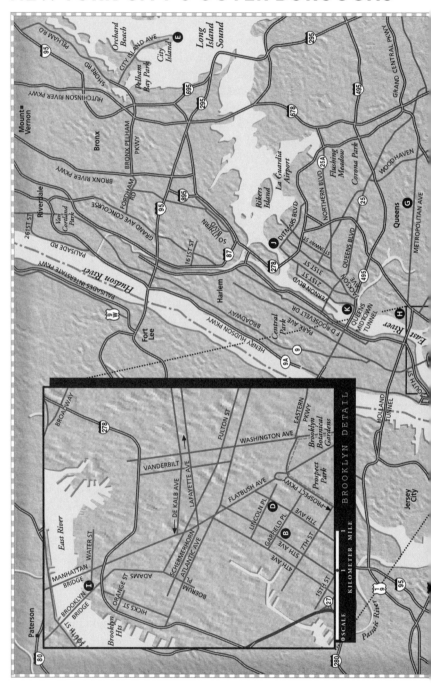

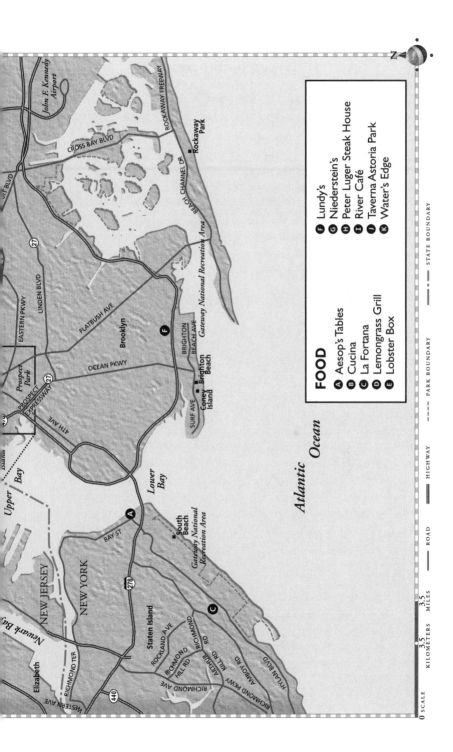

FOOD

- **Ⓐ** Aesop's Tables
- **Ⓑ** Cucina
- **Ⓒ** La Fortana
- **Ⓓ** Lemongrass Grill
- **Ⓔ** Lobster Box
- **Ⓕ** Lundy's
- **Ⓖ** Niederstein's
- **Ⓗ** Peter Luger Steak House
- **Ⓘ** River Café
- **Ⓙ** Taverna Astoria Park
- **Ⓚ** Water's Edge

SCALE

0   3.5 MILES

0   3.5 KILOMETERS

ROAD   HIGHWAY   ---- PARK BOUNDARY   ---- STATE BOUNDARY

N

SHOPPING IN BROOKLYN

Brooklyn is home to some of New York's funkier antique shops. The Attic, 220 Court St., 718/643-9535, specializes in Americana from the mid-1800s to the 1930s. Junk, 324 Wythe Ave., 718/388-8580, has a great selection of antique lamps, among other old trinkets. Victoria Station, 274 Court St., 718/522-1800, offers ceramics, china, and loads of vintage jewelry, all from the Victorian age. For vintage furniture, Ugly Luggage, 214 Bedford Ave., 718/384-0724, is a can't-miss. If they don't have it, they'll find it. Polka-dot beanbag chair, anyone?

Flatbush, Ocean, and Parkside Avenues) in Brooklyn was laid out by the same designers as Central Park and is located not that far from the Brooklyn Bridge. For a huge workout, go over the bridge, take a lap through Prospect Park, and cross back. In Queens between Grand Central Parkway and Van Wyck Expressway, Flushing Meadow Park, home to two New York World's Fairs, is a popular spot for locals. On Staten Island, South Beach has the 2.5-mile Franklin D. Roosevelt Boardwalk—a nice place to run, but stay out of the water. The 2,500-acre Greenbelt includes two major trails: the 8.5-mile Blue Trail and the White Trail. Both Staten Island parks are between Fort Wadsworth and Miller Field. At the Gateway National Recreation Area, park rangers lead nature tours. But really, who comes to New York City to hike? Pelham Bay Park, bounded by Bruckner Blvd., Eastchester Bay, Long Island Sound, and Hutchinson River Parkway in the Bronx, has two golf courses, but arrive early—they tend to jam up, especially on weekends. For more information about parks in all boroughs, call 888/NYParks or 212/360-3456.

FOOD

Brooklyn has two restaurants that consistently draw a Manhattan crowd. The **River Café**, One Water St., 718/522-5200, is perfectly situated under the Brooklyn Bridge. The elegant dining complements the dramatic view of the Manhattan skyline. **Peter Luger Steak House**, 178 Broadway, 718/387-7400, just rocks. But bring lots of cash: it's not cheap and it doesn't take credit cards.

Two Park Slope picks: **Cucina**, 256 Fifth Ave. at Garfield Pl., 718/230-0711, a favorite with locals, offers traditional Italian dishes in a rustic Tuscan atmosphere; and **Lemongrass Grill**, 61A Seventh Ave. at Lincoln Pl., 718/399-7100, boasts authentic Thai cooking. **Lundy's**, 1901 Emmons Ave. at Ocean Ave., Sheepshead Bay, 718/743-0022, is an old Brooklyn standby, serving huge portions of seafood. The **Water's Edge**, 44th Dr. at the East River, Long Island City, 718/482-0033, is a great spot in Queens, with an outside deck overlooking the Manhattan skyline. **Taverna Astoria Park**, 19-06 Ditmars Blvd., Astoria, 718/626-9035, has a tasty Greek menu, and **Niederstein's**, 69-16 Metropolitan Ave., 718/326-0717, serves traditional German dishes.

On Staten Island, **Aesop's Tables**, 1233 Bay St. just south of Hylan Blvd., 718/720-2005, has an outside patio for warm-weather dining on fresh fish, chicken, or chops. For Italian food, try **La Fortana**, 2879 Amboy Rd., 718/667-4343.

In the Bronx, you can watch the boats sail by while dining at the **Lobster Box**, City Island Ave. near Rochelle St., 718/885-1952. The restaurant is in a small white 1800s house where generations of the same family have been serving lobster some 10 different ways, along with other fresh seafood.

For dining in the outer boroughs, if you are staying in Manhattan note that the subways are not safe to ride after 10 or 11 p.m. Taxi fare from all restaurants, with the exception of the first two mentioned in Brooklyn, may cost you more than the actual meal. A car is more than a burden for those visiting Manhattan, and getting lost driving around the outer boroughs could land you in a dangerous neighborhood. If you're visiting friends or relatives in the area, they'll surely know where to dine.

LODGING

As mentioned above, taxi fare to the outer boroughs is outrageous. Although technically it is illegal for a cab driver to turn down a fare, in the real Manhattan it is very difficult to get a cab to take you over any bridge because chances are it will be forced to return empty. There really is no upside to lodging in any of the outer boroughs. The rates are no cheaper, and when you factor in the traveling expenses it might even cost you more. If you're visiting friends or relatives, stay with them. Free would be an upside to lodging in the outer boroughs.

For all lodging choices see the Lodging section in Chapter 1, Manhattan.

3
LONG ISLAND

Long Island is the largest and most varied island adjoining the continental United States. Technically, two of New York City's boroughs, Brooklyn and Queens, occupy Long Island's western section. However, the real Long Island begins only after leaving the city behind and crossing into Nassau County. East of Nassau is the more rural Suffolk County, with its two forks, north and south. From the Nassau/Queens border to the tip of Montauk Point, Long Island is 103 miles long.

There are many different Long Islands: the island of suburban sprawl and the notoriously congested Long Island Expressway; the rural island of farms and vineyards; the island of historic seaside villages; and the island of the rich and famous, on the North and South shores in the string of beachside villages known collectively as "the Hamptons," also called the "New York Riviera." The North Shore, home to a number of estates built by real-life Great Gatsbys, is lapped by Long Island Sound, which F. Scott Fitzgerald dubbed "the most domesticated body of salt water in the Western Hemisphere." Teddy Roosevelt's summer home at Sagamore Hill and Walt Whitman's birthplace are North Shore attractions.

Many of the South Shore attractions are beaches—at the grand oceanside Jones Beach State Park, on Fire Island, at the Hamptons, and at the end of the island at Montauk Point. Despite the monied summer visitors, most of the island's finest beaches are part of national, state, or county parks and are open to all. Many fishing world records have been set in the waters around Long Island.

A PERFECT DAY ON LONG ISLAND

Beach lovers have a wealth of choices on Long Island, and one of the best is Montauk Point. Located at the very tip of the island, it is bathed in a delicious feeling of remoteness. There are miles of beaches to explore in Montauk. For a breathtaking view of the sea, climb to the top of Montauk Point Lighthouse, the oldest in the state. This is also one of the prime areas for fishing, whether from the shore, on a party boat, or on a deep-sea fishing charter boat. Top off your day of fishing and beachcombing with fresh seafood at Gosman's Dock.

ORIENTATION

Car-ferry service is available year-round from Long Island between Connecticut and Rhode Island. **Cross Sound Ferry, Inc.**, Orient Point, 516/323-2743, provides service to New London, Connecticut. **Bridgeport & Port Jefferson Ferry Company**, Port Jefferson, 516/473-0286, provides service to Bridgeport, Connecticut. **Viking Ferry**, Montauk, 516/668-5709, provides passenger service to Block Island and Newport, Rhode Island, and to New London and Mystic, Connecticut.

Service to and from Shelter Island is available year-round for cars and passengers. **North Ferry Company**, Shelter Island, 516/749-0139, travels to Greenport. **South Ferry, Inc.**, Shelter Island, 516/749-1200, travels to North Haven, near Sag Harbor.

Several ferry companies travel to Fire Island—most during the April through October season. **Davis Park Ferry Co.**, Patchogue, 516/475-1665, www.pagelinx.com/ferries/, travels to Davis Park, Watch Hill, and Fire Island Seashore. **Fire Island Ferries**, Bay Shore, 516/665-3600, www.fireisland-ferries.com, travels to Saltaire, Ocean Beach, Atlantique, Kismet, Dunewood, Fair Harbor, Seaview, and Ocean Bay Park. **Sayville Ferry Service**, Sayville, 516/589-0810, www.pagelinx.com/ferries/, provides service to Fire Island Pines, Cherry Grove, Fire Island National Seashore, and Sailors Haven. **Sunken Forest Ferry Co.**, Sayville, 516/589-8980, wstg56a@prodigy.com, serves Sunken Forest and Sailors Haven.

SIGHTSEEING HIGHLIGHTS

★★★★ **FIRE ISLAND NATIONAL SEASHORE**
National Seashore Headquarters, 120 Laurel St., Patchogue, 516/289-4810, www.nps.gov/fiis

LONG ISLAND

N

Atlantic Ocean

Montauk Point State Park
D Montauk
Amagansett
East Hampton

Fishers Island

Gardiners Island

Plum Island

Orient
Greenport
Shelter Island
Sag Harbor
H (114)
Water Mill
Southampton
K

Shinnecock Indian Reservation

Long Island

Hampton Bays
Flanders
(24)
Westhampton
(27)

Mattituck

Wildwood State Park
Wading River
(25A)
(25)
Coram
(46)
Medford
(27)
Shirley
Smith Point County Park
A Fire Island National Seashore

Long Island Sound

Port Jefferson
(112)
Stony Brook
(347)
Hauppauge
(454)
Patchogue
C West Sayville
East Islip
Heckscher State Park
Robert Moses State Park

New London

New Haven

Bridgeport
(15)

King's Park
SUNKEN MEADOW
SAGTIKOS STATE PKWY
ROBERT MOSES PKWY

Sunken Meadow State Park
PKWY
West Islip

CONNECTICUT

Stamford
(95)

Centerport
L
Huntington Station
M
Bethpage
E
(110)
WANTAGH STATE PKWY
(135)
Merrick
B
Jones Beach State Park

NEW YORK

New Rochelle

Bayville
I (25A)
Oyster Bay
G
Westbury
Port Washington
(106)
F Garden City
Hempstead

White Plains

Sands Point
J
Port Washington
(101)
Jamaica
(25)
(678)

To New York
(295)
(95)

SCALE

0   17
KILOMETERS

0   17
MILES

→ POINT OF INTEREST

━━ HIGHWAY

──── PARK BOUNDARY

━━ ROAD

✈ POINT OF INTEREST

The National Seashore consists of four separate areas on Fire Island, comprising 32 miles of superb public beaches. Access to the Lighthouse area in the west and the Smith Point area in the east is by car. The National Seashore areas in the heart of the island, Watch Hill and Sailors Haven, can be reached only by water taxi, private boat, or ferry from Long Island in season. In between are clusters of small communities, but no roads. The National Park Service offers regular interpretive walks and programs ranging from lighthouse history to sing-alongs of old sea chanteys. There are Interpretive Centers at Sailors Haven, Watch Hill, and Smith Point.

The Sunken Forest in the Sailors Haven area of the seashore is the jewel of Fire Island. This forest is unlike any you have experienced. Imagine entering an eerie woodland of gnarled branches—a forest primeval and a botanical wonderland at the same time. A network of well-maintained boardwalks extends for a mile and a half through the forest. Ocean salt kills vegetation, so when the foliage reaches the height of the dunes it begins to grow horizontally instead of vertically. The result is a lovely, delicate canopy that forms a dark, cool respite from the hot sun. Elevated spots on the trail provide glimpses of ocean and bay, and from the boardwalk there's a trail to the beach. Farther east is Smith Point, the only federally designated wilderness area in the state. With the exception of a boardwalk trail for those with disabilities at Smith Point West, the wilderness is accessible only by foot.

Details: *Open daily. Free, but there is a charge for parking and for the ferries, which run May–Oct. (6 hours)*

★★★★ **JONES BEACH STATE PARK**
Ocean Dr., Wantagh, 516/785-1600 (516/221-1000 for concert schedules), www.nysparks.com

SIGHTS

Ⓐ Fire Island National Seashore
Ⓑ Jones Beach State Park
Ⓒ Long Island Maritime Museum
Ⓓ Montauk Point Lighthouse
Ⓔ Old Bethpage Village Restoration
Ⓕ Old Westbury Gardens
Ⓖ Planting Fields Arboretum and Coe Hall
Ⓗ Sag Harbor Whaling Museum
Ⓘ Sagamore Hill National Historic Site
Ⓙ Sands Point Preserve
Ⓚ Shelter Island
Ⓛ Vanderbilt Museum
Ⓜ Walt Whitman Birthplace State Historic Site

From its opening in 1929, everything about Jones Beach has been grand. It is the largest bathing facility complex in the world. It was the dream of Robert Moses, a man who loved to build and create. What can you say about a park with parking fields for 23,000 cars, a landmark water tower that holds 300,000 gallons of water, eight ocean bathing areas, 250 lifeguards, and two Olympic-sized pools? Five miles of ocean beach frontage and one-half mile of bay frontage have been developed for swimming. There are nearly 12,000 lockers and dressing rooms in the two bathhouses, 17 cafeterias and refreshment stands, three restaurants, and almost two miles of boardwalk.

Fishing is also popular here. The 11,200-seat Jones Beach Theatre opened in 1952 and hosts a variety of world-renowned performers each summer. The park can be very crowded on summer weekends, so arrive before 9 a.m. if possible. Otherwise, May and September can be beautiful and relatively uncrowded.

Details: *Open daily. $5 per car Memorial Day–Labor Day, weekends through mid-Oct. Free rest of year. (6 hours)*

★★★ MONTAUK POINT LIGHTHOUSE
Tip of SR 27, Montauk, 516/668-2544
www.montauklighthouse.com

This lighthouse is the oldest in the state, completed in 1796 on a spot where the British Royal Navy had maintained signal bonfires for its ships during the American Revolution. President George Washington authorized its construction. On November 5, 1797, Jacob Hand lit the wicks of 13 whale oil lamps and a light shone from the Montauk Point Lighthouse for the first time.

In 1987 the Coast Guard automated and leased the lighthouse to the Montauk Historical Society. The society maintains the lighthouse and the surrounding property, fighting an ongoing battle against erosion. Visitors can climb the 137 iron steps to the top of the old keeper's quarters. On a clear day the views of the East End, the distant shore of Connecticut, and Block Island off the coast of Rhode Island are breathtaking.

The Deep Hollow Ranch in Montauk, 516/668-2744, www.peconic.net/deephollow, claims to be the oldest cattle ranch in the country and offers horseback riding through four thousand acres of trails to the beach. There are lessons and pony rides for the young set.

WHALE-WATCHING TOURS

The Riverhead Foundation for Marine Research and Preservation, 516/369-9840, www.riverheadfoundation.org, offers day-long whale-watching cruises Wednesday through Sunday during July and August. The whale-watching boat sails from Montauk. While there are no guarantees, it is a rare boat that returns from the Atlantic Ocean without having spotted some whales. The foundation offers guided seal walks during the winter along the Montauk beaches.

Details: *Open Memorial Day–Columbus Day daily 10:30–6; Columbus Day–Nov weekends 10:30–5, Fri and Mon 10:30–4:30. $3 adults, $2.75 seniors, $1 children. Parking $4 Memorial Day–Labor Day, rest of year free. (1 hour)*

★★★ PLANTING FIELDS ARBORETUM AND COE HALL
Planting Fields Rd., Oyster Bay, 516/922-9201
coehall@worldnet.att.net

This was the home of William Robertson Coe, a British-born insurance magnate, from 1913 to 1955. The Arboretum encompasses 409 landscaped acres of greenhouses, gardens, and natural habitat. The Synoptic Garden's ornamental shrubs and small trees are arranged alphabetically and identified by botanical and common names and by family and country of origin. In the last years of his life, Coe planted the rhododendron park, one of the outstanding features of Planting Fields.

Coe Hall at Planting Fields, built in 1919, is one of the finest examples of Tudor Revival architecture in America. The home is furnished with sixteenth- and seventeenth-century pieces. The stained-glass windows came from Hever Castle, where British king Henry VIII's second wife, Anne Boleyn, once lived. The Buffalo Room contains murals of buffalo and Native Americans set against a Western landscape.

Details: *Arboretum open daily 9–5; Coe Hall open Apr–Oct daily 12:30–3:30. Admission Arboretum $4 per car; Coe Hall $3.50 adults, $2 seniors, $1 children. (2 hours)*

★★★ SAGAMORE HILL NATIONAL HISTORIC SITE
20 Sagamore Hill Rd., Oyster Bay, 516/922-4447
www.nps.gov/sahi

This rambling 23-room Victorian home was built by Theodore Roosevelt in 1884–85. He raised his six children here. "There could be no healthier and pleasanter place in which to bring up children than in that nook of old-time America around Sagamore Hill," he reflected. After overcoming childhood sickness, he loved tough physical challenges and joined his children in playing games, riding horseback, and hiking in the woods.

This was the summer White House during the Roosevelt presidential years and his permanent home from 1887 to his death in 1919. Roosevelt received his nomination for governor of New York, for vice president, and for president of the United States on the piazza of Sagamore Hill. In the library he met with ambassadors from two warring countries, Russia and Japan. When they emerged, they had agreed on a treaty ending the war. Roosevelt won the Nobel Prize for his role in the peace process. The house is filled with family possessions, including animal trophies shot during his world travels. The famous original teddy bear is in a place of honor in the nursery. The Orchard Museum, on the grounds, showcases family photos and shows a film about Roosevelt's life.

Details: Open mid-May–mid-Oct daily 9:30–5; rest of year Wed–Sun 9:30–4. $5 adults, free to children. Grounds and museum are free. Admission to house by guided tour only. Limited to 14 people. Reservations suggested on weekends. (2 hours)

★★ OLD BETHPAGE VILLAGE RESTORATION
Round Swamp Rd., Old Bethpage, 516/572-8400

This is a living-history museum that re-creates eighteenth- and nineteenth-century rural life. Homes, barns, stores, and other buildings from that period have been moved here from their original sites and restored. The buildings are populated with costumed interpreters who familiarize visitors with the domestic habits, social customs, and work styles of an earlier time. It's a veritable time machine.

When you enter the village you can exchange modern-day money for nineteenth-century paper scrip, which you can use to buy such old-fashioned items as birch beer, apple cider, pretzels, and penny candy in the tavern. Seasonal and holiday events are held throughout the year, including political campaigning, balloting, and victory celebrations in November for the 1848 elections.

Details: *Open Mar–Nov 15 Wed–Sun 10–5; rest of year Wed–Sun 10–4. Closed Jan–Feb. $6 adults, $4 seniors and children. (3 hours)*

★★ OLD WESTBURY GARDENS
70 Old Westbury Rd., Old Westbury, 516/333-0048
www.plantamerica.org/oldwestbury

This former home of financier-sportsman John S. Phipps and his family is one of the few intact great Long Island estates open to the public. It rivals the grandest manors in Europe with its splendid formal gardens, tree-lined avenues, and beautiful statuary. The Italian Garden boasts the largest expanse of herbaceous borders in the United States. The stately Georgian mansion, often the setting for movies and fashion layouts, reflects eighteenth- and nineteenth-century grandeur in architecture and furnishings.

Details: *Open Apr–Dec daily 10–5. $10 adults, $8 seniors, $6 children for mansion and gardens; $6 adults, $5 seniors, $3 children for gardens only. (2 hours)*

★★ SAG HARBOR WHALING MUSEUM
Main and Garden Sts., Sag Harbor, 516/725-0770

To get into this museum, visitors pass through the jawbones of a right whale. Once through the jaw, there are exhibits of whaling equipment, scrimshaw, oil paintings, ship models, fishing gear, logbooks, and other objects connected with Colonial eastern Long Island.

Details: *Open May–Sept Mon–Sat 10–5, Sun 1–5. $3 adults, $2 seniors, $1 children. (1 hour)*

★★ SANDS POINT PRESERVE
95 Middleneck Rd., Sands Point, 516/571-7900

This is one of the great estates of the North Shore. Built by Howard Gould, son of financier Jay Gould, this incredible property overlooking the Long Island Sound has many facets. It is a 216-acre nature preserve with six marked trails and one mile of beachfront. Falaise is a fully furnished French Normandy–style mansion that was the home of Captain Harry F. Guggenheim. Here, in the solitude of the ivy-covered villa, aviator Charles Lindbergh wrote *We*, an account of his historic adventures. Hempstead House is an English Tudor mansion.

FISHING ON LONG ISLAND

Captree State Park, 516/669-0449, is in the heart of the Long Island fishing grounds at the eastern tip of Jones Beach Island. It has been a fisherman's haven since the park opened in 1954. The park features a boat basin with charter boats available for fishing, as well as scuba diving, sightseeing, and excursion boats. There are also two wheelchair-accessible fishing piers. There are annual fishing contests and a bluefish surf-fishing tournament. There are many seabirds here as well as one of the largest nesting areas of herring gulls along the Atlantic coast.

Castlegould is an authentic 400-foot-long medieval castle with changing exhibits. A Medieval Festival is held on two weekends in mid-September.

Details: *Preserve open daily 8–5. $1 adults on weekends during the summer; free rest of year. Falaise open May–Oct for tours at noon, 1, 2, and 3. $5 adults, $4 seniors. No children under 10 allowed. Hempstead House open May–Oct Fri–Sun; $2. Castlegould open June–Labor Day; free. (2 hours)*

★★ SHELTER ISLAND
Shelter Island Chamber of Commerce, 516/749-0399 or 800/9-SHELTER

Nestled in the bay between Long Island's North and South Forks, Shelter Island has managed to remain sheltered from much of the development to the west. The island maintains a New England atmosphere and was one of the first areas of Long Island settled by the English. It was a haunt of eighteenth-century pirates and, during Prohibition, a favorite landing point for bootleggers who were smuggling in alcohol.

It is accessible by a ten-minute auto/passenger ferry ride from either Greenport to the north or from North Haven near Sag Harbor to the south. You can use the island as a scenic stepping stone to pass from one fork to another. There are white sandy beaches and protected harbors for boaters. The two-thousand-acre Mashomack Nature Preserve, with 12 miles of wild shoreline, occupies the entire southeast section of the island.

Details: *Ferry service is available year-round from N. Ferry Co., 516/749-0139, and S. Ferry Inc., 516/749-1200. (3 hours)*

★★ VANDERBILT MUSEUM
180 Little Neck Rd., Centerport, 516/854-5555
www.webscope.com/vanderbilt

The summer estate of William K. Vanderbilt II, the great-grandson of Commodore Cornelius Vanderbilt, is an ornate 24-room Spanish Revival mansion overlooking Northport Harbor and Long Island Sound. The Vanderbilt Museum is filled with specimens collected by Vanderbilt on three world cruises from 1926 to 1932, when he visited all of the world's seas and oceans. The planetarium, one of the

THE VILLAGE OF SAG HARBOR

The village of Sag Harbor retains the charm of its glory years in the 1800s, when it was one of the most productive whaling ports in the world. During this period the town was the source of many real and imagined heroes, including those of the sea stories of James Fenimore Cooper, who began his first novel here in 1824.

Its sheltered position between the North and South Forks of Long Island made Sag Harbor important from its earliest days. As early as 1707, it had assumed such stature as a port that the British Crown appointed an officer to stop the "running of illicit cargos into Sagg Harbour, the principal port of Long Island." In 1789 President George Washington signed the Act of Congress that created two ports of entry for the new nation. The first port was Sag Harbor; the second, New York City.

The stately homes of whaling merchants line Main Street, which terminates in the thousand-foot Long Wharf. Antique hunters have long since replaced whale hunters. Park your car and stroll down the back lanes. Stop at the Custom House on Main Street, the restored home of a customs officer and postmaster of Sag Harbor in the late 1700s and early 1800s.

LONG ISLAND

N

New London

Fishers Island

Montauk Point State Park

F Montauk

Plum Island

Gardiners Island

Orient

Greenport

Amagansett

G East Hampton

Shelter Island

J Shelter Island

Sag Harbor

M

(114)

C

N Southampton

Water Mill

H

Shinnecock Indian Reservation

Mattituck

Long Island

Hampton Bays

Flanders

(24)

O Westhampton

Atlantic Ocean

(27a)

Wildwood State Park

Wading River

Shirley

Smith Point County Park

Fire Island National Seashore

(46)

Coram

Medford

(27)

Patchogue

(25A)

D Port Jefferson

(112)

R

Stony Brook

(347)

E Hauppage

(495)

West Sayville

I King's Park

(454)

Hechscher State Park

B East Islip

ROBERT MOSES

Sunken Meadow State Park

I SUNKEN MEADOW

SAGTIKOS

STATE PKWY

PKWY

West Islip

PKWY

Robert Moses State Park

Centerport

Huntington Station

Bethpage

(110)

(25A)

K

(106)

Bayville

Oyster Bay

Old Westbury

(135)

Merrick

WANTAGH

STATE PKWY

Q

Jones Beach State Park

New Rochelle

Sands Point

A Port Washington

(101)

Garden City

P

Hempstead

(25)

White Plains

(95)

Jamaica

To New York

(295)

(678)

NEW YORK

CONNECTICUT

Bridgeport

New Haven

(15)

Stamford

(95)

Long Island Sound

largest in the country, is open to the public; its skyshows change three or four times a year.

Details: *Open Memorial Day–Labor Day Tue–Sun noon–5; rest of year noon–4. $8 adults, $6 seniors and students, $4 children. (2 hours)*

★★ WALT WHITMAN BIRTHPLACE STATE HISTORIC SITE
246 Old Walt Whitman Rd., Huntington Station
516/427-5240, www.nysparks.com/hist

Whitman, one of America's greatest poets, was born in 1819 in this humble farmhouse, built by his father in 1810. He spent his early childhood in this home, which is now a National Historic Landmark. Guided tours feature an audiovisual presentation. There's a good collection of nineteenth-century furnishings as well as changing exhibits of Whitman memorabilia, photographs, books, and excerpts from his writings and letters.

Details: *Open Wed–Fri 1–4, Sat–Sun 11–4. $3 adults, $2 seniors and students, $1 children. (1 hour)*

★ LONG ISLAND MARITIME MUSEUM
86 West Ave., West Sayville, 516/854-4974

Although the purpose of this museum is to protect and preserve the entire maritime heritage of Long Island, it highlights the history and lore of the oysterman. In an actual vintage oyster house, visitors can look at the gritty world of the Great South Bay oysterman, who

---

FOOD
- **Ⓐ** The Barge
- **Ⓑ** Chowder Bar
- **Ⓒ** Claudio's Restaurant
- **Ⓓ** Danford's Inn
- **Ⓔ** Gasho
- **Ⓕ** Gosman's Dock Restaurant
- **Ⓖ** Lobster Roll Restaurant
- **Ⓗ** Mirko's Restaurant
- **Ⓘ** Old Dock Inn
- **Ⓙ** Ram's Head Inn
- **Ⓚ** Steve's Pier I
- **Ⓛ** Three Village Inn

LODGING
- **Ⓜ** 1770 House
- **Ⓝ** Baron's Cove Inn
- **Ⓞ** Colonial Shores Resort
- **Ⓟ** Garden City Hotel
- **Ⓠ** Gateway Inn
- **Ⓡ** Gurney's Inn Resort & Spa
- **Ⓡ** Inn at Medford
- **Ⓢ** Montauk Yacht Club Resort & Marina
- **Ⓣ** Shelter Island Resort

Note: Items with the same letter are located in the same area.

culled and packed oysters along the bay from the late 1800s to the 1940s. There's a wonderful collection of small craft including oyster vessels, South Bay sailboats, and ice scooters. There's also an exhibit on the U.S. Life Saving Service, forerunner of the Coast Guard.

Details: *Open Wed–Sat 10–3, Sun noon–4. Donation. (1 hour)*

FITNESS AND RECREATION

Many sports can be enjoyed on Long Island, including surfing, scuba diving, canoeing, and kayaking. The miles of beaches beckon swimmers, runners, and walkers. The most challenging hiking trails are Long Island's two Greenbelt Trails. The Suffolk Greenbelt Trail snakes 34 miles along the shores of the Nissequogue and Connetquot Rivers, from Sunken Meadow State Park on Long Island Sound southward to Heckscher State Park on the Great Sound Bay. The Nassau Greenbelt Trail extends 22 miles from Cold Spring Harbor to Massapequa. On Fire Island, a 20-mile beachfront trail runs from Davis Park eastward to Smith Point. Known to hikers as the Fire Island Seashore Trail, local residents affectionately refer to this dirt road/sand trail as "the Burma Road."

FOOD

Long Island has restaurants that rival Manhattan's. More than four thousand dining establishments provide a wealth of choices. Many restaurants boast some of the freshest fish, oysters, and clams, and award-winning local wines. In the winter some restaurants operate on reduced schedules or close.

In Montauk, at the tip of the island, **Gosman's Dock Restaurant**, at the entrance to Montauk Harbor, 516/668-5330, offers a wide array of fish and a great view of the harbor. Lunch and dinner daily. On the road to Montauk, stop at the **Lobster Roll Restaurant** (locally known as LUNCH because of the big sign on the roof), 1980 Montauk Hwy., Amagansett, 516/267-3740, for great seafood, including the lobster roll. **Mirko's Restaurant**, Water Mill Square off Montauk Hwy., Water Mill, 516/726-4444, is one of the best in the Hamptons. Dinner daily. **Claudio's Restaurant**, Mina St., Greenport, 516/477-0627, in an 1840 National Historic Landmark building overlooking the waterfront, bills itself as the country's oldest same-family-run restaurant. Lunch and dinner daily. **The Barge**, 86 Orchard Beach Blvd., Port Washington, 516/944-9403, is located on a converted World War II munitions barge and offers great water views and food to match. Long Island duckling and other Continental fare are good choices at the **Ram's Head Inn**, 108 Ram Island Dr., Shelter Island, 516/749-0811, which is also a lovely country inn. Dinner daily. **Old Dock Inn**, 798 Old Dock Rd., Kings Park, 516/269-4118, is a seafood and steak house overlooking the Nissequogue River and the Long Island Sound. The food is indeed as good as the view. Lunch and dinner daily. **Danford's Inn**, 25 E. Broadway, Port Jefferson, 516/928-5200, adjacent to the ferry dock, offers fine dining overlooking the harbor. Lunch and dinner daily. The **Chowder Bar**, 123 Maple Ave., Bay Shore, 516/665-9859, next to the Fire Island Ferries, specializes in seafood. Open for lunch and dinner daily. **Gasho**, 356 Vanderbilt Motor Pkwy., Hauppauge, 516/231-3400, features Japanese hibachi cooking at your table in a replica of a four-hundred-year-old Japanese farmhouse (the real farmhouse is in Hudson Valley). Dinner daily. **Three Village Inn**, 150 Main St., Stony Brook, 516/751-0555, in a lovely Colonial inn overlooking the Stony Brook Harbor, features New England specialties. Lunch and dinner daily. **Steve's Pier I**, 33 Bayville Ave., Bayville, 516/628-2153, in the heart of Oyster Bay, specializes in fish and beef. Lunch and dinner daily.

LODGING

In resort communities, a two-night minimum stay is often required during summer weekends, and rates are usually higher during the summer season. Hotel, motel, bed-and-breakfast, and resort accommodations are plentiful throughout the island. In Montauk, **Gurney's Inn Resort & Spa**, 290 Old Montauk Highway, 516/668-2345, www.gurneysweb.com, offers a full spa and a magnificent oceanfront location. **Montauk Yacht Club Resort & Marina**, 32 Star Island, Montauk, 516/668-3100 or 888/MYC-8668, www.montaukyachtclub.com, boasts a full marina, resort facilities, and fine dining. The **1770 House**, 143 Main St., East Hampton, 516/324-1770, www.1770house.com, is a gem of a small inn, with a fine restaurant. **Colonial Shores Resort**, 83 W. Tiana Rd., Hampton Bays, 516/728-0011, has pool and waterfront cottages and suites with full kitchens. The **Shelter Island Resort**, 35 Shore Rd., Shelter Island, 516/749-2001, offers fine water views and a beach. **Baron's Cove Inn**, W. Water St., Sag Harbor, 516/725-2100, www.hamptonresorts.com, has its own marina. The **Garden City Hotel**, 45 Seventh St., Garden City, 516/747-3000 or 800/547-0400, is one of the most opulent on the island. The **Gateway Inn**, 1780 Sunrise Hwy., Merrick, 516/378-7100, is just minutes from Jones Beach and the Nassau Coliseum. The comfortable **Inn at Medford**, 2695 SR 112, Medford, 516/654-3000, is just five minutes from the Fire Island Ferries.

CAMPING

Most Long Island campgrounds beckon campers with the lure of the sea. Hither Hills State Park, SR 27, Montauk, 516/668-2554 or 800/456-CAMP, boasts 165 campsites just over the sand dunes from two miles of perfect white-sand beach. The 26-site Watch Hill campground on Fire Island, 516/597-6633, is accessible only by boat or ferry; contact Superintendent, Fire Island National Seashore, 120 Laurel St., Patchogue, NY 11772, 516/289-4810, for summer camping applications. The 69-site Hechscher State Park, East Islip, 516/581-4433 or 800/456-CAMP, promises more than three miles of frontage on Great Sound Bay. The 737-acre Wildwood State Park, Route 25A, Wading River, 516/929-4314 or 800/456-CAMP, has 322 sites, more than a mile of beach on Long Island Sound, and 10 miles of hiking trails.

4
THE HUDSON RIVER VALLEY

The river that Native Americans called "the water that runs two ways" has always exerted a powerful influence on people who live near it or travel along it. No other river in America, with the possible exception of the Mississippi, has played such a major role in the country's history. It formed the backdrop for critical battles of the Revolutionary War; it served as a major industrial waterway; it gave its name to an American school of landscape painting; it led to the birth of the first effective steamboat; and the river valley has probably inspired more ghost stories than any other part of the country. The Hudson has been designated an American Heritage River.

Native Americans had been thriving in this fertile valley for more than one thousand years when Henry Hudson sailed the *Half Moon* up the river in 1609 for the Dutch East India Company. From early Colonial days, the river's banks have been a setting for the display of wealth. Dutch patroons divided the valley into great estates. Later, other Europeans settled the area. The U.S. Military Academy was built at West Point in 1802 to train American army officers. The Vanderbilts, Rockefellers, Harrimans, and other moguls built massive country homes on the banks of the river. Much of this history is still visible today; visitors are invited to tour the grand estates of the "American aristocracy," to experience the special light that captivated artist Frederic Church, and to wander through the sleepy villages that inspired writer Washington Irving.

THE HUDSON RIVER VALLEY

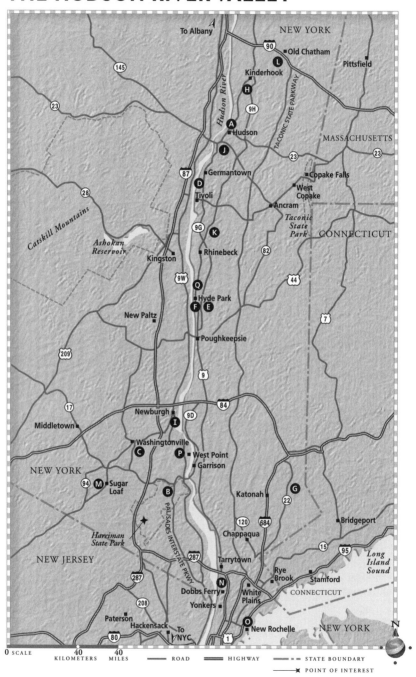

A PERFECT DAY IN THE HUDSON RIVER VALLEY

Start your day with a hike in Bear Mountain State Park. If the day is clear, walk or drive to the top of the mountain for spectacular river and mountain views. As you drive north there are a number of mansions and historic sites to visit—history buffs will enjoy Franklin D. Roosevelt's home at Hyde Park; those who want to revel in what wealth could buy in the late nineteenth century should be sure to see the nearby Vanderbilt Mansion. Stop for lunch at the Culinary Institute of America in Hyde Park. The Old Rhinebeck Aerodome stages wonderful shows on the weekends. Before or after the shows you can become a barnstormer yourself and take a ride in a 1929 open-cockpit biplane. The best choice for dinner and overnight is the Beekman Arms Hotel.

BOAT TOURS

The best way to appreciate the Hudson River is to take a ride on it. Half Moon Cruises offers river cruises daily from June through October from Verplanck, 914/736-0500. Riverboat Tours schedules sightseeing and dinner cruises from Poughkeepsie, 914/473-5211. Commander/Hudson Highlands Cruises and Tours offers cruises from West Point, 914/446-7171. Hudson River Adventures' two-hour cruises leave from Newburgh Landing, 914/782-0685.

SIGHTSEEING HIGHLIGHTS

★★★★ **FRANKLIN D. ROOSEVELT NATIONAL HISTORIC SITE**
U.S. 9, Hyde Park, 914/229-9115, www.nps.gov/hofr

SIGHTS

- **A** American Museum of Fire Fighting
- **B** Bear Mountain State Park
- **C** Brotherhood Winery
- **D** Clermont
- **E** Eleanor Roosevelt National Historic Site
- **F** Franklin D. Roosevelt National Historic Site
- **G** John Jay Homestead
- **H** Martin Van Buren National Historic Site
- **I** New Windsor Cantonment State Historic Site
- **J** Olana State Historic Site
- **K** Old Rhinebeck Aerodome
- **L** Shaker Museum
- **M** Sugar Loaf Art and Craft Village
- **N** Sunnyside
- **O** Thomas Paine Cottage
- **P** U.S. Military Academy
- **Q** Vanderbilt Mansion

Better known as Hyde Park, this is the 1826 home where Roosevelt was born and raised and later lived while he was president. FDR's home reveals much about this complex man. His bedroom is large and impressive, with sweeping views of the Hudson River and the distant Catskill Mountains. Reading material from his last days still rests on a desk in his bedroom. Within easy reach are two telephones, one secretly coded with a direct line to the White House. It was used many times during the dark days of World War II. The museum houses the original desk and chair used by FDR in the White House as well as drafts of some of his most famous addresses, including the "date which will live in infamy" speech after the Japanese attack on Pearl Harbor. The estate contains a walking trail and the graves of Franklin and Eleanor Roosevelt.

Details: Open daily 9–5. $10 adults, free to children under 17, $5 with Golden Pass, which is good for all national sites and parks. Pass costs $10 for 62 and older (lifetime membership); $50 for all other ages (one-year pass). Purchase at any national site. (1 ½ hours)

★★★★ **U.S. MILITARY ACADEMY**
SR 9W, West Point, 914/938-2638, www.usma.edu
West Point is America's oldest and most distinguished military academy. Situated on the bluffs overlooking the Hudson River, West Point has been the training ground for U.S. Army officers since 1802. Here you can walk the paths of Patton, Eisenhower, MacArthur, and Schwarzkopf. George Washington ordered a massive iron chain to be placed across the river at West Point to thwart the British during the American Revolution. Links of the Great Chain are preserved and on view at Trophy Point. Here also are cannons and relics of all American wars dating back to the Revolutionary War.

The best place to begin your visit to West Point is the visitors center, which includes displays on cadet life, a model cadet room (extremely neat), and a theater showing movies covering a cadet's four-year stay at the academy and the history of West Point. Just behind the visitors center is the West Point Museum, which contains an astounding collection of sixteenth- through twentieth-century arms, uniforms, flags, military art, and West Point memorabilia. A poster sums up the West Point experience: "At West Point, much of the history we teach was made by people we taught." The 4,500-seat Eisenhower Theatre is the second-largest theater in the East. Cadet parades are held throughout the spring and fall.

Details: Museum open daily 10:30–4:15; visitors center open daily 9–4:45. Free. (3 hours)

★★★ AMERICAN MUSEUM OF FIRE FIGHTING
125 Harry Howard Ave., Hudson, 518/828-7695
www.artcom.com/museums/vs/af/12534-b.htm
Your guide here will be one of the residents of the Volunteer Firemen's Home, on whose grounds this museum sits. The museum is filled with an amazing collection of firefighting equipment and paraphernalia, including the oldest piece of firefighting machinery in the United States: the Newsham engine, built in London in 1725. This contraption of wooden wheels and leather pipes arrived in New York in 1731 and served the people of Manhattan for 154 years. This is the oldest collection of firefighting equipment in the United States.
Details: Open daily 9–4:30. Free. (1 hour)

★★★ BEAR MOUNTAIN STATE PARK
Access via Pallisades Pkwy., Bear Mountain, 914/786-2731
www.nysparks.com
The large statue of Walt Whitman alongside the park's nature trail was erected to honor Mrs. E. H. Harriman, who rescued Bear Mountain and the surrounding lands from one of the most dunderheaded ideas ever: the state wanted to build a prison on top of Bear Mountain. Thankfully, the park was created instead, and the view has been preserved for all. Standing atop Bear Mountain on a very clear day, you can see Manhattan's skyline 45 miles to the south. Even if your view doesn't include Manhattan, it will include the Hudson River, Bear Mountain Bridge, and neighboring mountains and valleys. There's an extensive trail system here. Part of the Appalachian Trail passes through the Bear Mountain Nature Trail and Trailside Museum, which has the distinction of being the country's first state nature center. The self-guided Bear Mountain Trail is the oldest continuously run trail in the country. Other attractions include a lake with boats for rent, fishing, a zoo, a huge swimming pool set amidst gigantic boulders, sledding, ice skating, festivals, craft shows, and a lovely country inn.
Details: Take SR 9W south to Pallisades Pkwy. Open daily 8–dusk. $4 per car. (3 hours)

★★★ ELEANOR ROOSEVELT NATIONAL HISTORIC SITE
SR 9G, Hyde Park, 914/229-9115, www.nps.gov/elro

This converted factory is off a dirt road on the Hyde Park grounds. Even while her husband was president, Eleanor Roosevelt usually stayed overnight here rather than in FDR's home. Named Val-Kill for "valley stream," the building was converted into two apartments, one for Eleanor and the other for her secretary. After FDR's death she lived here full-time. Begin your visit by viewing the film *First Lady of the World*. Although the building is plain and simple on the outside, it is warm and comfortable inside. Here Eleanor entertained friends, family, and heads of state.

   Details: *Open May–Oct daily 9–5; Nov–Apr weekends 9–5. $5 adults, free to children under 17. (1 hour)*

★★★ **NEW WINDSOR CANTONMENT STATE HISTORIC SITE**
374 Temple Hill Rd., Vail's Gate, 914/561-1765
www.nysparks.com
This was the final encampment of Washington's army. More than 10,000 soldiers, cooks, blacksmiths, and other camp followers constructed the log cabins, outbuildings, and the meeting hall where Washington quelled a mutiny by troops who were upset over the slow payment of wages. The site features a visitors center, exhibits, artillery displays, and military demonstrations.

   Details: *Open Apr–Oct Wed–Sat 10–5, Sun 1–5. Free. (2 hours)*

★★★ **OLANA STATE HISTORIC SITE**
SR 9G, Hudson, 518/828-0135, www.nysparks.com
Olana is the dream home of Frederic Church, the most famous of the Hudson River School artists. It is also a fantastical 1870s Persian-style mansion on 250 acres. With his artist's eye Church pronounced "the views (from Olana) most beautiful and wonderful." Olana is derived from an Arabic word meaning "our place on high." Many of Church's best works are on display.

   Details: *Grounds open daily 8–dusk. House open for tours Apr 2–Nov 2 Wed–Sun 10–4. Reservations suggested for tours. $3 adults, $2 seniors, $1 children, grounds free and picnicking allowed. (1½ hours)*

★★★ **OLD RHINEBECK AERODOME**
42 Stone Church Rd., Rhinebeck, 914/758-8610
www.oldrhinebeck.org
Aviation buffs will love this place, which is filled with old planes dating back to the earliest days of aviation. If you visit the Aerodome

The Town of Hudson

Hudson, an historic river town, claims to be the oldest chartered city in the United States. In 1783, a group of seafaring men from Massachusetts and Rhode Island were seeking a safe harbor for their vessels because of attacks by the British navy. They purchased land and began settling the area. Despite its distance from salt water, it soon developed into a prosperous whaling center.

As befitting a port city, Hudson had a reputation as a very sinful place. In the 1950s, the city's image was so bad that Governor Dewey sent in the state police to clean up the town. With that mission accomplished, today Hudson is undergoing a revival as an antique center for the region. Antique-shop owners have been restoring the brick Federal period homes along Main Street. Banners proclaiming "antiques" flutter in the breeze.

This town is made for walking. An hour's worth of parking costs a nickel. Pick up a Hudson Walking Tour Guide at the Chamber of Commerce and take a walk down Warren Street, ending up at Promenade Hill, where you'll get a view of the river and Hudson-Athens Lighthouse.

Architectural historians have said that Hudson is one of the richest areas of architectural history in the state. Number 115 Warren Street is the Seth Jenkins House, built circa 1795. Seth Jenkins's father was the city's first mayor. Next door is the Robert Jenkins house, built in 1811. He also served as mayor. Stop at the beautifully restored Amtrak station just over the bridge from the river.

on weekends you can do more than admire the old planes. Air shows are held every Saturday and Sunday afternoon. Aircraft from the pioneer and Lindbergh eras show their stuff on some days, and on others Percy Goodfellow and the Black Baron engage in a mock dogfight and bombing raid in World War I aircraft. After the show the public is invited to take a ride in a 1929 open-cockpit biplane for a 15-minute spin over the Hudson Valley and a flashy series of wing-overs and dives.

Details: Open May 15–Oct 31 daily 10–5. Air shows mid-Jun–mid-Oct. $5 adults, $2 children; $10 adults for air show, $5 children. (3 hours for air show)

★★★ SUNNYSIDE
W. Sunnyside Lane, Tarrytown, 914/591-8763
www.hudsonvalley.org
This was the home of *The Legend of Sleepy Hollow* writer Washington Irving from 1835 to 1859. He called it his "little snuggery." The house was built in the late seventeenth century as a tenant farmer's cottage. Irving added Dutch-style stepped gables to the main part of the house, attached a Romanesque tower, and planted wisteria and ivy vines. The interior has features far advanced for their day, such as a bathtub with running water and a hot-water tank in the kitchen. Costumed guides explain the house and its furnishings, which include the author's library. Irving planted the trees and flowers on the grounds; picnicking is permitted.
Details: Open Apr–Sept Wed–Mon 10–5 (last tour at 4); Oct–Dec Wed–Mon 10–4 (last tour at 3). $8 adults, $7 seniors, $4 students and children. (1 hour)

★★★ VANDERBILT MANSION
U.S. 9, Hyde Park, 914/229-9115, www.nps.gov/vama
European royalty would feel at home in this "cottage" of Frederick William Vanderbilt, grandson of Commodore Cornelius Vanderbilt. The 54-room mansion, designed by Stanford White in 1895, was once described by *The New York Times* as "the finest place on the Hudson between New York and Albany." Like most prominent Hudson River families, the Vanderbilts used their retreat only for a few weeks in the spring and fall. Vanderbilt had a passion for tapestries, many of which adorn the walls. Mrs. Vanderbilt's bedroom is modeled after a French queen's bedroom of the Louis XV period. The white and gold railing around the bed recalls the custom of French queens and ladies of nobility, who would hold receptions in the morning while still in bed. The grounds provide sweeping views of the Hudson River.
Details: Open daily 9–5. $8 adults, free to children. (1 hour)

★★ CLERMONT
1 Clermont Ave., Germantown, 518/537-4240
www.friendsofclermont.org

This is the home of Robert Livingston, an early leader and the first chancellor of New York State. It is the focal point of a 450-acre state historic site. Originally built in 1730, the house was burned by the British during the Revolution and later rebuilt. Clermont is probably the only mansion to have a steamboat named after it—the very first steamboat that Robert Fulton docked at the chancellor's dock on its maiden voyage up the Hudson River in 1807. (Livingston and Fulton were partners in the steamboat business.) Seven generations of Livingstons lived here. There are formal gardens, and you can picnic along the banks of the river.

Details: Open Apr–Oct Tue–Sun 11–5; Nov–Dec 14 weekends 11–4. $3 adults, $2 seniors, $1 children. (1 hour)

★★ JOHN JAY HOMESTEAD
400 Jay St., Katonah, 914/232-5651

The Federal-style residence of the famous statesman and first chief justice of the U.S. Supreme Court is a State Historic Site. The restored period rooms tell the story of Jay, his family, and lifestyles in the new republic.

Details: Open Apr 15–Oct Wed–Sat 10–4, Sun and holidays that fall on Mon noon–4. $3 adults, $2 seniors, $1 children. (1 hour)

★★ SHAKER MUSEUM
88 Shaker Museum Rd., Old Chatham, 518/794-9100
www.shakermuseumoldchat.org

This museum displays the diversity of the Shaker genius. The vast majority of the collection was acquired by John S. Williams Sr. between 1935 and 1965, with the help of the Shaker leadership. The goal was to provide a complete picture of Shaker life and culture from as many Shaker communities as possible. On display are furniture, oval boxes, baskets, buckets, stoves, and machinery. Ann Lee, spiritual founder of the Shakers, directed her believers to "do all your work as though you had a thousand years to live on earth, and as you would if you knew you must die tomorrow."

Details: Open Apr 24–Oct Thu–Mon 10–5. $8 adults, $7 seniors, $4 children, $18 family. (2 hours)

★★ SUGAR LOAF ART AND CRAFT VILLAGE
Woods Rd. to White Oak Dr. on Kings Hwy. (County Rd. 13)
914/469-9181

This tiny village, founded in 1749, is a community of craftspeople. More than 65 shops, galleries, and restaurants, in buildings dating back to the 1700s and 1800s, line Main Street. Many craftspeople work in their shops, so visitors can watch works of art being created. Throughout the year there are special seasonal events, including concerts, a spring and fall festival, and a Christmas caroling and candle-lighting service complete with Santa.

Details: Most shops open Tue–Sun. (2 hours)

★★ THOMAS PAINE COTTAGE
983 North Ave., New Rochelle, 914/632-5376
www.mediapro.net/cdadesign/paine

In 1784, the year after the American Revolution ended, New York State granted Thomas Paine three hundred acres of land as a reward for his role in the war. The author of *Common Sense* was famous for his statement, "These are the times that try men's souls." The Thomas Paine Cottage was built in 1793 and originally stood atop a hill, but was relocated to its current site. Several authentic Franklin stoves are on display that were presented to Paine by Ben himself.

Details: Open May–Oct Fri–Sun 2–5. $3 adults, $1 seniors and children. (1 hour)

★ BROTHERHOOD WINERY
Brotherhood Plaza Dr., Washingtonville, 914/496-9101
www.wines.com/brotherhood

More than 160 years old, this winery bills itself as America's oldest. Guided tours of its cavernous underground cellars end in a wine-tasting; hors d'oeuvres are also served.

Details: Winery outlet open daily 11–6; tours May–Oct 11–5; Jan–Apr and Nov–Dec weekends noon–5. $4 adults, free to children. (1 hour)

★ MARTIN VAN BUREN NATIONAL HISTORIC SITE
1013 Old Post Rd., off SR 9H, Kinderhook, 518/758-9689
www.nps.gov/mava

Van Buren, the nation's eighth president, was born in the tiny village of Kinderhook and retired to Lindenwald, his home, after his defeat for a second term. He has the distinction of being the first president born under the U.S. flag. The mansion was built in 1797, and Van Buren enjoyed making home improvements. He was most proud of the indoor plumbing, complete with a Wedgwood porcelain toilet bowl.

Details: Open mid-May–Oct 31 daily 9–4:30; Nov–Dec 5 Wed–Sun 9–4:30. $2 adults, free to children. (1 hour)

FITNESS AND RECREATION

Runners who need inspiration should head for the U.S. Military Academy at West Point, where all the cadets seem to run rather than walk. Visitors can jog along the campus paths and trails. Bear Mountain State Park and adjoining Harriman State Park are good choices for hiking, running, cross-country skiing, snowshoeing, and swimming. Lake Taghkanic State Park is popular for hiking, swimming, and boating. Stony Kill Farm Environmental Education Center is a 756-acre center with a variety of programs as well as hiking and ski-touring trails.

FOOD

There is a wealth of fine dining establishments in this region. Two of the best are at the Culinary Institute of America, 433 Albany Post Rd., Hyde Park: the **American Bounty**, 914/471-6608; and **Escoffier**, 914/471-6608. Both serve lunch and dinner Tuesday through Saturday. **Crabtree's Kittle House**, 11 Kittle Rd., Chappaqua, 914/666-8044, in a two-hundred-year-old country house, is a delightful restaurant with an award-winning wine cellar of 10,000 bottles. Lunch and dinner daily. **Gasho of Japan**, 2 Saw Mill River Rd., Hawthorne, 914/592-5900, is a Japanese restaurant housed in an authentic four-hundred-year-old Japanese farmhouse (moved here from Japan) surrounded by lush Oriental gardens. Dinner daily. In Sugar Loaf, the **Barnsider Tavern**, Kings Hwy. (County Rd. 13), 914/469-9810, offers a simple menu in a rustic taproom with a glass-enclosed patio overlooking the crafts community. The historic **Beekman Arms**, 4 Mill St., Rhinebeck, 914/876-7077, has four dining areas, including the 1766 Tap Room where Washington and Jefferson dined; American regional fare dominates the menu by noted chef Larry Forgione. Lunch and dinner daily. In Kinderhook, the **Old Dutch Inn**, 8 Broad St., 518/758-1676, is in the heart of the village in an old-fashioned country inn serving lunch and dinner daily. The **Bird and Bottle Inn**, 1123 Old Albany Post Rd., Garrison, 914/424-3000, is another historic inn and dining room. All dinners are five courses and fixed price.

LODGING

The Hudson River Valley offers a wide variety of accommodations, including many historic inns and hotels. At the **Beekman Arms Hotel**, 4 Mill St.,

THE HUDSON RIVER VALLEY

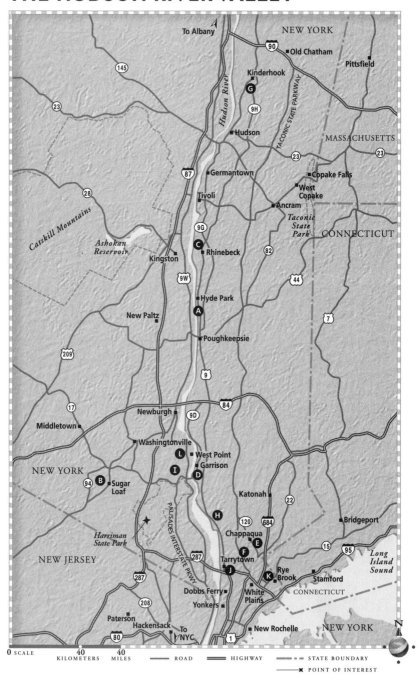

To Albany
NEW YORK
90
Old Chatham
Pittsfield
145
Kinderhook
G
23
9H
Hudson River
Hudson
MASSACHUSETTS
23
23
87
Germantown
Copake Falls
28
Tivoli
West Copake
Ancram
9G
Taconic State Park
CONNECTICUT
Catskill Mountains
Ashokan Reservoir
C
Rhinebeck
82
Kingston
9W
44
Hyde Park
New Paltz
A
7
Poughkeepsie
209
9
17
Newburgh
9D
84
Middletown
Washingtonville
L
West Point
I
Garrison
NEW YORK
94
B
Sugar Loaf
D
Katonah
22
H
Bridgeport
120
684
Harriman State Park
Chappaqua
15
95
NEW JERSEY
287
E
F
Long Island Sound
Tarrytown
J
Rye Brook
K
Stamford
287
Dobbs Ferry
White Plains
CONNECTICUT
208
Yonkers
Paterson
Hackensack
80
To NYC
New Rochelle
NEW YORK
1
N

0 SCALE   40   40
KILOMETERS MILES   ROAD   HIGHWAY   STATE BOUNDARY
                                          POINT OF INTEREST

Rhinebeck, 914/876-7077, www.beekmanarms.com, guests can stay in the original inn or choose from rooms in motel units, a house, a carriage house, or a restored townhouse. The **Hotel Thayer**, on the grounds of West Point, SR 9W, West Point, 914/446-4731 or 800/247-5047, www.hotelthayer.com, is an elegant historic hotel·steeped in tradition. Many rooms have views of the Hudson River, and the entire hotel recently underwent an extensive renovation. Nearby is the **Bear Mountain Inn**, in Bear Mountain State Park, SR 9W, Bear Mountain, 914/786-2731. There are rooms in the original chalet-style main inn overlooking Hessian Lake and in five newer lodges on the opposite side of the lake. **Doral Arrowwood**, Anderson Hill Rd., Rye Brook, 914/939-5500 or 800/22-DORAL, www.arrowwood.com, is in a country-club setting on 114 wooded acres with full resort facilities, including indoor and outdoor pools, tennis courts, and a golf course. The **Tarrytown Hilton**, 455 S. Broadway, Tarrytown, 914/631-5700 or 800/HILTONS, is in a 10-acre garden setting with full resort facilities including a jogging trail. In Croton-on-Hudson, the **Alexander Hamilton House**, 49 Van Wyck St., 914/271-6737, www.alexanderhamiltonhouse.com, is an historic bed-and-breakfast with a pool and always-available, chocolate-chip cookies. The **Tarrytown House**, E. Sunnyside Lane, Tarrytown, 914/591-8200 or 800/678-8946, is a member of Historic Hotels of America and has complete meeting and resort facilities. The **Castle at Tarrytown**, 400 Benedict Ave., Tarrytown, 914/631-1980 or 800/616-4487, www.castleattarrytown.com, is a Norman-style structure that was originally the

George Washington really did sleep here, and so did Thomas Jefferson and Franklin D. Roosevelt. Beekman Arms Hotel has welcomed travelers since 1766 and bills itself as America's oldest hotel.

FOOD

- Ⓐ American Bounty
- Ⓑ Barnsider Tavern
- Ⓒ Beekman Arms
- Ⓓ Bird and Bottle Inn
- Ⓔ Crabtree's Kittle House
- Ⓐ Escoffier
- Ⓕ Gasho of Japan
- Ⓖ Old Dutch Inn

LODGING

- Ⓗ Alexander Hamilton House
- Ⓘ Bear Mountain Inn
- Ⓒ Beekman Arms Hotel
- Ⓙ The Castle at Tarrytown
- Ⓚ Doral Arrowwood
- Ⓛ Hotel Thayer
- Ⓙ Tarrytown Hilton
- Ⓙ Tarrytown House

Note: Items with the same letter are located in the same area.

estate of Spanish-American War general Howard Carroll. The 31 luxury units, including suites and many rooms, have woodburning fireplaces. The castle is a member of Relais & Chateaux and offers fine dining.

CAMPING

Several state and private campgrounds dot the Hudson River Valley; call 800/456-CAMP for reservations at state campgrounds. The Beaver Pond Campground at Harriman State Park, SR 106, Bear Mountain, 914/947-2792, has two hundred campsites and boating, swimming, and fishing. Lake Taghkanic State Park, SR 82, Ancram, 518/851-3631, has 60 campsites, swimming, fishing, and boating. Taconic State Park, SR 22, Copake Falls, 518/329-3993, offers 112 campsites, swimming, and fishing. Oleana Campground, SR 22, West Copake, 518/329-2811, features 325 campsites, swimming, and fishing.

5
THE CATSKILLS

Although the Catskills are not the highest of American mountain ranges, they are the most visited, painted, and written about. Much of their fame is a result of their proximity to New York City and to the millions of people who leave the city looking for a nearby respite.

The Catskills have many faces: the "Borscht Belt" Catskills, home to enormous Jewish resorts where many stars, including Danny Kaye, Sid Caesar, and Jerry Lewis, got their first breaks (most of these resorts have now closed); the fly-fishing Catskills, home to some of the country's most renowned trout streams; the hiking Catskills; and the Catskills of old, filled with history and romance. Washington Irving brought the romance of the region to the world in his 1819 tale of Rip Van Winkle. "These fairy mountains," as Irving called them, took on a new image because of his story. Rock 'n' roll fans and the '60s generation still make pilgrimages to Bethel, home of the Woodstock Festival.

Like the Adirondacks, part of the Catskills are "forever wild," and, since 1885, they have been maintained as the Catskill Forest Preserve. Today the Catskill Park encompasses 705,500 acres and includes the Forest Preserve and towns and villages within the park boundaries. South of the Catskill Mountains are the Shawangunk Mountains, commonly called "the 'Gunks." Five lakes are hidden here, along with hundreds of miles of hiking trails. Geologically, the Shawangunks are not part of the Catskills—they are 100 million years older. But the 'Gunks are one with the region.

THE CATSKILLS

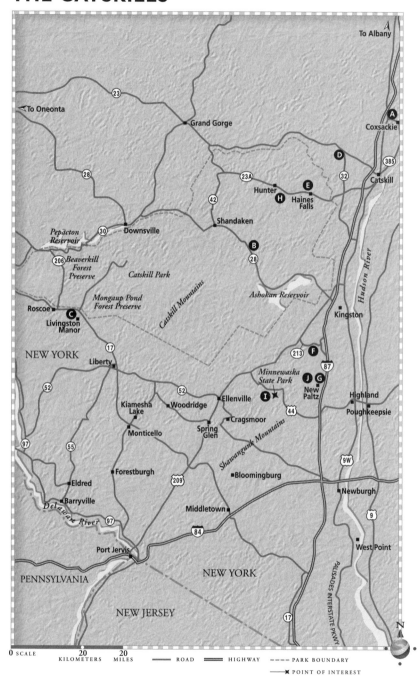

To Albany

To Oneonta

23

Grand Gorge

A Coxsackie

D

385

28

23A

42

Hunter

H Haines Falls

E

32

Catskill

Pepacton Reservoir

30

Downsville

Shandaken

206 Beaverkill Forest Preserve

Catskill Park

B

28

Mongaup Pond Forest Preserve

Catskill Mountains

Ashokan Reservoir

Hudson River

Roscoe

C

Livingston Manor

Kingston

NEW YORK

17

Liberty

213

F

87

52

52

Minnewaska State Park

J

G

Kiamesha Lake

Woodridge

Ellenville

I

New Paltz

Highland

44

Poughkeepsie

Monticello

Spring Glen

Cragsmoor

97

55

Shawangunk Mountains

9W

Forestburgh

209

Bloomingburg

Newburgh

Eldred

Barryville

Middletown

9

Delaware River

97

84

West Point

Port Jervis

PENNSYLVANIA

NEW YORK

PALISADES INTERSTATE PKWY

NEW JERSEY

17

N

0 SCALE   20 KILOMETERS   20 MILES   ——— ROAD   ═══ HIGHWAY   ---- PARK BOUNDARY   —✕ POINT OF INTEREST

A PERFECT DAY IN THE CATSKILLS

Fly-fishing enthusiasts will surely want to start their day at one of the many famed Catskill trout streams. On a clear day head for one of the celebrated lookout points; Catskill Mountain House Site is certainly spectacular. The Mohonk Mountain House is like a fairy-tale castle and befits the romantic aura of the Catskills. It's a favorite with most everyone who has seen it. The miles and miles of trails at Mohonk offer wondrous views around almost every turn. Nearby Huguenot Street in New Paltz is a testament to the seventeenth-century settlers of the region and their ability to create homes for the ages.

SIGHTSEEING HIGHLIGHTS

★★★★ CATSKILL CORNERS
SR 28, Mount Tremper, 914/688-2451, 888/303-3936
www.catskillcorners.com
This amazing complex is the brainchild of Dean Gitter, who has been called the P.T. Barnum of the Catskills. The centerpiece of this development is the Kaatskill Kaleidoscope, the world's largest kaleidoscope, as certified by the *Guinness Book of World Records*. The kaleidoscope is inside a 60-foot-high silo. There's a 40-foot tube of mirrors onto which a video of three thousand images drawn from American history, ranging from the Pilgrims to Elvis, blend and multiply into streams of geometric patterns. Leaving the silo, visitors will find themselves in the Kaleidostore with a dazzling display of . . . kaleidoscopes, of course—ranging in price from 50 cents to $2,500. Kaleidoworld consists of hundreds of additional viewing devices including "The Amazing Dondoakahedron," a 50-foot horizontal scope in which a 60-point star suspended in space reflects video images of galaxies and stars that are furnished by the Hubble Space Telescope.

SIGHTS

- **A** Bronck Museum
- **B** Catskill Corners
- **C** Catskill Fly Fishing Center and Museum
- **D** Catskill Game Farm
- **E** Catskill Mountain House Site
- **F** Delaware and Hudson Canal Museum
- **G** Huguenot Street
- **H** Hunter Mountain
- **I** Minnewaska State Park
- **J** Mohonk Mountain House

Bald Eagle Watching

If you are visiting during the winter from December through March, some wondrous sights await you if you travel north on SR 55 in Sullivan County—bald eagles.

Great wings outstretched, a bald eagle soars over the open water of the Mongaup Reservoir, giving the group of observers a brief sighting before it dives behind the tall pines. The number of eagles wintering here in the Upper Delaware watershed has grown steadily in recent years, and Sullivan County now boasts the largest wintering population of bald eagles in the Northeast. The phenomenon of eagle watching has grown accordingly.

The eagles migrate here primarily from Canada, attracted by the sight of open fresh water. They can have their fill of fresh fish, then perch in the pines among large tracts of undisturbed land, including 12,000 state-owned acres managed strictly for the eagles' protection. Bald eagles have even been known to fly over Wendy's Restaurant in downtown Monticello. **The Eagle Institute** was founded in 1998 to work for the protection of the bald eagle and other birds of prey. Institute-trained volunteers are available each weekend during the prime viewing season—January through March—to assist visitors and to remind them of good eagle etiquette. Remember that movement, noise, loud colors, and car lights are upsetting to the birds. In 1999 a record 179 bald eagles were counted in the Upper Delaware watershed. **The Mongaup Valley Wildlife Management Area**, just below Monticello, was created in 1990 when the state bought the 12,000 acres as a reserve for the bald eagle. It is the best place to see eagles in New York State.

The complex also contains Tom's Crystal Palace, a mirrored room with interactive kaleidoscopes geared to kids and an exhibition of light sculptures using fiber optics and neon. All of these are housed in a collection of lovingly restored nineteenth-century structures.

The Festival Marketplace sells works created by Woodstock-area artists and has a pair of themed restaurants: the family-oriented Spotted Dog Firehouse Restaurant and the spectacular Catamount Café with a deck nestled over the Esopus Creek, one of the country's best trout-fishing streams. Visitors may stay overnight at The Lodge at Catskill Corners.

Details: *Open daily June–Labor Day 11–7, rest of year closed Tue. $6 for Kaleidoscope, $10 adults for Kaleidoworld (which includes Kaatskill Kaleidoscope), $8 seniors and children. (2 hours)*

★★★★ CATSKILL MOUNTAIN HOUSE SITE
Haines Falls

One of the most spectacular views in all the Catskills is from this site, a hotel that is no more. James Fenimore Cooper called it "the greatest wonder of all creation." Artist Thomas Cole, founder of the Hudson River School, felt that this "grand diorama" was far too sublime for him to paint. They were talking about the view from the then world-famous Catskill Mountain House, one of the most beloved hotels in nineteenth-century America. Everyone who was anyone stayed here. The hotel lasted into the twentieth century but then fell into slow decline and was burned to the ground by the state in 1963. Today all that is left is a commemorative marker on the site. But the view remains. Walk along the escarpment to enjoy the vistas.

Details: *At Haines Falls take a right on SR 18 at the sign for North Lake State Campsite. There you can get a map to the Mountain House Site. (1 hour)*

★★★ BRONCK MUSEUM
Pieter Bronck Rd. off SR 9W, Coxsackie, 518/731-8862

This was once home to nine generations of the Bronck family, who gave their name to the Bronx. The original structure is a 1663 stone house. The 1738 brick house is connected to the stone house and is now used to display paintings by eighteenth- and nineteenth-century artists including Frederic Church and Thomas Cole. Each of the three barns represents a different era. A walk through the family cemeteries can bring you closer to the people who made the Bronck complex a working farm.

Details: *Open last Sun in June–Sun before Labor Day Tue–Sat 10–5, Sun 2–6; Labor Day–Oct 15 Tue, Sat, and Sun noon–4. $4 adults, $3.50 seniors, $2 children. (1 hour)*

★★★ CATSKILL GAME FARM
400 Game Farm Rd., Catskill, 518/678-9595
www.catskillgamefarm.com

One of the oldest and most popular game farms in the country, the Catskill Game Farm is home to more than two thousand animals, including lions, tigers, and bears. Special shows feature pigs, elephants, and monkeys. The petting zoo is a popular area for young children. A small train transports visitors from one section to another, including an amusement park and picnic and play area.

Details: *Open Memorial Day–Labor Day daily 9–6, May 1– Memorial Day and day after Labor Day–Oct 31 weekends 9–6, weekdays 9–5. $13.95 adults, $11.75 seniors, $9.95 children. (3 hours)*

★★★ HUGUENOT STREET
Visitors center, 18 Broadhead Ave., New Paltz
914/255-1889

Considered the oldest street in America with its original houses, Huguenot Street's stone houses were built between 1692 and 1712. The Huguenots were French Protestants who were persecuted in their native country by the Catholic majority. They came here in pursuit of freedom and tolerance. In 1677, 12 of their number purchased these lands from the Esopus Indians and built log huts. As they prospered they decided to build more permanent dwellings. And permanent they were.

The six houses and the 1717 stone church are owned by the Huguenot Historical Society. The dark rooms of the 1692 Abraham Hasbrouck House include a cellar kitchen and a built-in Dutch bed. The Jean Hasbrouck House once served as a store and tavern. Four of the six homes are wheelchair accessible.

Details: *Visitors center open June–Oct Tue–Sun 9–3. $7 adults, $6 seniors, $3.50 children. (2 hours)*

★★★ HUNTER MOUNTAIN
SR 23A, Hunter, 518/263-4223 or 800/775-4641
www.huntermtn.com

Hunter Mountain bills itself as the "snowmaking capital of the world." The ski resort was born January 9, 1960, defying expert advice that the mountain would never become a major ski center. Despite these dire predictions, the average ski season here is 162 days, with skiing on 47 slopes and trails. Skiboarding, tubing, and snowshoeing are other popular winter activities. Hunter Mountain is a multiple-season center of activity, hosting the Patriot Festival, the German Alps Festival, the Hunter Country Music Festival, Rockstalgia, the International Celtic

CALLICOON CENTER

Callicoon Center is home to Apple Pond Farming Center on Hahn Rd., 914/482-4764, an educational and working farm that uses old-fashioned horse-drawn equipment and organic farming methods. The farm is located on a rocky hillside with lovely views of neighboring mountains and valleys. Visitors ride around the site on a wagon, and sleigh rides may be arranged in the winter. The farm is stocked with sheep, draft horses, goats, cows, and border collies whose dedication to their task of sheepherding is a wonder to behold. There are workshops and clinics on carriage driving and wool spinning, a petting farm, and a gift shop with Native American crafts and lambskin products. A guest house is available for overnights, weekends, or longer. Families can arrange for a family farm vacation.

Festival, the National Polka Festival, the Mountain Eagle Indian Festival, and Oktoberfest during the summer/fall season. The Skyride, the longest and highest chair lift in the Catskills, operates from spring through the fall to offer splendid views.

Details: Open daily 9–4. $44 adult ski-lift ticket on weekends, $37 adult ski-lift ticket mid-week (packages available). (6 hours)

★★★ MOHONK MOUNTAIN HOUSE
Lake Mohonk, New Paltz, 914/256-2197
www.mohonk.com

Twins Alfred and Albert Smiley established the Mohonk Mountain House in 1869. More than 7,500 acres in the heart of the Shawangunk Mountains surrounding the fairy-tale castle-hotel have been preserved. The property has numerous skiing and hiking routes that are open to non–hotel guests on a day-pass basis. Cross-country skis can be rented. The sprawling Victorian hotel sits on trout-stocked Lake Mohonk, a half-mile-long lake. From the observation point known as Sky Top Tower, there are stunning panoramic views. The hotel and surrounding lands were named a National Historic Landmark in 1986.

Details: Open 7–one hour before dusk. $9 adults ($12 weekends and holidays), $25 for family ($32 for family weekends and holidays). (5 hours)

★★ CATSKILL FLY FISHING CENTER AND MUSEUM
5447 Old Rt. 17, Livingston Manor, 914/439-4810
flyfish@velacom.com

This place is for fly fishermen and -women. At the library and Hall of Fame of Fly Fishing, learn about the people who made Catskill dry fly-fishing famous. The art gallery showcases the many paintings of fly-fishing scenes, rods, reels, and examples of hand-tied flies. Special appearances by well-known anglers and craftspeople take place during the high season. Wheelchair accessible.

Details: Open Apr–Sept daily 10–4; Oct–Mar Mon–Fri 10–1. $3 adults, $1 seniors and children. (1 hour)

★★ MINNEWASKA STATE PARK
SR 44, Minnewaska, 914/255-0752, www.nysparks.com

This 11,000-acre preserve is in the heart of the Shawangunk Mountains. There's a superb network of 50 miles of walking and hiking trails. Just a few minutes from the park's information booth is Awosting Falls, where the foaming waters of the Peters Kill tumble over a sheer cliff into a deep pool. Lake Minnewaska itself is surrounded by a network of woodland trails and carriageways that are excellent for hiking, horseback riding, and cross-country skiing. The paved carriageways are great for biking. Swimming is permitted at the sandy beach area of the lake and on Lake Awosting.

Details: Open daily 9–dusk. $5 per car from late June–Labor Day; $4 per car during spring and fall. During the winter, charges per person for skiers are $4 adults, $2 seniors, $3 children. On weekends and holidays, charges are $5 adults and seniors, $4 children. (4 hours)

★ DELAWARE AND HUDSON CANAL MUSEUM
23 Mohonk Rd., High Falls, 914/687-9311
www.canalmuseum.org

This museum is dedicated to the history and lore of the 108-mile Delaware and Hudson Canal, built in the early nineteenth century. The canal was used to ship coal from the mines of Pennsylvania to the factories of New York. Conceived by the designer of the Erie Canal, the locks were an engineering wonder of their day. Exhibits depict life along the canal and activity on the canal boats. A self-guided tour of the locks is available.

Details: Open May 30–Labor Day Mon and Thu–Sat 11–5, Sun 1–5; May 1–29 and the day after Labor Day–Oct Sat 11–5 and Sun 1–5. $2 adults, $1 children. (1 hour)

FISHING

It has been said that God created the Catskills for the trout fisherman. This is the birthplace of dry fly fishing. There are more than five hundred miles of prime trout streams in the Catskills. Esopus Creek, with its excellent trout water, is a tributary of the Hudson. Schoharie Creek flows into the Mohawk. The Neversink, Beaverkill, Willowemoc, East Branch, and West Branch belong to the Delaware River drainage system. These are the main trout streams of the Catskills. In addition to the extraordinary trout streams, the Catskills boast another unique fishing resource: New York City's water reservoirs. Six bodies of water make up this unusual reservoir system. They are the Ashokan, Cannonsville, Neversink, Pepacton, Rondout, and Schoharie reservoirs. Bathing, swimming, and wading are prohibited in the reservoirs, as are all boats except rowboats with a special permit. The Beaverkill Angler School of Fly-Fishing, in Roscoe, which calls itself "Trout Town USA," 607/498-5194, offers classes along the banks of the legendary Willowemoc and Beaverkill rivers.

FITNESS AND RECREATION

The Catskills offer a rich array of hiking, walking, and skiing opportunities. The Mohonk Mountain House has 128 miles of paths and carriage roads to hike and cross-country ski. Minnewaska State Park also has many miles of excellent trails. The trails in the North Lake area in Greene County are renowned for their fantastic views of the Hudson Valley. Kaaterskill Falls and the Catskill Mountain House are particularly scenic hiking trails. More experienced hikers enjoy Devil's Path, named for its steepness. The path passes over rugged terrain, particularly Indian Head Mountain and the West Kill Mountain Range Trail. At 4,040 feet Hunter Mountain is the second-highest peak in the Catskills and has good hiking trails.

FOOD

Dining opportunities are plentiful in the Catskills region. Hotels that operate on all-inclusive plans also welcome meal guests. During the off-season some

THE CATSKILLS

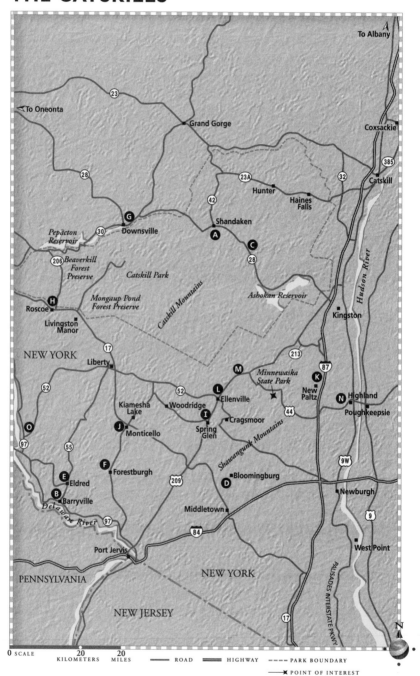

To Albany

To Oneonta

23

Grand Gorge

Coxsackie

28

385

23A

32

Catskill

Hunter

42

Haines
Falls

G

Downsville

Shandaken

A

C

Pepacton
Reservoir

30

28

Hudson River

206 Beaverkill
Forest
Preserve

Catskill Park

Ashokan Reservoir

H

Mongaup Pond
Forest Preserve

Catskill Mountains

Kingston

Roscoe

Livingston
Manor

NEW YORK

17

213

Liberty

M

Minnewaska
State Park

87

K

52

52

L

Ellenville

New
Paltz

N

Highland

Kiamesha
Lake

Woodridge

I

44

Poughkeepsie

J

Spring
Glen

Cragsmoor

O

Monticello

Shawangunk Mountains

9W

55

F

Forestburgh

209

D

Bloomingburg

97

E

Eldred

Newburgh

B

Barryville

Middletown

9

Delaware River

97

84

West Point

Port Jervis

PENNSYLVANIA

NEW YORK

PALISADES INTERSTATE PKWY

N

NEW JERSEY

17

0 SCALE   20   20
           KILOMETERS   MILES   ——— ROAD   ═══ HIGHWAY   ---- PARK BOUNDARY
                                                          ——✕ POINT OF INTEREST

operate with restricted hours and days. The **Roscoe Diner**, Old Rt. 17, Roscoe, 607/498-4405, is a long-time favorite that offers Greek specialties and delicious homemade desserts. Breakfast, lunch, and dinner daily. **Eldred Preserve Restaurant**, SR 55, Eldred, 914/557-8316 or 800/557-FISH, specializes in fresh trout. Open for lunch and dinner daily June through August and limited days in the off-season. The **Inn at Lake Joseph**, 400 St. Joseph Rd., Forestburgh, 914/791-9506, offers fine dining in a lovely setting. Lunch and dinner daily. **Eagle's Nest Hotel**, Mountain Rd., Bloomingburg, 914/733-4561, specializes in German and Continental cuisines. Lunch and dinner daily. The **Bridge Restaurant**, SR 97, Barryville, 914/557-6088, overlooks the Delaware River at Roebling's Bridge. Lunch and dinner daily. The **Old Schoolhouse Restaurant**, Main St., Downsville, 607/363-7814, serves traditional fare in a former schoolhouse. The bar is in the former first-grade classroom. Lunch and dinner daily. **Auberge des 4 Saisons**, SR 42, Shandaken, 914/688-2223, serves fine French country cuisine for dinner daily. The **Catamount Cafe**, SR 28, Mt. Tremper, 914/688-7900, part of the Catskill Corners development, offers fine dining overlooking the famed Esopus Creek. Dinner daily and Sunday brunch.

LODGING

From small rustic inns to dude ranches to huge sprawling resorts, the Catskills have it all. It's hard to match the wonder of the **Mohonk Mountain House**, Lake Mohonk, New Paltz, 914/255-1000 or 800/772-6646, www.mohonk.com, which is a mountaintop Victorian castle and National Historic Landmark. It has welcomed guests since 1869. There are 85 miles of hiking and skiing trails and other activities including horseback riding and golf. The **Nevele Grand Hotel**, Nevele Rd., Ellenville, 914/647-6000 or 800/647-6000, www.nevele.com, is

---

FOOD

Ⓐ Auberge des 4 Saisons
Ⓑ Bridge Restaurant
Ⓒ Catamount Cafe
Ⓓ Eagle's Nest Hotel
Ⓔ Eldred Preserve Restaurant
Ⓕ Inn at Lake Joseph
Ⓖ Old Schoolhouse Restaurant
Ⓗ Roscoe Diner

LODGING

Ⓘ Gold Mountain Chalet Resort
Ⓙ Kutsher's Country Club
Ⓚ Lodge at Catskill Corners
Ⓚ Mohonk Mountain House
Ⓛ Nevele Grand Hotel
Ⓜ Pinegrove Dude Ranch
Ⓝ Rocking Horse Ranch
Ⓞ Villa Roma Resort Hotel

Note: Items with the same letter are located in the same area.

another legendary resort with a complete range of activities and entertainment. **Rocking Horse Ranch**, 600 SR 44–55, Highland, 800/647-2624, www. rhranch.com, has 120 rooms and a wide array of activities including horseback riding, a private lake, archery and rifle ranges, an indoor shooting range, and downhill skiing. It's popular with families. **Kutsher's Country Club**, Anawana Lake Rd., Monticello, 914/794-6000 or 800/431-1273, www.kutshers.com, is another grand 450-room resort with a wide range of activities from horseback riding to skiing to fishing and children's and teen programs. **Pinegrove Dude Ranch**, Lower Cherrytown Rd., Kerhonkson, 914/626-7345 or 800/925-7634, www.pinegrove-ranch.com, is an award-winning dude ranch that welcomes children. The **Gold Mountain Chalet Resort**, Tice Rd., Spring Glen, 914/647-4332 or 800/395-5200, www.goldmtnresort.com, is a romantic resort and spa offering chalets with woodburning fireplaces. Pets are warmly welcomed and the resident dog will even sleep over in your chalet if invited. **Villa Roma Resort Hotel**, 340 Villa Roma Rd., 914/887-4880 or 800/533-6767, www.villaroma.com, has expansive facilities including golf, indoor and outdoor pools and tennis, bowling, a spa and fitness center, top-name entertainment, and a supervised children's program. Menus in the two dining rooms emphasize Italian specialties. The **Lodge at Catskill Corners**, SR 28, Mt. Tremper, 914/688-2828 or 877/688-2828, www.catskillcorners.com, is a comfortable rustic log structure that is part of the growing Catskill Corners empire, which includes "the world's largest kaleidoscope."

CAMPING

Camping is popular in the Catskills region. The state North and South Lake Campground, SR 23A, Haines Falls, 518/589-5058, is a multi-use 219-site campground and recreational area with breathtaking scenery that includes Kaaterskill Falls (wheelchair accessible). Beaverkill Campground, RR 1, Roscoe, 914/439-4281, offers swimming, fishing, and 46 campsites. Yogi Bear's Jellystone Park, Woodridge, 800/552-4724, has 252 sites and a full range of facilities. Mongaup Pond State Campsite, Livingston Manor, 914/439-4233, has 163 campsites, a small sandy beach, and well-marked hiking trails.

6
ALBANY AND
SARATOGA SPRINGS

Albany was founded as Fort Orange in 1609, when Henry Hudson sailed up the river that would later bear his name. It has long been a popular pastime to malign Albany, the state capital. H. H. Richardson, a famed architect, had this to say in 1870: "Of all the most miserable, wretched, second-class, one-horse towns, this is the most miserable." But the city, which has sent more presidents to Washington than any other city, has undergone a transformation in recent decades; Pulitzer Prize-winning Albany author William Kennedy called his hometown an "improbable city of political wizards, fearless ethnics, spectacular aristocrats, splendid nobodies and underrated scoundrels."

When the State Capitol was completed in 1898, at the then-staggering cost of $25 million, it was the most expensive building in the country and one of the lengthiest public-works projects in the state. This expense proved to be relatively small compared with the Nelson A. Rockefeller Empire State Plaza. Governor Rockefeller was inspired to build the mammoth structure in 1962, after he was embarrassed by the slums he and Dutch Queen Juliana passed through while she was visiting the city.

Since the opening of the Erie Canal, Albany has served as a gateway to the west and the north. Especially during August, when thoroughbred horses are racing, "north" means Saratoga Springs, a place long associated with elegance, horse racing, mineral springs, and a famous Revolutionary War battle. In the nineteenth century, Saratoga was the place to be in the summer, and people

ALBANY

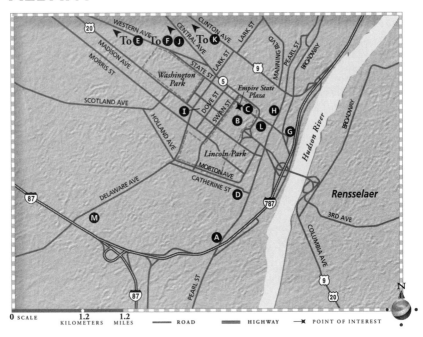

SIGHTS

- **A** Historic Cherry Hill
- **B** Nelson A. Rockefeller Empire State Plaza
- **C** New York State Capitol
- **B** New York State Museum
- **D** Schuyler Mansion State Historic Site

FOOD

- **E** Coco's
- **F** Grandma's Restaurant
- **G** Jack's Oyster House
- **H** Ogden's
- **I** Yono's

LODGING

- **J** Albany Marriott Hotel
- **K** Desmond
- **L** Omni Albany Hotel
- **M** Ramada Inn Downtown

---

came from as far away as the Deep South to summer at the "Queen of Spas." More than eight hundred structures in town are listed on the National Register of Historic Places.

A PERFECT DAY IN SARATOGA SPRINGS

If you are in Saratoga during August, start the day with a longtime tradition: have breakfast at the racetrack, where you will be served by tuxedoed waiters

---

while champion equines work the stretch. Visit the Saratoga Battlefield, site of the battle that turned the tide in favor of the colonists, and immerse yourself in Revolutionary War history. Reserve the afternoon for the thoroughbred races at the nation's oldest and most beautiful track. The bugler's "call to post" announces the beginning of the races. After the races, many jockeys and visitors head for the soothing therapy of the Roosevelt and Washington bathhouses in Saratoga Spa State Park. You can picnic in the park before the evening concert at the Saratoga Performing Arts Center or dine at one of the nearby restaurants or at the Gideon Putnam Hotel in the park.

ALBANY SIGHTSEEING HIGHLIGHTS

★★★★ NELSON A. ROCKEFELLER EMPIRE STATE PLAZA
Bounded by Eagle St., S. Swan St., Madison Ave., and Swan St., Albany, 518/474-2418
When this plaza was built in 1962, at a cost of $1 billion, Governor Rockefeller predicted in his characteristic grandiose style that it would be "the most spectacularly beautiful seat of government in the world." Not everyone would agree, but the complex certainly dominates downtown Albany. The center for festivities and entertainment in the city, the plaza is a public square with reflecting pools, a skating rink in winter, flowers, fountains, and parks. The plaza is also the site of the New York State Vietnam Memorial and has a convention center and performing-arts facility, a gallery featuring modern painting and sculpture, a state museum devoted to the cultural and natural environment, a library, a covered quarter-mile concourse, a 42-story tower with an observation gallery overlooking the Hudson River Valley (wheelchair accessible), and the headquarters for nearly 50 state agencies.

Details: *Open daily 10–5; Observation Deck in Corning Tower open Mon–Fri 9–3:45, Sat–Sun 10–3:45. Free. (2 hours)*

★★★ NEW YORK STATE CAPITOL
Empire State Plaza, bounded by Eagle St., S. Swan St., Madison Ave., and Swan St., Albany, 518/474-2418
The seat of the New York State government, built between 1867 and 1899 at a total cost of $25 million, was at the time the most expensive building in the country. The building is adorned with intricate and elaborate woodwork; carvings on the staircase depict famous

---

ALBANY: PATH TO THE WHITE HOUSE

Being the governor of New York State has launched the presidential careers of Martin Van Buren, Millard Fillmore (he was a state comptroller), Grover Cleveland, and Theodore and Franklin Roosevelt. Several gubernatorial job holders tried—but failed—to secure the Oval Office; among them were Samuel Tilden, Charles Evans Hughes, Al Smith, Tom Dewey, Averell Harriman, and Nelson Rockefeller, who made it to the vice presidency.

---

people in American history as well as friends and relatives of the sculptors. The tour includes the Million-Dollar Staircase and the legislative and executive chambers. Wheelchair accessible.

Details: *Open daily. Guided tours Mon–Fri hourly 9–11, 1–4; Sat–Sun 10, noon, 2, 3. Free. (1 hour)*

★★★ SCHUYLER MANSION STATE HISTORIC SITE
32 Catherine St., Albany, 518/434-0834
www.nysparks.com

Built in 1761, this is the Georgian home of Revolutionary War general Philip Schuyler. George Washington, Benjamin Franklin, Benedict Arnold, and Alexander Hamilton visited these rooms; Hamilton wed Schuyler's daughter Elizabeth at the mansion in 1780. General Burgoyne was a prisoner here after his defeat at Saratoga. An architectural gem, the house contains an excellent collection of Colonial- and Federal-period furnishings, many original to the home. Following the war Schuyler served in the New York and U.S. senates.

Details: *Open mid-Apr–Oct Wed–Sat 10–5, Sun 1–5. $3 adults, $2 New York State resident seniors, $1 children. (1½ hours)*

★★ HISTORIC CHERRY HILL
523 1/2 S. Pearl St., Albany, 518/434-4791

This is the Georgian-style home of Philip Van Rensselaer, and it was once the center of a Colonial farm. It was home to five generations of the family, from 1787 through 1963. The site offers guided

---

tours, which depict the changes experienced by the family and highlight the Van Rensselaer's 20,000 objects.

Details: *Guided tours on the hour Tue–Sat 10–3, Sun 1–3; closed January. $3.50 adults, $3 seniors, $2 college students, $1 children. (1 hour)*

★★ NEW YORK STATE MUSEUM
Empire State Plaza on Madison Ave., Albany
518/474-5877, www.nysm.nysed.gov

This is the oldest and largest state museum in the country. It is dedicated to researching and preserving the state's natural and cultural resources. Multimedia exhibits focus on the Adirondacks, New York City, and Native Americans in the state. There is also a hands-on discovery area for children. Wheelchair accessible.

Details: *Open daily 10–5. Free. (2 hours)*

SARATOGA SPRINGS SIGHTSEEING HIGHLIGHTS

★★★★ SARATOGA NATIONAL HISTORIC PARK
648 SR 32, Stillwater, 518/664-9821, www.nps.gov/sara

About nine miles from Saratoga Springs are the park and the Saratoga Battlefield, according to some historians the most significant battlefield of the Revolutionary War. Every American schoolchild learns of the surrender of General John "Gentleman Johnny" Burgoyne to the colonists at Saratoga on October 17, 1777. It was a vital and sweet colonist victory that turned the course of history.

Stop at the visitors center to see the film *Checkmate on the Hudson*, which explains the strategy and political implications of the battle. There are 10 stops on the well-marked nine-mile auto tour of the battlefield. The road is one-way, so you can't change your mind and turn back, but you can skip stops. Living-history encampments are regularly scheduled at Nielson Farm, which American generals used as their headquarters. The "boot monument" marks the spot where General Benedict Arnold was wounded in the leg. There's no name on the monument, reflecting Arnold's later traitorous switch to the British side.

Details: *Open daily 9–5, closed early Dec–early Apr. $4 per car, $2 per person for hiking trails (free with driving tour). (3 hours)*

★★★★ SARATOGA SPA STATE PARK
19 Roosevelt Dr., Saratoga Springs, 518/584-2535
www.nyparks.com

For centuries people have come to Saratoga Springs to "take the waters." The Iroquois were the first to pronounce the springs therapeutic. In 1803 doctors began touting this elixir as a cure for a laundry list of ailments, and Gideon Putnam opened a boardinghouse. A spa was born, and Saratoga soon became the nation's leading resort. Visitors can still take to the state-operated baths at the Roosevelt (named after FDR, who sought relief from his polio at Saratoga) and Lincoln bathhouses, both in the two-thousand-acre park.

Also in the park is the Saratoga Performing Arts Center, the July home of the New York City Ballet and the August home of the Philadelphia Orchestra. The center is nestled in a superb natural amphitheater. The park also contains tennis courts, two golf courses, two swimming pools, and the Gideon Putnam Hotel. Baths are wheelchair accessible.

Details: Open daily 8–dusk. Free. Parking $4 Memorial Day–Labor Day, free rest of year; charge for concerts varies; call 518/587-3330 for concert information. (3 hours)

★★★ CASINO AND CONGRESS PARK
Congress Park, bounded by Circular, Broadway, and Spring Sts., Saratoga Springs, 518/584-6920

For many years tourists came from all parts of the country, especially the South, to enjoy the delights of this three-story gambling casino facing Congress Park in the center of the city. Built by John

FOR THE KIDS
The Children's Museum of Saratoga, 36 Phila St., Albany, 518/584-5540, was created from an old fruit and vegetable warehouse and is conveniently located next door to Ben & Jerry's Ice Cream, one of the company's first franchise locations. This fun and interactive museum is for the 2- to 12-year-old set. Closed on Sundays during July and August.

AT THE RACES

Jockeys have been saddling up in Saratoga since 1863 and, though the world has changed much in all these years, there is still something very special about Saratoga during the racing season. There is electricity in the air. Edna Ferber described it in the book *Saratoga Trunk*, which is now out of print: "There's nothing like it in the whole country. Races every day, gambling, millionaires and pickpockets and sporting people and respectable family folks and politicians and famous theater actors and actresses, you'll find them all in Saratoga."

Morrissey, who also built the first racetrack, it was often called "Morrissey's Elegant Hell," and it attracted the likes of "Diamond Jim" Brady. It just may be the only gambling den that is a National Historic Landmark.

Gambling ended here in 1907, and today the casino houses the Historical Society of Saratoga Springs. Poker chips and dice remain, but they are now in display cases, along with other exhibits that trace the growth of the town from rural village to flamboyant resort. In Congress Park, in front of the building, is Congress Spring (the one that started it all), under a Greek Revival pavilion. *The Spirit of Life*, by sculptor Daniel Chester French, creator of the Seated Lincoln in the Lincoln Memorial, is on display here.

Details: *Open June–Aug Mon–Sat 10–4, Sun 1–4; Rest of year Wed–Sun 1–4. $2 adults, $1.50 seniors and students. (1 hour)*

★★★ **NATIONAL MUSEUM OF RACING AND HALL OF FAME**
Union Ave. and Ludlow St., Saratoga Springs
518/584-0400
Across the street from Saratoga's racetrack, this museum features a unique collection of racing artifacts, memorabilia, and lore. Paintings by the world's most renowned equine artists hang on the walls. In a simulated racetrack, videotapes of well-known trainers and jockeys explain training and racing techniques. The Hall of Fame honors horses,

ALBANY AND SARATOGA SPRINGS

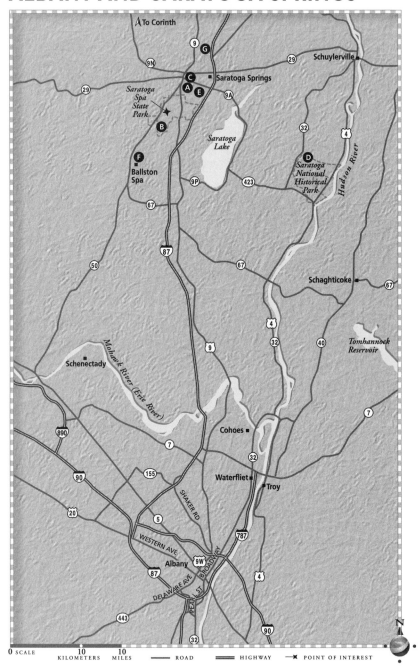

À To Corinth

9

G

9N

29

Schuylerville

C

Saratoga Springs

A E

Saratoga
Spa
State
Park

9A

29

32

4

B

Saratoga
Lake

Hudson River

F

Ballston
Spa

9P

423

D

Saratoga
National
Historical
Park

67

87

67

Schaghticoke

67

50

4

32

40

Tomhannock
Reservoir

9

Mohawk River (Erie River)

Schenectady

7

890

Cohoes

7

90

155

32

20

Waterfliet

Troy

SHAKER RD

5

WESTERN AVE

787

9W

Albany

BROADWAY

87

4

DELAWARE AVE

PEARL ST

443

90

32

N

0 SCALE   10   10
         KILOMETERS   MILES   ━━━ ROAD   ══ HIGHWAY   ✕ POINT OF INTEREST

jockeys, and trainers. Its most colorful feature is the brilliant display of two hundred of the world's most renowned racing silks, including those of Queen Elizabeth and Sir Winston Churchill. Wheelchair accessible.

Details: Open during racing season (late July–Labor Day) daily 9–5; rest of year Mon–Sat 10–4:30, Sun noon–4:30. $3 adults, $2 seniors and students. Free on off-season Sundays. (1 hour)

★★★ SARATOGA RACE COURSE
Union and East Aves., Saratoga Springs, 518/584-6200
www.nyra.com

This is the nation's oldest and, most would say, most beautiful thoroughbred racetrack. The first races were held in town in 1863. Many of the world's most famous horses, including Secretariat, raced here. The Travers Stakes, horse racing's oldest stakes race, is run yearly at Saratoga. The action starts at sunrise, when breakfast is served at the track. Guided tours of the backstretch and stables and how-to workshops on handicapping are offered during the morning hours. There are general-admission seats for the daily races (a limited number go on sale daily at 8 a.m.), as well as seats in the clubhouse or restaurants. The grounds are dotted with booths and kiosks, and jazz combos play for passersby. The atmosphere at the track is a unique blend of country fair and garden party. A huge area is set aside for picnickers.

Details: Open late July–Labor Day Wed–Mon, post time 1 p.m. $4 clubhouse, $2 general admission. (4 hours)

SIGHTS
- **Ⓐ** Casino and Congress Park
- **Ⓑ** National Museum of Dance
- **Ⓒ** National Museum of Racing and Hall of Fame
- **Ⓓ** Saratoga National Historic Park
- **Ⓔ** Saratoga Race Course
- **Ⓑ** Saratoga Spa State Park

FOOD
- **Ⓐ** Inn at Saratoga
- **Ⓐ** Lillian's Restaurant
- **Ⓕ** Little Czechoslovakia
- **Ⓐ** Pennell's Restaurant
- **Ⓐ** Professor Moriarty's

LODGING
- **Ⓐ** Adelphi Hotel
- **Ⓑ** Gideon Putnam Hotel
- **Ⓖ** Sheraton Saratoga Springs Hotel

Note: Items with the same letter are located in the same area.

★★ NATIONAL MUSEUM OF DANCE
99 S. Broadway, Saratoga Springs, 518/584-2225
www.dancemuseum.org
Located in the Saratoga Spa State Park in a handsome building that once housed the Washington baths, this is the only museum devoted exclusively to professional American dance. With videos, costumes, and photos, it salutes just about every great name in twentieth-century dance. Visitors can watch dance classes in session at the studios.

> *Details: Open Mon–Fri 10–5. $3.50 adults, $2.50 seniors and students, $1 children. (1 hour)*

FITNESS AND RECREATION

Saratoga Spa State Park, in Saratoga Springs, has walking trails as well as bikes for rent, tennis courts, golf courses, and a swimming pool. Nearby Saratoga National Historic Park has hiking trails as well as a 10-mile tour of the Battle of Saratoga. John Boyd Thacher State Park, in Voorheesville, 15 miles southwest of Albany, contains the Indian Ladder Geological Trail, one of the richest fossil-bearing formations in the world, as well as cross-country skiing and hiking trails. Five Rivers Environmental Education Center, in Delmar, five miles from Albany, has outdoor educational programs as well as hiking and ski trails. Erastus Corning Riverfront Preserve, along the Hudson River in Albany, features hiking trails and paths for biking.

FOOD

Albany and Saratoga Springs enjoy a surprisingly diverse selection of restaurants, helped in part by graduate chefs from the nearby Culinary Institute of America. **Jack's Oyster House**, 42 State St., Albany, 518/465-8854, an Albany landmark since 1913, is open 365 days a year for lunch and dinner. Also downtown is **Ogden's**, 42 Howard St., Albany, 518/463-6605, which is located in a 1903 building. In the summer there's dining outside overlooking the Empire State Plaza. Lunch Monday through Friday, dinner Monday through Saturday. **Yono's**, 289 Hamilton St., Albany, 518/436-7747, is located in historic Robinson Square; the menu combines Continental and Indonesian cuisines. Dinner Monday through Saturday. **Coco's**, 1470 Western Ave., Albany, 518/456-0297, is a fun restaurant with four huge salad bars and a large menu selection. Lunch and dinner daily. For some down-home cooking 6 a.m. to midnight daily try **Grandma's Restaurant**,

1273 Central Ave., 518/459-4585. There's chicken with biscuits, meatloaf, and 22 kinds of pies.

In operation since 1922, **Pennell's Restaurant**, 284 Jefferson St., Saratoga Springs, 518/583-2423, is a longtime favorite with locals and visitors. **Lillian's Restaurant**, 408 Broadway, Saratoga Springs, 518/587-7766, offers good food at reasonable prices. Lunch and dinner daily. The **Inn at Saratoga**, 231 Broadway, Saratoga Springs, 518/583-1890, is one of the town's oldest inns and features seafood, pasta, and beef. Lunch and dinner daily. **Professor Moriarty's**, 430 Broadway, 518/587-5981, offers casual dining in a Victorian atmosphere, and patio dining in the summer. Lunch and dinner daily. **Little Czechoslovakia**, 437 Geyser Rd., Ballston Spa, 518/885-2711, bills itself as the only Czechoslovakian restaurant between New York and Montreal and has received many awards for its food. Dinner daily.

LODGING

The **Desmond**, 660 Albany-Shaker Rd., Albany, 518/869-8100 or 800/448-3500, calls itself a "one-of-a-kind hotel," and its Old World indoor courtyards and Colonial manor house support the claim. Near the airport, the 320-room hotel comes with such modern amenities as indoor pools, saunas, and whirlpools. The **Albany Marriott Hotel**, 189 Wolf Rd., Albany, 518/458-8444 or 800/443-8952, http://marriotthotels.com/ALBNY/, is also convenient to the airport. Downtown, the 386-room **Omni Albany Hotel**, State and Lodge Sts., Albany, 518/462-6611 or 800/THE-OMNI, www.omnihotels.com, is close to the State Capitol. Also downtown in an historic building is the **Ramada Inn Downtown**, 300 Broadway, Albany, 518/434-4111 or 800/333-1177, www.ramada.com.

In Saratoga Springs, hotel rates often double or even triple during the late July through Labor Day racing season, so some visitors stay in Albany to the south or Lake George to the north. Bed-and-breakfasts are popular, and some residents leave town and rent their homes during the season. The 37-room **Adelphi Hotel**, 365 Broadway, 518/587-4688, or www.adelphihotel.com, in the middle of downtown, is a small-scale version of the three huge hotels that once flanked it. Built in 1877, it has been restored and all rooms are filled with Victorian furnishings. The historic **Gideon Putnam Hotel**, Saratoga Spa State Park, 518/584-3000 or 800/732-1560, www.gideonputnam.com, offers all the park facilities. The 240-room **Sheraton Saratoga Springs Hotel**, 534 Broadway, Saratoga Springs, 518/584-4000 or 800/325-3535, www.sheraton.com, is a short walk from the track.

CAMPING

Most area campgrounds are open from May through October. South of Saratoga National Historic Park is the 368-site Deer Run Campground, off SR 67, Schaghticoke, 518/664-2804, which offers swimming and fishing. The 400-site Alpine Lake Camping Resort, 78 Heath Rd., Corinth, 518/654-6260, offers swimming, fishing, and a boat launch. Northampton Beach is a 224-site New York State Environmental Conservation Campground with swimming and fishing.

7
THE ADIRONDACKS

To say that Adirondack Park is big is something of an understatement. Established in 1892, the park covers 6.1 million acres of public and private land, or much of the northern third of New York State. The largest park outside of Alaska, it contains more than 1,000 miles of rivers, 30,000 miles of brooks and streams, and more than 2,500 lakes and ponds. Some 46 Adirondack peaks are more than four thousand feet in elevation. Mount Marcy, a source of the Hudson River at the poetically named Lake Tear-of-the-Clouds, is the highest and most celebrated of the Adirondack peaks.

The park continues to grow. In the summer of 1998 the 14,700-acre William C. Whitney area in Long Lake opened to the public, marking a victory for conservationists who battled to save the historic Whitney property from development. The state bought the estate area including Little Tupper Lake for $17.1 million. It opens up many miles of new canoe routes and provides unspoiled opportunities for wilderness camping, swimming, and fishing. No motorized vehicles of any kind are allowed in the area.

People actually live in the Adirondacks, making the area far more diverse than any national park. Instead of civilization outside and wilderness inside, there's a living mixture here. The interior of the park remained silent in its splendor until after the Civil War, when a tourist boom began and changed the region forever. An entire industry grew up, spawning inns with guides who took the "city sports" hunting and fishing. Lavish hotels followed. The

THE ADIRONDACKS

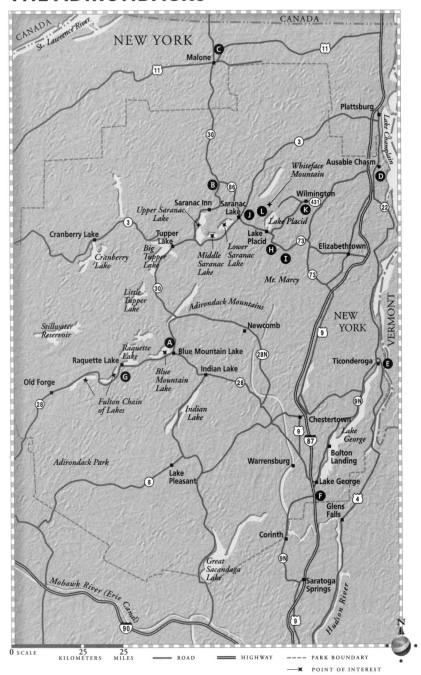

Adirondack region became one of the major playgrounds for the rich and famous of the Gilded Age in American history, between the end of the Civil War and the beginning of World War I. Lake Placid has hosted two Winter Olympics and still serves as an Olympic training center. Lake George, the largest in the park, has been called the "queen of American lakes."

A PERFECT DAY IN THE ADIRONDACKS

Originally, the only way to explore the Adirondacks was by water. It is still one of the best ways. Canoeing, especially, is a longtime tradition. A popular area is the St. Regis Wilderness Canoe Area, the only specially designated canoe management area in the state. But the best lake for canoeing or just visiting is Blue Mountain Lake, the geographical center of the area. The tiny town by the same name is one of those jewels that manages to remain true to itself despite the thousands of visitors each year. After a morning on the lake, spend some time hiking one of the many trails and then visit the Adirondack Museum, both for its exhibits and its spectacular views. Spend the evening at a concert at the Adirondack Lakes Center for the Arts in the village of Blue Mountain Lake.

BOAT TOURS

Various boat tours and guides are offered throughout the Adirondacks. The **Lake George Steamboat Cruise Company**, Lake George, 518/668-5777 or 800/553-BOAT, claims to be the oldest boat-excursion company in the country and has been giving rides since 1817. **Lake Placid Marina**, Lake Placid, 518/523-9704, has one-hour narrated boat tours of Mirror Lake. *Norridgewock III* **River Boat**, Eagle Bay, 315/376-6200, offers a unique boat tour on the Stillwater Reservoir to remote Beaver River Lodge. The

---

SIGHTS

- **Ⓐ** Adirondack Museum
- **Ⓑ** Adirondack Park Visitor Interpretive Centers
- **Ⓒ** Almanzo Wilder Homestead
- **Ⓓ** Ausable Chasm
- **Ⓔ** Fort Ticonderoga
- **Ⓕ** Fort William Henry
- **Ⓖ** Great Camp Sagamore
- **Ⓕ** Great Escape Fun Park
- **Ⓗ** John Brown Farm
- **Ⓘ** Mt. Van Hoevenberg Recreation Area
- **Ⓙ** Robert Louis Stevenson Cottage
- **Ⓚ** Santa's Workshop
- **Ⓛ** Whiteface Mountain

Note: Items with the same letter are located in the same area.

Blue Mountain Lake Boat Livery, Blue Mountain Lake, 518/352-7351, takes tours of this lovely lake in a 1916 wooden launch. **St. Regis Canoe Outfitters**, Lake Clear, 518/891-1838, offers day paddle trips and extended overnight trips as well as guide services.

SIGHTSEEING HIGHLIGHTS

★★★★ ADIRONDACK MUSEUM
SR 30, Blue Mountain Lake, 518/352-7311
www.adkmuseum.org

Rated one of the finest regional museums in the country, this institution aims to chronicle the entire Adirondack experience. The 22 exhibit buildings are spread over a 30-acre compound on a peninsula nearly surrounded by Blue Mountain Lake. The award-winning film *The Adirondacks: The Lives and Times of an American Wilderness*, shown at regular intervals, provides a good overview of the region. In the main building, exhibits highlight the land and history of the area. Detailed dioramas are accompanied by "hearphones," headsets that provide explanations of the scenes before you.

One building contains nothing but boats—Adirondack guide boats, sail canoes, polished teak speedboats, a naphtha-fueled launch that looks like a truncated steamboat, and a Colonial-era bateau. Another building is given over to stagecoaches, buckboard wagons, carriages, and horse-drawn sleighs—one with a fox-fur lap robe that E. H. Harrison gave to tuberculosis pioneer Dr. Edward Trudeau. If you admire fine craftsmanship, you'll marvel at the eight hundred wooden miniatures made by one local man—everything from an elegant circus wagon to 407 chairs, no two the same. Wheelchair accessible.

Details: *Open Memorial Day weekend–mid-Oct daily 9:30–5:30. $10 adults, $9 seniors, $6 children. (4 hours)*

★★★★ WHITEFACE MOUNTAIN
Whiteface Mountain Veterans' Memorial Highway
Wilmington, 518/523-1655, 888-WHITEFACE
www.whiteface.net

This is the highest skiing peak in the East and the only Adirondack high peak accessible by car. Ice has shaped the mountain, and its distinctive white slash was created by avalanches. President Franklin D.

Diving on the Sunken Fleet

Lake George offers scuba divers a rare experience—diving on the Sunken Fleet of 1758. Some 260 bateaux were sunk in Lake George by the British in the fall of 1758 to prevent their capture or destruction by French forces by sealing them under winter ice. Seven of the bateaux now make up a unique dive site. They range from 25 to 36 feet in length and 4 to 5 feet in width. They are aligned and roughly perpendicular to the shore, suggesting they were all scuttled at once. Only the bottom planks, the lower parts of ribs, and some cleats and garboards remain. Stones, apparently used to sink them, can be seen overlying the bottom planks. Because the bateaux are in 25 to 40 feet of water they are accessible to intermediate-level divers. A mooring buoy marks the spot, and only one dive boat at a time can be tied to the buoy.

There's another wreck from 1758 that claims the distinction as the oldest intact wreck in the United States. It's the *Land Tortoise*, which appears to be the sole survivor of a class of military vessels unique to Lake George and Lake Champlain in the eighteenth century. Researchers say the ship, 105 feet under water near the southern end of Lake George, is a remarkably well-preserved artifact from another time. The fresh, cold water has helped to preserve the ship. But this dive is for advanced divers only. It is cold down below—35 to 45 degrees—105 feet deep, and dark. A safety/decompression stop is recommended. Contact the Department of Environment Conservation (DEC) at 518/891-1370 for diving information.

Roosevelt, disabled by polio and standing with the aid of crutches, dedicated this high peak to New York's war dead.

The highway terminates just five hundred feet short of the summit. A stone castle near the main parking area at the top houses historic and scientific exhibits, a cafeteria, a gift shop, and many windows for viewing the countryside. To reach the summit, most visitors take the elevator. Hardier individuals climb the quarter-mile **Whiteface Mountain Nature Trail**—be sure to wear good walking shoes. On a clear day, the view from the top is unsurpassed, encompassing the Montreal skyline, Lake Champlain, Vermont's Green Mountains, and hundreds of Adirondack peaks and lakes. World traveler and writer Lowell Thomas described it as "one of the great scenic vistas of the world."

Two aerial chairlifts take summer and fall visitors to the summit of Little Whiteface. The **Stag Brook Falls** nature trail, descending from the mid-station, offers a relatively easy hike down alongside the waterfalls and pools of Stag Brook. Mountain bikes are available for rent, and trails wind from the chairlift mid-station through the valley and along the river to nearby Wilmington. Highway and elevator are wheelchair accessible.

Details: *Highway open June 26–Labor Day daily 8:30–5; May 15–Jun 26 and day after Labor Day–Oct 11 daily 9–4. Road open only in good weather. $8 per driver, $4 per passenger. Chairlifts SkyRide open June 12–Oct 11 9–4. $7 adults, $5 seniors and children. Mountain biking June 12–Oct 11 9–4. $5 adults, $3 children. (3 hours)*

★★★ **ADIRONDACK PARK VISITOR INTERPRETIVE CENTERS**
SR 30, Paul Smiths, 518/327-3000; SR 28N, Newcomb 518/582-2000, www.nyparks.com
These two centers offer exhibits and tourist information in large buildings modeled after one of the park's legendary Great Camps.

BOLTON LANDING

In the early decades of the twentieth century, Bolton Landing on Lake George was a mecca for opera stars and composers. From 1921 to 1935 Marcella Sembrich, a Polish soprano, made her home here. A member of the Metropolitan Opera, she founded the vocal departments of the Juilliard School and the Curtis Institute. The **Marcella Sembrich Memorial Studio**, Lakeshore Dr., 518/ 644-2492, now houses a collection of music, furniture, and costumes from her brilliant career. It is open daily during the summer, and music-history lectures and concerts are held on afternoons and evenings.

At **Paul Smiths**, the **Butterfly House** is a showcase for native species. The center's five-and-one-half miles of trails are designed to allow visitors to complete one loop or all six at their own pace. The crushed-stone surface of the **Easy Access Trail**, less than one mile, is suitable for wheelchairs or strollers.

The **Newcomb Center** is adjacent to the Santanoni Preserve, with its Great Camp complex. Winter visitors can borrow snow-shoes at no charge to explore the miles of trails. The 12,000-acre Santanoni Preserve, now deserted and empty, is owned by the state. Occasionally, the Newcomb Center sponsors guided tours of the preserve. More than one hundred special events, workshops, and lectures are conducted annually at each center through the support of the Adirondack Park Institute.

Details: *Open daily 9–5. Free. (2 hours)*

★★★ AUSABLE CHASM
U.S. 9, Ausable Chasm, 518/834-7454, 880/537-1211
www.ausablechasm.com

A tourist attraction since 1870, this chasm is a huge cleft with towering sandstone cliffs, formed about 500 million years ago. Visitors travel by foot, following stone steps up and down and crossing steep bridges that span the gorge. The three-quarter-mile walk through the chasm ends at Table Rock; from there you travel by boat. The highlight of the 10-minute boat journey is a bouncing ride through rapids into the Whirlpool Basin. When the boat ride is over, a bus takes you back to the main souvenir shop.

Details: *Open mid-May–early Oct daily 9–4. $19 adults, $17 children. (2 hours)*

★★★ FORT TICONDEROGA
SR 74, Ticonderoga, 518/585-2821
www.fort-ticonderoga.org

The French built the original fort in 1755. Because it is perched on a promontory overlooking both Lake Champlain and an outlet of Lake George, whoever controlled the fort also controlled travel between Canada and the American colonies. For this reason, the fort has been nicknamed the "Key to the Continent." Between 1755 and 1777, it was attacked six times. Three times it was successfully held, and three times it fell—a record no other fort can match. You can wander through the fort independently or join a guided tour. During the summer there are dress parades, cannon firings, and fife-and-drum concerts.

Details: *Open Jul–Aug daily 9–6; May–June and Sept–Oct 20 daily 9–5. $8 adults, $7.20 seniors, $6 children. (3 hours)*

★★★ FORT WILLIAM HENRY
End of Canada St., Lake George, 518/668-5471
800/234-0267, www.fortwilliamhenry.com

This fort was originally constructed by England to block an anticipated French advance from Canada into the colonies along the Lake Champlain–Hudson River Valley route. In the summer of 1757, the Marquis de Montcalm mustered a force of 10,000 French and Indians and swept south over Lake Champlain and Lake George. For six days and nights the French mercilessly pounded the log fort. Finally, the colonists and British surrendered, the fort was burned, and hundreds who surrendered were slaughtered. The tragedy is the subject of James Fenimore Cooper's *The Last of the Mohicans.*

The fort has been completely rebuilt, and artifacts recovered from the ashes of the fort and from the lake below are on display in the fort museum. Tours include a musket-firing demonstration, a grenadier bomb-toss demonstration, a cannon firing, and a musket-molding demonstration. The fort looks down the length of Lake George, and the view alone is worth the stop. An audiovisual program recounts the fort's history.

Details: *Open July–Aug daily 9–10; May, June, and Sept–mid-Oct daily 9–5. $8 adults, $6 seniors and children. (2 hours)*

★★★ GREAT CAMP SAGAMORE
Sagamore Rd. off SR 28, Raquette Lake, 315/354-5311
www.sagamore.org

When the twentieth century was young, it was a real journey to this Great Camp. Guests came by a relay of motor launch and private train, chugging along the half mile that made up the shortest track in the country to join the party at Alfred Vanderbilt's summer retreat. The massive main lodge was built along the lines of a Swiss music box. The 29 structures were grouped into a family and guest complex on a wooded promontory on Sagamore Lake, and a servant and service area was one-quarter mile away.

A National Historic Site, the camp is now operated by the nonprofit Sagamore Institute. Tours are offered, but guests can also stay

The Point

The Point, 800/255-3530 or 518/891-5674, www.thepointresort.com, on the shores of Upper Saranac Lake, recaptures the gracious lifestyle of a bygone age. Visiting The Point is rather like visiting your rich, indulgent uncle—if your uncle were a Rockefeller. The Point is one of the region's famed "Great Camps" and was originally Camp Wonundra, the home of William Avery Rockefeller.

Today, this member of Relais & Chateaux and the Historic Hotels of America continues to collect numerous awards, and guests agree that there aren't enough superlatives to capture the atmosphere, the rooms, and the food. It is quite simply the most enchanting lakefront sanctuary in the country. There are no signs to The Point (guests are given directions when they make reservations and visitors generally are not allowed), and no TVs or telephones in the rooms. Everything, including the gourmet meals, is included in the room rate, which tops $1,000 a night per couple—two nights minimum on weekends. In the style of elegant Adirondack living, guests in the 11 rooms dress for dinner, and black tie is suggested on Wednesdays and Saturdays. A flotilla of boats is available for guests, and fishing equipment is provided. During the winter, skis are available for cross-country skiing.

overnight at the camp and participate in workshops and special programs, which include Elderhostel offerings. One of the most popular programs is the Grandparents and Grandchildren's Summer Camp, held during three one-week periods in the summer.

Details: *Open July 4th weekend–Labor Day daily for two-hour tours, at 10 and 1:30; Labor Day–Columbus Day tours on weekends, 10 and 1:30. $6 adults, $4.50 seniors, $3 children. (2 hours)*

★★★ MT. VAN HOEVENBERG RECREATION AREA
Bobrun Rd. off SF 73, Lake Placid, 518/523-1655
800/462-6236, www.orda.org
Located on Lake Placid, this area is best known as the home of the 1932 and 1980 Winter Olympics and is the site of the only dedicated bobsled run in the country. The folks who operate the course for the public call it "the champagne of thrills." The reassuring thing about

CAMP TOURS
White Pine Camp, one of the famed Adirondack "Great Camps," was the 1926 summer White House for President Calvin Coolidge. It is a complex of 18 buildings in the village of Paul Smiths. Visitors take a two-hour tour and a videotape is shown before the tour. Open from Memorial Day through Labor Day. Call 518/327-3030.

the bobsled ride is that a professional driver and brakeman is on board, whereas on a luge there is no such security. During the winter two bobsled rides are open to the public—a half-mile ride that reaches speeds of 60 to 75 miles per hour and a one-mile ride for the ultra brave or the speed demon. It reaches speeds of 80 miles per hour. There are two luge rides, a traditional luge ride (on your back steering with your feet), and a luge rocket ride.

If you want to try the bobsled without the cold, you can ride down the runs on wheels during the warmer months. Hitting speeds of 45 to 50 miles per hour from the half-mile start, riders quickly reach the bottom, with plenty of thrills along the way. There are rollover bars, seat belts, and helmets for the passengers. Professional bobsledders drive and brake on the sleds in the summer months, too. There are also more than 30 miles of cross-country ski trails here as well as mountain-bike trails and rentals and an Olympic biathlon target-shooting range open to the public, with guns and ammunition provided.

Details: Open Apr–Nov daily 9–4; rest of year Tue–Sun 9–4. $4 adults, $3 seniors, $2 children; cross-country ski area $12 adults, $10 seniors and children. Bobsled ride $30 for half mile, $100 for one mile, $25 in summer. Reservations suggested. Call for schedule. Traditional luge ride $15, capsule luge ride $30. (2 hours)

★★ ALMANZO WILDER HOMESTEAD
Stacy Rd., Malone, 518/483-1207, sallar@slic.com
Fans of writer Laura Ingalls Wilder will enjoy a pilgrimage to the real home of Almanzo Wilder, "Farmer Boy" in the "Little House" books. The simple home has been restored. Furnishings include

original family items and memorabilia. A visitors center displays family photographs and a model of the farm, where young Alonzo sheared sheep and milked cows, as it is described in the book. Wheelchair accessible.

Details: *Open Memorial Day weekend–Labor Day Tue–Sat 11–4, Sun 1–4. $2 adults, $1 children. (1 hour)*

★★ GREAT ESCAPE FUN PARK
SR 9, Lake George, 518/792-3500
www.thegreatescape.com

Great Escape Fun Park is one of the state's largest amusement parks. One of the main attractions is the famous Comet Roller Coaster, which delighted generations at Crystal Beach, Ontario, and has been rated one of the best roller coasters in the country. The park has more than one hundred rides, including an alpine bobsled ride, the Splashwater Kingdom Water Park, and puppet, circus, and magic shows, stage performances, high divers, and Western shoot-outs. Wheelchair accessible.

Details: *Open Memorial Day–Labor Day daily 9:30–6. Open summer weekends until 10 and summer weekdays until 8. Sept–Oct weekends 9:30–5. $25.99 48 inches and over, $18.99 under 48 inches and seniors. (6 hours)*

★★ JOHN BROWN FARM
2 John Brown Rd., Lake Placid, 518/523-3900
www.nysparks.com

Many might be surprised to learn that the home and grave site of abolitionist John Brown, immortalized in song—"John Brown's body lies a-mouldering in the grave"—are just outside Lake Placid Village. Brown is best known for leading an assault on the United States Arsenal at Harpers Ferry, West Virginia, in 1859. Trying to capture arms for use in the campaign to free Southern slaves, Brown was apprehended, convicted, and hanged for his participation in the raid. He and two sons who were killed in the raid are buried on his farm, now a state historic site.

The house has been restored to its original appearance and is furnished in the style of a typical mid-nineteenth-century Adirondack farmhouse.

Details: *Open late May–late Oct Wed–Sat 10–5, Sun 1–5. Free. (1 hour)*

THE ADIRONDACKS

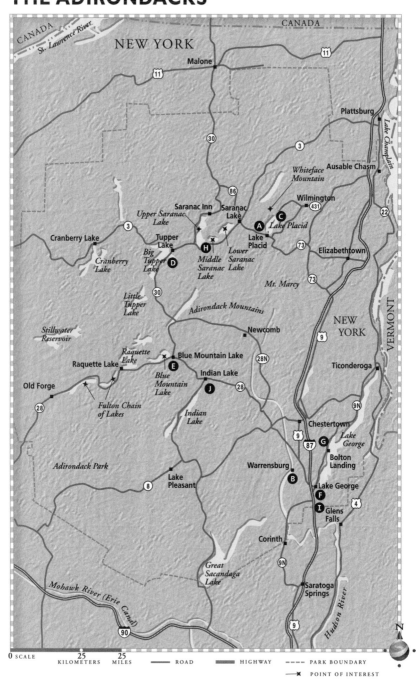

CANADA
St. Lawrence River
NEW YORK
CANADA

Malone
11
11

Plattsburg

30
3

Whiteface Mountain
Ausable Chasm

Wilmington
431
22

86

Saranac Inn
Saranac Lake
Upper Saranac Lake

C
A Lake Placid
Lake Placid

3
Cranberry Lake
Tupper Lake
H
73
Elizabethtown

Cranberry Lake
Big Tupper Lake
D
Middle Saranac Lake
Lower Saranac Lake

Mt. Marcy
73

Little Tupper Lake

30
Adirondack Mountains

Newcomb
NEW YORK

Stillwater Reservoir
9

Raquette Lake
Blue Mountain Lake
28N

Raquette Lake
E
Indian Lake
Ticonderoga

Old Forge
Blue Mountain Lake
J
28

28
Fulton Chain of Lakes
Indian Lake
Chestertown
9N

9
87
G
Lake George

Adirondack Park
Lake Pleasant
Warrensburg
Bolton Landing

8
B
Lake George
F
I Glens Falls
4

Corinth

9N

Great Sacandaga Lake
Saratoga Springs

Mohawk River (Erie Canal)
90
9
Hudson River

VERMONT

Lake Champlain

N

0 SCALE   25   25
KILOMETERS   MILES   ROAD   HIGHWAY   PARK BOUNDARY
POINT OF INTEREST

★★ SANTA'S WORKSHOP
Memorial Hwy., North Pole, 518/946-7838, 800/488-9853
www.northpoleny.com
Young children love this place, billed as the North Pole and complete with live reindeer, Santa Claus (of course), crafts demonstrations, rides, storybook characters, live entertainment, and a gift shop with personalized magic wands for sale. Wheelchair accessible.

Details: *12 miles from village of Lake Placid. Open July–Labor Day daily 9:30–4:30; June and the day after Labor Day–Columbus Day daily 10–3:30; weekend before Thanksgiving to weekend before December 25 weekends 10–3. Summer $11.95 adults, $6.95 seniors, $7.95 children; spring, fall, and December $9.95 adults, $6.95 children. (3 hours)*

★ ROBERT LOUIS STEVENSON COTTAGE
11 Stevenson Ln., Saranac Lake, 518/891-1462
Saranac Lake was a major tuberculosis treatment center during the late 1800s and early 1900s. Stevenson spent the winter of 1887–88 here in a futile attempt to regain his health. He began *The Master of Ballantrae* during his stay in this cottage.

Details: *Open July–mid-Sept Tue–Sun 9:30–noon and 1–4:30. $5 adults, free children under 12. (30 minutes)*

FITNESS AND RECREATION

Nowhere else east of the Mississippi boasts such opportunity for a variety of sports: wilderness canoeing, hiking, rock and ice climbing, downhill and cross-

---

FOOD
- Ⓐ Alpine Cellar
- Ⓑ Anthony's Ristorante Italiano
- Ⓐ The Boathouse
- Ⓒ Lake Placid Resort
- Ⓓ Park Restaurant
- Ⓔ Potter's Restaurant
- Ⓕ Shoreline Restaurant
- Ⓖ The Trillium
- Ⓗ The Wawbeek

LODGING
- Ⓘ Fort William Henry Motor Inn
- Ⓔ The Hedges
- Ⓔ Hemlock Hall
- Ⓒ Lake Placid Resort
- Ⓐ Mirror Lake Inn
- Ⓕ Roaring Brook Ranch & Tennis Resort
- Ⓖ Sagamore Hotel
- Ⓙ Timberlock
- Ⓗ The Wawbeek

Note: Items with the same letter are located in the same area.

hunting, golfing, mountain biking, kayaking, luging and bobsledding, horseback riding, swimming, white-water rafting—it's all here, with expert instructors, guides, and equipment to buy or rent. There is even a specially designated canoe management area—the St. Regis Wilderness Canoe Area—where canoeists can paddle in the wilderness for days. More than three hundred professional outdoor guides are licensed in the state and are available to teach and demonstrate their specialties. Many work in the Adirondacks. Contact the New York State Outdoor Guides Association at 518/798-1253.

FOOD

Most hotels and lodges welcome non-guests to their dining rooms. Lake Placid and Lake George have the largest variety of restaurants. **The Boathouse**, 89 Mirror Lake Dr., Lake Placid, 518/523-4822, is in a lovely spot overlooking Mirror Lake. **Lake Placid Resort**, 518/523-2700, Whiteface Inn Rd., Lake Placid, offers sophisticated porch dining specializing in fish and game. Lunch and dinner daily. **Alpine Cellar**, SR 86, Lake Placid, 518/523-2180, is a friendly German restaurant in the heart of the village that is open for lunch and dinner daily. **The Trillium**, at the Omni Sagamore Hotel, Sagamore Rd., Bolton Landing, 518/644-9400, offers elegant and expensive dining. Dinner daily. Not far from Lake George is **Anthony's Ristorante Italiano**, U.S. 9, Warrensburg, 518/623-2162, with some of the best Italian food outside of New York City, at reasonable prices. Dinner daily. The **Shoreline Restaurant**, 4 Kurosaka Ln., 518/668-2875, overlooking Lake George, offers good casual American fare for lunch and dinner daily and outdoor lakeside dining in season.

On Blue Mountain Lake, **Potter's Restaurant**, SR 30 and 28N, 518/352-7664, has a lofty log dining room and an old-fashioned menu, serving breakfast, lunch, and dinner daily during the May to October season. The **Park Restaurant**, 320 Park St., Tupper Lake, 518/359-7556, offers good family fare and is one of the few places you can enjoy fresh bullhead (the fish). Lunch and dinner daily. **The Wawbeek**, 555 Panther Mountain Rd., Upper Saranac Lake, 518/359-2656, offers a gorgeous view of the lake and food befitting the setting. Lunch and dinner daily.

LODGING

The villages of Lake Placid and Lake George have the highest concentrations and variety of lodgings. Only in the Adirondacks could the word "camp" mean both a cabin and a 68-building complex. **Lake Placid Resort**, Whiteface Inn Rd., Lake Placid, 518/523-2700, www.lakeplacidresort.com, operated by the same family as The Point, could be called a "Point for mortals." It is also a member of the elite Relais & Chateaux group. Each of the 34 guest rooms and cabins evokes the legacy of the Adirondacks. Most feature enormous stone fireplaces and views of the lake and Whiteface Mountain. Another Lake Placid classic is the **Mirror Lake Inn**, 5 Mirror Lake Dr., Lake Placid, 518/523-2544, www.mirrorlakeinn.com, complete with an indoor pool and spa. There's a private beach, fine dining, and a superb location on Mirror Lake.

Hemlock Hall, Maple Lodge Road, Blue Mountain Lake, 518/352-7706, is a longtime favorite, with a motel unit and rustic cabins. A favorite Blue Mountain Lake resort is **The Hedges**, SR 28, Blue Mountain Lake, 518/352-7325, where you can stay in a one-hundred-year-old stone house or one of 14 cottages and hop on a canoe whenever you wish. Breakfast and dinner are included. At **Timberlock**, Sabael Rd., Indian Lake, 518/648-5494, where guests stay in log cabins, "rustic" is the operative word. **The Wawbeek**, 555 Panther Mountain Road, Upper Saranac Lake, 518/359-2656 or 800/953-2656, has lovely Adirondack-style rooms in the lodge or 11 cabins, as well as boats for guest use.

The **Sagamore Hotel**, 110 Sagamore Rd., Bolton Landing, 518/644-9400 or 800/358-3585, www.thesagamore.com, is on its own island on Lake George. It has attracted guests for more than one hundred years and underwent a $72 million restoration and expansion in 1985. It's a member of the Historic Hotels of America. There are indoor and outdoor pools, a golf course, a spa, fine dining in six restaurants, and expansive rooms. The Sagamore also offers a well-organized children's program. For more than 130 years there's been a hotel named "Fort William Henry" on this bluff overlooking Lake George next to the fort. Currently it's the **Fort William Henry Motor Inn**, 48 Canada St., Lake George, 518/668-3081 or 800/234-0267. It's open April through October, with higher rates during the summer. Some rooms have refrigerators. The **Roaring Brook Ranch & Tennis Resort**, Luzerne Rd. (half mile outside village), Lake George, 518/668-5767 or 800/882-7665, www.adirondack.net/tour/roaring, has three pools (including one indoors), five tennis courts, and horseback riding. Breakfast and dinner are included.

CAMPING

There are literally hundreds of campgrounds in this region, both public and private. In addition, camping is permitted year-round on most of the 2.5 million acres of state land. Along the Northville-Lake Placid Trail and on popular canoe routes you'll find lean-tos for free camping. These three-sided log structures are a trademark of the Adirondack wilds. The Department of Environment Conservation (DEC) operates more than 40 public campgrounds, most of which are on beautiful lakes and ponds. Some are on islands, accessible only by boat. Some are also wheelchair accessible. Contact the DEC office in Warrensburg, 518/623-3671, for information. Reservations at state campgrounds can be made by calling 800/456-CAMP.

In Lake Placid, the Adirondack Mountain Club operates the Adirondack Loj Campground, Adirondack Loj Rd., 518/523-3441. In the Lake George area, there are DEC campgrounds on Glen Island, 518/644-9696, Narrow Island, 518/499-1288, and Long Island, 518/656-9426. On Cranberry Lake, the DEC operates Cranberry Lake, SR 3, 315/848-2315. On Saranac Lake, the DEC runs Fish Creek Pond, SR 30, 518/891-4560, and Rollins Pond, 518/891-3239. In the Fulton Chain of Lakes area at Old Forge, the Old Forge KOA, Route 28, 315/369-6011, offers complete facilities year-round.

Scenic Route: Adirondack Park

This circular route travels through some of the Adirondack Park's most scenic vistas. Begin the trip in the village of North Creek, which gained international fame in September 1901 when Vice President Teddy Roosevelt, who had been vacationing in the mountains, was summoned to return to Buffalo after President William McKinley was assassinated. Roosevelt made his harrowing nighttime ride down the mountain in a buckboard to reach the train station in **North Creek**. There's an historic marker between Minerva and Newcomb that commemorates the fateful ride and Roosevelt's ascendancy to the presidency. The road has been renamed the Roosevelt-Marcy Memorial Highway in his honor.

Gore Mountain, just outside North Creek, is the second-largest ski area in the state. Nonskiers can get a view from the top of Gore in the summer and fall, when the gondola operates for sightseers. The town is also the whitewater hub of the Adirondacks and the site of the annual Whitewater Derby during the first full weekend in May.

The drive between North Creek and Long Lake is one of the prettiest in the Adirondacks. The mountains and valleys are covered with beech, spruce, birch, and maples. The lake and mountain views are awesome, especially in late September when the mountains are usually at their peak of color. Adirondack author William

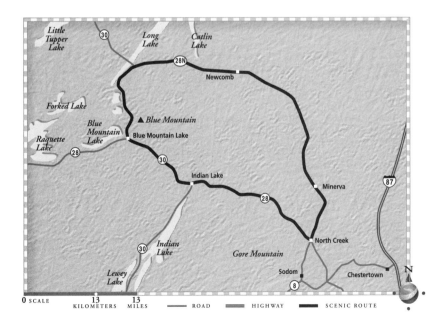

Chapman described the colors of the woods and mountains: "On highland and lowland, the world is red, with all the reds from . . . madder and vermilion flaring in the sun. A hillside of maples will have 50 shades."

At Long Lake, SR 28N heads south along the east side of the lake following the Adirondack Trail. Just north of **Blue Mountain Lake**, SR 28N becomes SR 30 and continues into the village of Blue Mountain Lake, considered by many to be the most beautiful village in the Adirondacks. Blue Mountain Lake is home to the **Adirondack Museum** and the **Adirondack Lakes Center for the Arts**, SR 28, 518/352-7715, which hosts concerts, films, theater, workshops on various crafts, and numerous programs for kids. This is also a good place to stop for a hike. There are hundreds of hiking trails in the region. One of the most popular and accessible trails is the route to the summit of the 3,759-foot **Blue Mountain**. The average hiking time for the four-mile round trip on this trail is less than four hours. From the fire tower on the top, the views of lakes, ponds, and mountains are spectacular and hard to match in the park. From Blue Mountain Lake continue east along SR 28, past Lake Durant, Indian Lake, Lake Adirondack, and Lake Abanakee to North Creek.

8
THE THOUSAND ISLANDS

"Garden Place of the Great Spirit"—Native Americans conferred this poetic name on the area now known as the Thousand Islands. An Iroquois Indian legend holds that when God summoned Eden to heaven, a thousand flowers fell and settled on the narrow channel of the St. Lawrence River between the United States and Canada; these became the Thousand Islands.

The name "Thousand Islands" is less than accurate. There are, in fact, nearly twice that number, depending on who's doing the counting and what's considered an island. "Any clump of land that could support two trees" was the definition the National Geographic Society used when it counted "1,800 or so islands." Once a summer playground of the wealthy, the islands are an appealing vacationland for families, fishing enthusiasts, and boat lovers.

The coastline runs for more than one hundred miles southwest from Massena to Cape Vincent, where the river meets Lake Ontario. When the St. Lawrence Seaway project was completed in 1959, it meant the formation of the longest navigable inland passage, more than 2,300 miles, in the world. The historic village of Sackets Harbor, on the shores of Lake Ontario, was the major naval port during the War of 1812; the battlefield and barracks have been restored. Napoleon's chief of police built a home for the emperor in Cape Vincent in anticipation of his escape from the island of St. Helena. Napoleon never made it to the Thousand Islands, but the village celebrates its French heritage each summer.

THE THOUSAND ISLANDS

Massena

11

458

Potsdam

56

Raquette River

To D

To Cornwall

345

68

Canton

St. Lawrence River

Iroquois

16

Prescott

37

Ogdensburg

E

812

Gouverneur

58

11

Smiths Falls

29

Brockville

26

Watertown

15

15

42

Lansdowne

Alexandria Bay

C A

37

81

12

43

Elgin

32

Seeleys Bay

Gananoque

H

K

B

Clayton

180

12

10

15

J

12E

3

Sackets Harbor

G

Perth

10

Verona

Kingston

96

95

F

I

12E

Sharbot Lake

509

38

Collins Bay

401

CANADA

NEW YORK

Napanee

Odessa

2

Lake Ontario

509

Kaladar

7

41

33

Picton

N

SCALE   18   18
0   KILOMETERS   MILES

ROAD   ——— HIGHWAY   —··— INTERNATIONAL BOUNDARY

A PERFECT DAY IN THE THOUSAND ISLANDS

The best way to start the day is on the river, fishing. Licensed fishing charter captains offer an easy way for newcomers to be where the fish are biting, although it's also possible to catch fish right from the shore. After a morning of successful fishing, it's time for the shore lunch, a longtime tradition with charter captains. The menu always includes bacon and tomato sandwiches, fresh fish fillets, salad, and salt potatoes, topped off with French toast, real maple syrup, and freshly brewed coffee. There's time for a visit to Boldt Castle, an awesome structure on Heart Island. If it's a clear day, an ideal way to get a sense of the islands and river is to take a tour with 1000 Islands Helicopters. For dinner, pick an Alexandria Bay or Clayton restaurant that overlooks the water to enjoy the river traffic while dining.

SIGHTSEEING HIGHLIGHTS

★★★★ BOLDT CASTLE
Alexandria Bay, 315/482-2501 or 800/8-ISLAND
www.boldtcastle.com

At the beginning of this century, financial barons vied with one another in building sumptuous summer estates on their own private islands in the region. The grandest of all is the signature structure of the islands, Boldt Castle. Hollywood could not have dreamed up a more tragically romantic story than the tale of the castle and its creator. George C. Boldt came to the United States from Prussia in 1864 at age 13. In time he became the most famous hotel magnate in the world, owner of the Waldorf-Astoria in New York and the Bellevue-

SIGHTS

- **A** 1000 Islands Helicopter Tours
- **B** Antique Boat Museum
- **C** Boldt Castle
- **C** Boldt Yacht House
- **D** Dwight D. Eisenhower Lock
- **E** Frederic Remington Museum
- **F** Horne's Ferry
- **G** Madison Barracks
- **F** Sackets Harbor Battlefield State Historic Site
- **B** Thousand Islands Museum
- **H** Thousand Islands Skydeck
- **I** Tibbett's Point Lighthouse
- **J** Uncle Sam Boat Tours
- **K** Wellesley Island State Park

Note: Items with the same letter are located in the same area.

Stratford in Philadelphia. He and his beloved wife, Louise, came to the Thousand Islands on vacation and fell in love with the area.

Boldt decided to buy an island and create a full-sized Rhineland castle to show his love for his wife. He even had the island re-shaped to resemble a heart. Hearts are integrated into design elements throughout the castle. Boldt spent more than $2.5 million before tragedy struck and his wife died in January 1904. Heartsick, he ordered the three hundred workers to leave, and he never returned.

The unfinished 120-room structure still stands in all its haunting majesty. For 73 years the castle and its buildings were left to the mercy of the wind, rain, ice, snow, and vandals. Since 1977 millions of dollars have gone into the restoration of Heart Island structures. Several rooms have been finished as they were intended, but most are empty. The castle is a symbol of what might have been had a death not cut short a man's dream.

There is a snack bar and continuous showings of a movie on Boldt's life in the castle. The castle is accessible by private boat or tour boats from the United States and Canada. Wheelchair accessible.

Details: *Open mid-May–Columbus Day 10–6, July–Aug 10–7. $3.75 adults, $2 children. (2 hours)*

★★★★ UNCLE SAM BOAT TOURS
47 James St., Alexandria Bay, 315/482-2611 or 800/ALEXBAY, www.usboattours.com

Since 1926 Uncle Sam has taken visitors for rides along the St. Lawrence River. There are lunch and dinner cruises as well as a variety of tours. The best way to get a feel for the river is to take a two-nation tour that includes an unlimited stopover at Boldt Castle (two-nation tour is wheelchair accessible). A guide tells you the history of the region and points out unusual features—Zavicon Island, for instance, which boasts the shortest international footbridge in the world. There are 45 Canadian and New York State parks in the region, several accessible only by boat. Check out *The Price Is Right* Island, which was given away in 1964 by Bill Cullen on *The Price Is Right* television program. Of course, Thousand Island salad dressing originated in the islands; it gained fame when George Boldt began using it in his hotels.

Details: *Open May–Oct daily 10–6. $13 adults, $6.50 children for two-nation tour. Also, ferry to Boldt Castle, evening cruises. (3 hours)*

ZEBRA MUSSELS, DIVERS' FRIENDS

In recent years tiny zebra mussels have invaded the St. Lawrence River. They are believed to have originally been brought here on a European cargo ship. While they cause many problems for water systems, their presence has resulted in remarkably clear water in much of the area, and the St. Lawrence River has become a mecca for scuba divers. Nearly two hundred wrecks, many dating back to the War of 1812, can be seen in the area. All About Scuba, 800/DIVE-NYS, in Clayton has dive charters and equipment rentals.

★★★ ANTIQUE BOAT MUSEUM
750 Mary St., Clayton, 315/686-4104, www.abm.org

The country's oldest and one of the largest collections of freshwater antique boats and engines is on display in this series of buildings. The museum is noted for its St. Lawrence Skiff and classic powerboat collection, including the world's largest runabout, the *Pardon Me*. Boats are rebuilt and refurbished here, and visitors can watch craftsmen and -women at work. Every summer during the first weekend in August the nation's oldest antique-boat show brings together a magnificent collection of classic freshwater boats. Rides on two special boats are also offered—on the *Seagull*, a 1935 40-foot antique cruiser, and a 1929 Hacker Craft reproduction speedboat.

Details: Open May 17–Oct 14 daily 9–4. $6 adults, $5 seniors, $2 children. (2 hours)

★★★ BOLDT YACHT HOUSE
Fern Island, 315/482-9724, www.boldtcastle.com

Opened in the summer of 1996 after undergoing restoration, this is George Boldt's boathouse, reachable by car from Wellesley Island or by free shuttle from Boldt Castle. Looking more like a castle than a boathouse, it was built in 1899 to hold a houseboat, two steam yachts, a sailing yacht, and several racing boats. Today it holds 15 antique boats, including three originally owned by Boldt; all are on loan from Clayton's Antique Boat Museum.

Details: Open June–Sept 10–6. $2 adults, $1 children. (1 hour)

★★★ **HORNE'S FERRY**
Lower James St., Cape Vincent, 315/783-0638 or 613/385-2262
This is the only international car and passenger ferry that crosses the St. Lawrence River; it travels back and forth between Cape Vincent, New York, and Ontario's Wolfe Island, the largest of the Thousand Islands. After crossing the island you can connect with Wolfe Island Ferry to Kingston, Ontario. Though it's faster to cross the river by bridge, it's certainly more fun to take the ferry. Be sure to bring identification and proof of citizenship.
Details: Open May–Oct 25 daily 8–7:30. $6 car and driver, $1 per passenger. (10 minutes)

★★★ **MADISON BARRACKS**
85 Worth Rd., Sackets Harbor, 315/646-3374
www.imcnet.net/madison
This is a living museum of military architecture. The barracks played a part in every war involving the United States from the War of 1812 to World War II. It is unique as an early example of a designed military complex and for the rich diversity of its stone and brick buildings. With a sweeping parade ground and wide view of Lake Ontario, the barracks forms a National Register Historic District. Ulysses S. Grant served a four-year tour of duty here in the early 1800s. The barracks has been renovated into a country inn, apartments, a health club, and a restaurant. Walking tours are available daily.
Details: Open daily. Free. (1 hour)

★★★ **SACKETS HARBOR BATTLEFIELD STATE HISTORIC SITE**
505 W. Washington St., Sackets Harbor, 315/646-3634
www.1000islands.com/sacketsharbor
During the War of 1812, Sackets Harbor was an important military and naval base. There are guided and self-guided tours of this site, which overlooks Lake Ontario. There's also a restored Navy Yard and the Commandant's House. During the summer, guides dressed in military uniforms reenact the camp life of the common soldier. Down the street on West Main Street is the former Augustus Sacket House, built in 1802. It is now the visitors center. During the War of 1812, it served as an officers' headquarters and makeshift hospital. Now renovated, it houses exhibits of the village's role in the war.
Details: Open May 15–Oct 15 daily. Free. (1 hour)

★★★ WELLESLEY ISLAND STATE PARK
Wellesley Island, 315/482-2722, www.nysparks.com
This 2,636-acre park near Alexandria Bay is on the western shore of Wellesley Island and is accessible by car. A highlight of the park is the **Minna Anthony Common Nature Center**, which includes a museum and wildlife sanctuary. The sanctuary encompasses a six-hundred-acre peninsula on the southeast end of the park, with spectacular views of the St. Lawrence River. The nature center, housed in a high-ceilinged, modern building, is dedicated to conserving natural resources, promoting environmental awareness, and providing recreational programs. Interpretive naturalists conduct various activities during the summer, including a voyageur canoe program, guided hikes, workshops, and a concert series. The quarter-mile Friendship Trail is designed for use by the visually impaired and those using wheelchairs. During winter the trails are maintained for cross-country skiing and snowshoeing. There's also a golf course and marina.
Details: *Open daily. $5 per car Memorial Day–Labor Day. Free rest of year. (3 hours)*

★★ DWIGHT D. EISENHOWER LOCK
180 Andrews St., Massena, 315/769-2422
Huge cargo ships pass through this lock on their way from the Atlantic to the heartland of the United States and Canada. The process of getting a ship through the lock takes about 45 minutes, and the statistics are quite amazing: Raising or lowering a ship by more than 40 feet requires the displacement of 22 million gallons of water in the lock, and that amount can be flooded or drained in only 10 minutes. There's a viewing deck and interpretive center.
Details: *Open May–Oct daily 7 a.m.–11 p.m. Call to find out when a ship is scheduled to go through the lock. Free. (1 hour)*

★★ FREDERIC REMINGTON MUSEUM
303 Washington St., Ogdensburg, 315/393-2425
www.northnet.org/broncho
Although Frederic Remington gained fame as a painter of the American West, he was born in nearby Canton. This museum houses more than two hundred of his works, the largest collection in the United States. Additional collections include Dresden china, cut glass, and Victorian furnishings.

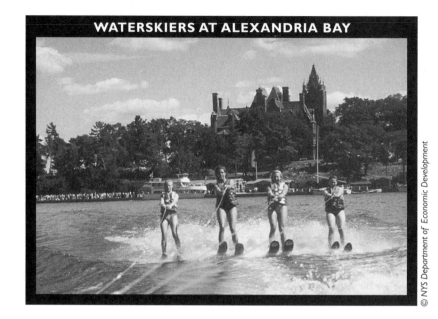

© NYS Department of Economic Development

Details: *Open May–Oct Mon–Sat 10–5, Sun 1–5; rest of year Wed–Sat 11–5, Sun 1–5. $4 adults, $2.50 seniors and students. (1 hour)*

★★ 1000 ISLANDS HELICOPTER TOURS
Rt. 12, Alexandria Bay, 315/482-4024

These helicopters offer the best way to get a real sense of the river and the islands. The chopper flies slowly over the islands, offering views of the spectacular island homes, Boldt Castle, and the ever-changing river traffic.

Details: *Open May–Oct daily, 10–sunset. $32 per person for a 20-minute tour. Longer tours available.*

★★ THOUSAND ISLANDS SKYDECK
Hill Island, Lansdowne, Ontario, 613/659-2335

Except for going up in a helicopter, this tower, four hundred feet above the St. Lawrence River, offers the best view of the islands and the river. On a clear day visibility is more than 40 miles. High-speed elevators take visitors to three observation decks, one of which is enclosed. The tower is located between the spans of the Thousand Islands International Bridge.

Details: Open May–Oct daily 8:30–7. $6.95 (Canadian) adults, $3.95 (Canadian) children. Bridge toll $2 per vehicle. (1 hour)

★★ TIBBETT'S POINT LIGHTHOUSE
33435 County Route 6, Cape Vincent, 315/654-2700
www.thousandislands.com/capechamber

Standing where Lake Ontario and the St. Lawrence River meet, the Tibbett's Point Lighthouse's automated beam of light reaches 14 nautical miles and has been a beacon to sailors and ship captains since 1827. The former lighthouse-keeper's house is used by American Youth Hostels.

Details: Grounds open daily, hostel open May 15–Oct 24. Free (hostel charge for overnight). (30 minutes)

★ THOUSAND ISLANDS MUSEUM
405 Riverside Dr., Clayton, 315/686-5794
www.1000islands.com/clayton

This museum is filled with artifacts and photos depicting life as it was in the golden years of the region, in the late nineteenth and early twentieth centuries. The Muskie Hall of Fame, which pays homage to the mighty muskellunge, is here, as is the Decoy Hall of Fame.

Details: Open Memorial Day–Labor Day daily 10–5. Free. (1 hour)

FISHING

Legendary for its ever-elusive muskie and trophy pike and walleye, the Thousand Islands region is considered one of the world's premier fishing destinations. The world record for muskellunge—69 pounds, 15 ounces—was set in the waters just off Clayton. Charter captains are licensed, and many belong to associations in Alexandria Bay, Clayton, and Cape Vincent. For fishing in U.S. waters, a New York State fishing license is necessary. A Canadian license is needed in Canadian waters. For fishing and travel information, contact the Thousand Islands International Tourist Council, 43373 Collins Landing, Alexandria Bay, 800/8-ISLAND. The Salmon River is also world famous for fishing, largely because of the New York State Salmon River Fish Hatchery. Thousands of anglers come to fish the river during the September–October salmon spawning season and the March–April steelhead spawning season. The village of Pulaski is one of the hot spots. For current information on Salmon River fishing conditions, call the Oswego County FISH-N-FUN line, 800/248-4FUN or 315/349-8322.

THE THOUSAND ISLANDS

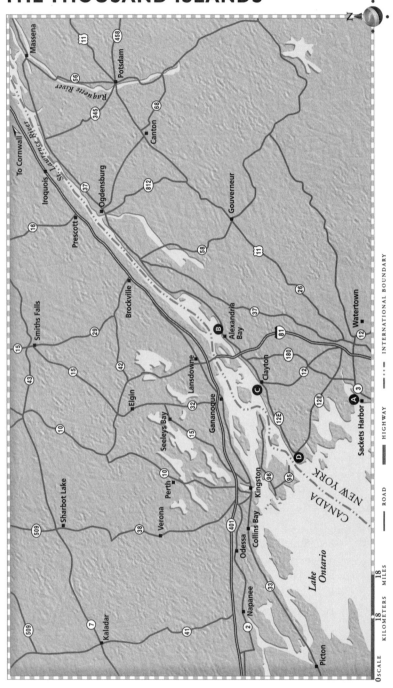

FITNESS AND RECREATION

Wellesley Island State Park has miles of hiking and cross-country ski trails as well as a special trail for the disabled and a golf course. In the early 1900s, Boldt, Rockefeller, Pullman, and other tycoons enjoyed golf at the Thousand Islands Golf Club on Wellesley Island. Now the public can play this 18-hole course. Selkirk Shores State Park has miles of hiking and cross-country ski trails. The Clayton Recreation Park and Arena has lighted tennis, basketball, and softball facilities, a heated pool and diving tank, and a one-mile exercise trail.

FOOD

In Alexandria Bay, **Cavallario's Steak and Seafood House**, 26 Church St., 315/482-9867, is a deservedly popular restaurant, open May through November for lunch and dinner. The Riveredge Resort Hotel, 17 Holland St., 315/482-9917, has two restaurants open year-round: **Jacques Cartier Fine Dining** (dinner only) and **Windows on the Bay**, open for breakfast, lunch, and dinner with good food and a view that can't be beat—the river. Bonnie Castle Manor houses the **Crystal Dining Room**, Holland St., 315/482-4511, which overlooks the river and Boldt Castle. Open year-round, it serves all meals. The **Thousand Islands Inn**, 335 Riverside Dr., Clayton, 315/686-3030 or 800/544-4241, serves breakfast, lunch, and dinner daily in its award-winning dining room that overlooks the river.

In Sackets Harbor, the **1812 Steak and Seafood Company**, 212 Main St., 315/646-2041, is popular year-round, although hours are limited in winter.

FOOD
- Ⓐ 1812 Steak and Seafood Company
- Ⓐ Barracks Inn
- Ⓑ Cavallario's Steak and Seafood House
- Ⓑ Crystal Dining Room
- Ⓑ Jacques Cartier Fine Dining
- Ⓒ Riverside Café
- Ⓒ Thousand Islands Inn
- Ⓑ Windows on the Bay

LODGING
- Ⓑ Bonnie Castle Resort
- Ⓑ Capt. Thomson's Resort
- Ⓑ Edgewood Resort
- Ⓑ Fisherman's Wharf Motel
- Ⓓ Hosteling International-
  Tibbetts Point Lighthouse Hostel
- Ⓐ Old Stone Row Country Inn Hotel
- Ⓐ Ontario Place Hotel
- Ⓑ Riveredge Resort Hotel
- Ⓒ Thousand Islands Inn

Note: Items with the same letter are located in the same area.

Open for lunch and dinner. The **Barracks Inn**, Madison Barracks, Sackets
Harbor, 315/646-2376, is open May 15 through September 15 and specializes
in Italian food as well as steaks and seafood. Open daily for dinner. In Clayton,
the **Riverside Café**, 506 Riverside Dr., 315/686-3030, features Greek specialties and is open April through September, serving three meals daily.

LODGING

Alexandria Bay has the largest concentration of accommodations in the area,
including island homes and bed-and-breakfasts. The large hotels are open year-
round, and prices are lower in the winter. Many offer special packages in the off-
season. Smaller facilities are generally open May through October. **Riveredge
Resort Hotel**, 17 Holland St., Alexandria Bay, 315/482-9917 or 800/EN-
JOYUS, www.riveredge.com, is a 129-room resort on the river with a great view
of Boldt Castle, indoor and outdoor pools, and two thousand feet of dock
space. Next door is the popular 128-room **Bonnie Castle Resort**,
Holland St., Alexandria Bay, 315/482-4511 or 800/955-4511, and www.
bonniecastle.com. It also offers commanding river views. The 68-room **Capt.
Thomson's Resort**, 43 James St., Alexandria Bay, 315/482-9961 or 800/ 253-
9229, is open from May through October 15. The **Edgewood Resort**, One
Edgewood Park Dr., Alexandria Bay, 315/482-9922 or 888/EDGEWOOD,
www.edgewoodresort.com, has 150 rooms on the river, horseback riding, a
spa, pool, and a beach, and offers nightly entertainment and various package
plans. **Fisherman's Wharf Motel**, 15 Sisson St., Alexandria Bay, 315/482-
2230, fwharf@1000islands.com, overlooks Alexandria Bay Harbor and provides
free boat dockage for guests and a popular fishing dock.

In Sackets Harbor, the **Old Stone Row Country Inn Hotel**, 315/646-
1234, is in the historic Madison Barracks and has been beautifully restored.
The **Ontario Place Hotel**, 103 General Smith Dr., Sackets Harbor,

315/646-8000, www.imcnet.net/Ontario_Place/Hotel.htm, overlooks the harbor in the center of the village. In Clayton, the **Thousand Islands Inn**, 335 Riverside Dr., 315/686-3030 or 800/544-4241, www.1000-islands.com, is in a renovated, century-old building across the street from the river; it's open May 17 through September. The **Hosteling International-Tibbetts Point Lighthouse Hostel**, 33439 CR 6, Cape Vincent, 315/654-3450 or 800/909-4776, www.hiayh.org, is a hostel in the lighthouse keeper's home on Lake Ontario, open May 15 to October 24.

CAMPING

Camping is popular in the Thousand Islands. If you have a boat or rent one, you can even camp on one of the state park islands. Wellesley Island State Park is, despite the name, accessible by car. One of the area's premier parks on the St. Lawrence River, it has 429 sites; call 315/482-2722 or 800/456-CAMP for reservations. In the Clayton area, Canoe-Picnic Point State Park, Cedar Island State Park, and Mary Island State Park are island campgrounds accessible only by boat; call 315/654-2522 or 800/456-CAMP for reservations. Selkirk Shores State Park, in Pulaski, is bordered by Lake Ontario, the Salmon River, and Grindstone Creek. Visitors here enjoy the expansive sandy beach, trails, great salmon fishing on the Salmon River, and one hundred sites to choose from; call 315/298-5737 or 800/456-CAMP for reservations.

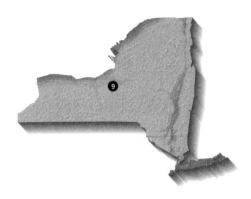

9
SYRACUSE

Syracuse, known as "Salt City," is located in the geographic center of New York. The Indian chief Hiawatha chose this location as the capital of the Iroquois Confederacy in the sixteenth century. The Onondaga Indian Reservation at Nedrow is now the seat of the Indian Confederacy. Father Simon LeMoyne, a French missionary, recorded in his journal of August 16, 1654, that he had found a salt spring near the head of Onondaga Lake. Salt brought the Indians, the French, and subsequent settlers to Syracuse, and for many years Syracuse was the source of most salt in the United States. Naturally enough, there's a Salt Museum in Syracuse, which demonstrates old-time salt processing, and another museum re-creates the early days of the French and Iroquois.

Syracuse is home to Syracuse University, with more than 12,000 undergraduate and 4,500 graduate students. The university's highly regarded NCAA Division I football, basketball, and lacrosse teams play in the striking Carrier Dome. Since 1841 Syracuse has been home to the New York State Fair, which operates for 12 days in late August, closing on Labor Day. The fair usually attracts more than 850,000 fairgoers. The fairgrounds are used for a variety of other shows during the year. The Syracuse area usually receives a bountiful snowfall each year, and winter is celebrated in January with a Winterfest. During the Christmas season, Lights on the Lake illuminates a two-mile area along Onondaga Lake in a dazzling display.

A PERFECT DAY IN SYRACUSE

The Museum of Science & Technology, or MOST, as locals call it, is a fascinating hands-on science museum located in an old armory building. MOST is in the Armory Square historic district, the perfect place for lunch and shopping for antiques and crafts. Visitors can travel back in time at Sainte Marie among the Iroquois, a living history compound that re-creates the lifestyles of the seventeenth-century French explorers and Iroquois natives. The museum is in Onondaga Lake Park, which features walking trails and picnic areas. If your timing is right, you might catch a concert or play on stage in the Landmark Theater. Opened in 1928, it is the last remaining Depression-era movie palace in central New York and is lavishly adorned with ornate carvings and decorations.

ORIENTATION

Many of Syracuse's downtown attractions are within easy walking distance of one another—anchored by the Armory Square District and Syracuse University. Attractions are well-marked. Erie Boulevard cuts through the middle of the city and Onondaga Lake Parkway borders Onondaga Lake. Traffic is not usually a problem and all attractions are within a 20-minute drive of one another. Syracuse is located just off the New York Thruway, the major east-west route across the state, and Rt. 81, the state's major north-south route.

SIGHTSEEING HIGHLIGHTS

★★★★ ARMORY SQUARE DISTRICT
Bounded by W. Fayette St., S. Clinton St., S. Salina St., and Onondaga Creek, http://armorysquare.com
Located in downtown Syracuse, the Armory Square District was originally settled in 1804. Most of the historic buildings were built between 1860 and 1890 as factories or warehouses. The original character of the buildings has been maintained even as they have been transformed into office, residential, restaurant, and retail spaces. The district is considered an outstanding example of urban renaissance and was designated a National Historic Landmark in 1984. A popular place for dining and entertainment, it's the city's liveliest night spot. There are art galleries, craft boutiques, antique shops, free lunchtime concerts, and festivals, including Winterfest. Both the Museum of Science & Technology and the **Landmark Theatre** are within the

SYRACUSE

FLY RD

East Syracuse

THOMPSON RD

JAMES ST

690

5

MEADOWBROOK DR

EUCLID AVE

LANCASTER AVE

COMSTOCK AVE

298

GRANT BLVD

Syracuse

ADAMS ST

Syracuse University

E

COURT ST

BREWERTON RD

DANFORTH ST

SALINA ST

STATE ST

81

G

STATE ST

111

111

H

F

SALINA ST

WOLF ST

CLINTON ST

A

Onondaga Creek

FRANKLIN ST

ERIE BLVD

FAYETTE ST

SEYMOUR ST

BEAR ST

GEDDES ST

SYRACUSE ST

81

Burnet Park

C

GRAND AVE

90

To Baldwinsville

Onondaga Lake County Park

ONONDAGA LAKE PARKWAY

WILBUR AVE

BRYANT AVE

690

OSWEGO ST

Liverpool

Onondaga Lake

AVERY AVE

5

STATE FAIR BLVD

MILTON AVE

Solvay

GENESEE ST

5

B

I

695

State Fairgrounds

To Camillus

5

D

To D

ERIE BLVD

5

481

N

0 SCALE

1.5 KILOMETERS MILES

1.5

★ POINT OF INTEREST

━━ HIGHWAY

━━ ROAD

district. A National Historic Landmark, the 2,922-seat theater hosts touring Broadway shows, classic films, and concerts.

Details: *Landmark Theatre is at 362 S. Salina St., 315/475-7979. (3 hours)*

★★★★ SAINTE MARIE AMONG THE IROQUOIS
Onondaga Lake Pkwy., Liverpool, 315/453-6767
www.co.onondaga.ny.us

"You must have had a long journey." That's the friendly welcome you'll receive as you walk into the mission and the seventeenth century at Sainte Marie, situated high above Onondaga Lake. This museum portrays the cultures of two seventeenth-century peoples, the Iroquois and the French missionaries. Outside the museum but within the fort walls, the lives of the French occupants of the fort in 1657 are depicted. The original fort on this site was erected in 1656 by Father Simon LeMoyne. Staff wear the clothing of middle-class Frenchmen, bake bread in beaverback ovens, and respond to the chapel bells calling them to daily vespers. Blacksmithing, carpentry, and farming are also portrayed. Inside, visitors can walk through a series of interactive museum galleries that depict the culture and customs and the flora and fauna of the Native American world. Visitors can also view the interior of a typical European ship used to transport immigrants to the New World. Wheelchair accessible.

Details: *Located just before Onondaga Lake Park. Open May–Nov Tue–Sun 10–5; Dec–Apr Wed–Sun 10–5. $3.50 adults, $3 seniors, $1.50 children 5–14. (2 hours)*

★★★ BEAVER LAKE NATURE CENTER
E. Mud Lake Rd., Baldwinsville, 315/638-2519
www.co.onondaga.ny.us

SIGHTS

Ⓐ Armory Square District
Ⓑ Beaver Lake Nature Center
Ⓒ Burnett Park Zoo
Ⓓ Camillus Erie Canal Park
Ⓔ Carrier Dome
Ⓕ Erie Canal Museum

Ⓖ Everson Museum of Art
Ⓗ Museum of Automobile History
Ⓐ Museum of Science & Technology (MOST)
Ⓘ Sainte Marie among the Iroquois
Ⓙ Salt Museum

Note: Items with the same letter are located in the same area.

This two-hundred-acre wilderness lake is surrounded by forests and meadows. The wheelchair-accessible visitors center, the hub of Beaver Lake's extensive interpretive programming, houses a variety of hands-on exhibits. Visitors enjoy guided nature walks, canoe tours, films, slide programs, natural history courses, and arts and crafts workshops. During the spring and fall, the nature center is a major resting place for thousands of Canada geese. Eight trails range from one-quarter mile to three miles in length.

Details: *Open dawn–dusk; winter until 10 p.m. for cross-country skiing. $1 per vehicle. (3 hours)*

★★★ BURNETT PARK ZOO
One Conservation Pl., Syracuse, 315/435-8511
www.co.onondaga.ny.us

This zoo provides a habitat for more than one thousand animals, including a popular group of elephants, members of a very successful breeding program. Visitors can trace the origins of life from 600 million years ago, learn about the unique adaptations that help animals survive, and hike the "Wild North." They can also walk through a prehistoric cave, view a rainstorm in a tropical forest, walk along a treetop boardwalk, and explore the wildlife of North America. Wheelchair accessible.

Details: *Open daily 10–4:30. $5 adults, $3 seniors, $2 children, $12 family. (2 hours)*

★★★ ERIE CANAL MUSEUM
318 Erie Blvd., Syracuse, 315/471-0593

This museum is housed in the 1850 Weighlock Building. It is the only surviving canal-boat weighing station on the Erie Canal and is a National Historic Landmark. Visitors can explore the history of Syracuse as it grew from a salt marsh to a city and view the story of Syracuse narrated by E. G. Marshall. They can also board a 65-foot canal boat, the *Frank Thomson*, to experience life and work on the Erie Canal. The orientation theater provides an historical overview of the world's most successful canal. Participatory exhibits allow the visitor to operate a bilge pump and try on a diving helmet. The Erie Canal took seven years to build and was the engineering marvel of its day. Finished in 1825, it spurred the first great westward migration of American settlers, opened the only trade route west of the Appalachians, and helped make New York City the commercial capital of the country.

Details: *Open daily 10–5. Free. (1 hour)*

A SAFE HAVEN

Because of its strategic location, Syracuse played a prominent role in the abolitionist movement. The **Wesleyan Methodist Church**, Columbus Circle, 315/428-1864, was founded by a group who seceded from the Methodist Episcopal Church over the issue of slavery. The Methodist Church served as a safe haven for escaping slaves on their way to Canada. A unique display of art survives in the basement consisting of a series of clay faces sculpted on the walls during the Underground Railroad days.

★★★ EVERSON MUSEUM OF ART
401 Harrison St., Syracuse, 315/474-6064
www.everson.org
Built in 1968, this museum is the first in the world to be designed by internationally renowned architect I. M. Pei. Ten galleries on three levels showcase a range of work with an emphasis on American art by such artists as Winslow Homer, Andrew Wyeth, and Gustav Stickley. The museum is also the home of the Syracuse China Center for the Study of Ceramics, with one of the nation's most comprehensive displays of American ceramics as well as ceramics from around the world. Wheelchair accessible.

 Details: *Open Sun and Tue–Fri noon–5, Sat 10–5. Suggested $2 donation. (2 hours)*

★★★ MUSEUM OF SCIENCE & TECHNOLOGY (MOST)
500 S. Franklin St., Syracuse, 315/425-9068
www.most.org
Officially named the Milton J. Rubenstein Museum of Science & Technology, this is a hands-on science museum with exhibits that explain scientific and technological phenomena. The MOST has three levels filled with hundreds of exhibits. The museum contains displays on color, computers, gravity, light, sound, and the stars. The planetarium, a 24-foot domed star theater, offers regular shows. The IMAX theater showcases nature and science movies on a giant screen. Wheelchair accessible.

Details: Open daily 9:30–5, Fri until 9. $4.50 adults, $3.50 seniors and children. Additional fee for IMAX theater and planetarium. (2 hours)

★★ CARRIER DOME
Syracuse University, Syracuse, 315/443-4634
888/DOMETIX, www.syracuse.edu
The Carrier Dome, at Syracuse University, is the only major domed stadium in the country on a college campus. The 50,000-seat multipurpose facility can accommodate both sporting and entertainment events. The Teflon-coated roof weighs 220 tons, and 16 fans produce the necessary air pressure to inflate it. Once inflated, two fans keep it aloft. Wheelchair accessible.
Details: Open Mon–Fri 8:30–4. Free tours available. Call for event times and prices. (1/2 hour)

★★ MUSEUM OF AUTOMOBILE HISTORY
321 N. Clinton St., Syracuse, 315/478-CARS
www.autolit.com/Museum
Visitors can walk through a time machine of the Automobile Age in this, the largest museum of its kind in the world. More than 10,000 objects are devoted to the history of automobiles, trucks, and motorcycles from the nineteenth century to the present.
Details: Open Wed–Sun 10–5. $4.75 adults, $3.75 seniors, $2.75 children. (1½ hours)

★★ SALT MUSEUM
Onondaga Lake Park, DR 370, Syracuse, 315/453-6767
www.co.onondaga.ny.us
This museum, located in Onondaga Lake Park, illustrates the Onondaga salt industry during the nineteenth century, when Syracuse earned the name "Salt City" as the country's leading salt manufacturing community. Exhibits include a full-size reconstruction of an 1856 boiling block, re-created crafts shops, and a "sights and sounds" tour of an 1800s salt workers neighborhood.
Details: Open May–Sept daily noon–5. Free. (1 hour)

★ CAMILLUS ERIE CANAL PARK
DeVoe Rd., Camillus, 315/488-3409, jsettin937@aol.com
This is a three-hundred-acre park with seven miles of navigable canal

SIDE TRIP: SKANEATELES

Skaneateles is both a lovely village and a lake south of Syracuse. (An Iroquois word meaning "long lake," it is pronounced "skinny-ata-less.") The village is on the northern tip of Skaneateles Lake, just 17 miles from Syracuse. The lake is the bluest of the Finger Lakes, and, according to legend, the sky spirits used to lean out of their home to admire themselves in the lake's reflection when the heavens were nearer to the earth than they are now. The lake spirits fell in love with the sky spirits and absorbed the color of the sky spirits' robes into the water, thus giving the lake its beautiful deep blue color.

After traveling around the world, William H. Seward, secretary of state under presidents Abraham Lincoln and Andrew Johnson, proclaimed Skaneateles Lake "the most beautiful body of water in the world." His description still rings true today, especially when you're on board the Barbara S. Wiles, *a restored wooden tour boat that also delivers the U.S. mail around the 16-mile-long lake. The boat tour is operated by* **Mid-Lakes Navigation Co.**, *11 Jordan St., 315/685-8500 or 800/545-4318, which offers various lake cruises on several tour boats from May through September. In the summer of 1999, the village received international attention when President Clinton and his family vacationed there.*

Polo matches take place every Sunday afternoon during July and August, and the highly acclaimed Skaneateles Festival, a series of chamber-music concerts, is held every August, 315/685-7418. Overlooking the lake is the **Sherwood Inn**, *26 W. Genesee St., 315/685-3405 or 800/3SHERWOOD, a comfortable rambling country inn that has welcomed travelers since 1807. Down the street is* **The Krebs**, *53 W. Genesee St., 315/686-5714, which has served hungry diners since 1899. It's open from April 30 through October and features a home-cooked, plate-passing feast. Another popular eatery is* **Doug's Fish Fry**, *8 Jordan St., 315/685-3288. The fish is flown in every day from Boston.*

The village promotes itself with the motto, "Relax, you're in the village." Even the meter maids are helpful. They carry extra nickels to place in the meters so visitors won't get a parking ticket.

SYRACUSE

FLY RD

East Syracuse

B

To J ▼

481

5

THOMPSON RD

To K ◢

JAMES ST

D

690

5

ERIE BLVD

MEADOWBROOK DR

EUCLID AVE

LANCASTER

M

298

COMSTOCK AVE

O

GRANT BLVD

H

Syracuse

ADAMS ST

Syracuse University

COURT ST

BREWERTON RD

81

DANFORTH ST

SALINA ST

STATE ST

F

N

81

STATE ST

111

I

111

G

SALINA ST

111

CLINTON ST

WOLF ST

A

Onondaga Creek

FRANKLIN ST

E

81

90

To Baldwinsville

ERIE BLVD

FAYETTE ST

SEYMOUR ST

BEAR ST

GEDDES ST

SYRACUSE ST

Onondaga Lake County Park

ONONDAGA LAKE PARKWAY

690

BURNET PARK

GRAND AVE

Liverpool

Onondaga Lake

BRYANT AVE

WILBUR AVE

C

Burnet Park

OSWEGO ST

STATE FAIR BLVD

AVERY AVE

5

MILTON AVE

Solvay

5

GENESEE ST

To Camillus

5

State Fairgrounds

695

L

0 SCALE
1.5 KILOMETERS   MILES
1.5

★ POINT OF INTEREST   ▬ HIGHWAY   ━ ROAD

and towpath trails. At Camillus Landing, the Lock Tender's Shanty Museum and the Sims' Store Museum, filled with artifacts and memorabilia, are authentic replicas of buildings from the Erie Canal era.

Details: Park open daily. Sims' Store open Sat 9–1. Free. Canal boats operate May–Oct Sun 1–5. $2 adults, $1 children. (2 hours)

FITNESS AND RECREATION

Onondaga Lake Park boasts a five-mile, vehicle-free recreational trail adjacent to the marina and boat launch. In-line skates and bicycles are available for rent. Baltimore Woods, in Marcellus, is a 160-acre preserve with a four-mile trail system. Beaver Lake Nature Center has eight trails, guided nature walks, and cross-country skiing. Camillus Erie Canal Park is a three-hundred-acre park with seven miles of towpath trails. Highland Forest, in Fabius, has miles of trails for horseback riding, cross-country skiing, hiking, hayrides, and sleigh tours.

FOOD

Several popular restaurants are located in the downtown Armory Square area. They include the award-winning **Pascale Wine Bar & Restaurant**, 204 W. Fayette St., 315/471-3040, which offers fine food for lunch and dinner Monday through Saturday. It has an excellent selection of wines. **Lemon Grass**, across from the Armory at 238 W. Jefferson St., 315/475-1111, serves Thai food in an elegant, understated setting. Dinner daily, lunch Monday through Saturday. **238 Bistro**, also at 238 W. Jefferson St., 315/475-9463, serves Continental cuisine in a casual atmosphere for lunch and dinner Monday through Saturday. **Pastabilities**, 311 S. Franklin St., 315/474-1153, is a popular Italian eatery for

FOOD
- **A** 238 Bistro
- **B** Captain Ahab's Seafood & Steaks
- **C** Coleman's Authentic Irish Pub
- **D** Grimaldi's
- **E** Lemon Grass
- **F** Ling Ling on the Square
- **E** Pascale Wine Bar & Restaurant
- **G** Pastabilities
- **H** Weber's Restaurant

LODGING
- **I** Bed & Breakfast Wellington
- **J** Craftsman Inn
- **K** Embassy Suites Hotel–Syracuse
- **L** Holiday Inn–Syracuse State Fair
- **M** Hosteling International–Downing International Hostel
- **N** Hotel Syracuse/The Radisson Plaza
- **O** Sheraton University Hotel

Note: Items with the same letter are located in the same area.

NEW YORK STATE FAIR

© NYS Department of Economic Development

lunch and dinner daily. **Coleman's Authentic Irish Pub**, 100 S. Lowell Ave., 315/476-1933, serves Irish favorites (even green beer for St. Patrick's Day) in the Irish-dominated Tipperary Hill area, where the green light is at the top of the traffic light. Menu items at Coleman's are written in both English and Gaelic. Lunch and dinner daily. **Weber's Restaurant**, 820 Danford St., 315/472-0480, serves ample portions of German food at reasonable prices. Lunch and dinner daily. **Grimaldi's**, 2950 Erie Boulevard E., 315/445-0012, has been serving Italian specialties since 1943. **Ling Ling on the Square**, 218 W. Genesee St., 315/422-2800, is a popular downtown Chinese restaurant. Lunch and dinner daily. **Captain Ahab's Seafood & Steaks**, 3449 Erie Boulevard, E. Syracuse, 315/446-3272, attracts seafood and steak lovers. Lunch and dinner daily.

LODGING

Hotel Syracuse/The Radisson Plaza, 500 S. Warren St., Syracuse, 315/422-5121 or 800/333-3333, www.radisson.com, has 420 rooms in the center of downtown and is one of the Historic Hotels of America. The **Sheraton University Hotel**, 801 University Ave., Syracuse, 315/475-3000 or 800/325-3535, is on the Syracuse University campus, with 232 rooms and an indoor pool and health club. The closest hotel to the State Fairgrounds is the **Holiday Inn–Syracuse State Fair**, 100 Farrell Rd., Syracuse, 315/457-8700

SYRACUSE IS ONTRACK

OnTrack, 800/FOR-TRAIN, is a unique passenger rail service that operates throughout downtown Syracuse and offers both historic excursion and shuttle services. Travel back in time with the steam engine and visit the restored Susquehanna train station.

or 800/HOLIDAY. The **Embassy Suites Hotel–Syracuse**, 6646 Old Collamer Rd., E. Syracuse, 315/446-3200 or 800/EMBASSY, is another good option for fair attendees. **Craftsman Inn**, 7300 E. Genesee St., SR 5, Fayetteville, 315/637-8000 or 800/797-4464, is a traditional country inn across from the Fayetteville Mall and ten minutes from the Carrier Dome. **Bed & Breakfast Wellington**, 707 Danforth St., Syracuse, 315/474-3641 or 800/472-5006, www.flbba.com/WELLINGTON, is an historic city home, with five guest rooms, listed on state and national historic registers. **Hosteling International–Downing International Hostel**, 535 Oak St., Syracuse, 315/472-5788 or 800/909-4776, www.hiayh.org, is open year-round.

CAMPING

Green Lakes State Park, 7900 Green Lakes Road, Fayetteville, 315/637-6111 or 800/456-CAMP for reservations, has 137 sites including cabins, as well as hiking, biking, and nature trails, a beach, fishing, a golf course, and cross-country skiing and snowshoeing in the winter. Fillmore Glen State Park, RD 3, Moravia, 315/497-0130 or 800/456-CAMP, has 70 sites and features swimming and fishing. It is named in honor of Millard Fillmore, thirteenth president of the United States, who was born about six miles southeast of the park. There is a replica of his birthplace in the park. For those who prefer to camp without clothes, Empire Haven, RD 3, Moravia, 315/497-0135, is a nudist camp with swimming, fishing, and 50 sites.

NIGHTLIFE

The Armory Square area, which has several restaurants and night spots, is popular with the younger crowd, especially on weekends. Syracuse Stage, 820 Genesee St., Syracuse, 315/443-3275, performs seven main plays during the season that runs from September through May. The Salt City Center for the Performing Arts, 601 South Crouse Ave., Syracuse, 315/474-1122, presents musicals, dramas, and comedies year-round. The Syracuse Symphony Orchestra, John H. Mulroy Civic Center, 411 Montgomery St., Syracuse, 315/424-8200 or 800/724-0113, performs classical music, popular music concerts, family series, and other productions during its 36-week season. The Famous Artists Series, Hotel Syracuse, 465 South Salina St., Syracuse, 315/424-8210, has brought great stage artists, concerts, and cinema to Syracuse for more than 50 years. The Syracuse Opera, the third-largest opera company in the state, performs at the John H. Mulroy Civic Center, 411 Montgomery St., 315/475-5915.

10
ROCHESTER

The third-largest city in the state, Rochester owes its existence to the Genesee River and its growth and development to the Erie Canal. The city is named after Colonel Nathaniel Rochester, who built and developed flour mills by Genesee River's High Falls. After construction of the Erie Canal, Rochester became the country's first "boom town," as long lines of barges loaded with flour, lumber, and other goods moved along the canal. Originally called the "Flour City" because of its flour mills, the city later became known as "Flower City" for its many flower nurseries. Home to the world's largest collection of lilacs, the city celebrates its flower heritage every May with the Lilac Festival.

Today the city calls itself "the world's image center" because of the University of Rochester's Institute of Optics, the Rochester Institute of Technology's College of Imaging Arts and Sciences, and many imaging and optics firms, including Bausch & Lomb, Xerox, and Eastman Kodak. Surely it is George Eastman, creator of Eastman Kodak, who has brought the most fame to the city. His donations made possible the University of Rochester's Eastman School of Music and the Eastman Theatre, as well as the internationally renowned collection of photographs and cameras on display at the International Museum of Photography and Film. During his lifetime, he donated more than $100 million to various charities and schools, many of which were in his hometown.

ROCHESTER

N

Cobbs Hill Park

To C

To C

To Mumford

SCALE

KILOMETERS MILES

ROAD

HIGHWAY

PARK BOUNDARY

University
of Rochester

Genesee River

Erie Canal

Erie Canal

Highland County Park

Streets and Avenues:

CLIFFORD AVE
BAY ST
CULVER RD
SOUTH WINTON RD
ATLANTIC AVE
UNIVERSITY AVE
EAST AVE
GOODMAN ST
PORTSMOUTH TERR
ELMWOOD AVE
HIGHLAND AVE
PORTLAND AVE
CENTRAL PKWY
MONROE AVE
CLEVELAND
NORTH ST
LOOP
CHESTNUT ST
CLINTON AVE
GOODMAN ST
UPPER FALLS BLVD
CLINTON AVE NORTH
SOUTH AVE
SAINT PAUL ST
INNER
BROAD ST
MT HOPE AVE
BAUSCH ST
STATE ST
PLYMOUTH AVE
EXCHANGE BLVD
FORD ST
LAKE AVE
DEWEY AVE
BROWN ST
MAIN ST
JEFFERSON AVE
PLYMOUTH AVE SOUTH
WOODSIDE AVE
LYELL AVE
WEST AVE
BROOKS AVE
MT READ BLVD
CHILI AVE
BUFFALO RD
EMERSON ST
LEE ST

490 390 31 15 33 33A 204

A PERFECT DAY IN ROCHESTER

If you time your visit for May, start the day with a walk through Highland Park, home of the world's largest collection of lilacs, where the ten-day Lilac Festival is held annually in mid-May. Nearby is the stately George Eastman House and the International Museum of Photography and Film, with one of the world's finest collections of photographs. The Eastman House is in the East Avenue Preservation District, an avenue filled with grand homes from the nineteenth and early twentieth centuries. For lunch, go to the High Falls area, where you can enjoy the Genesee River and the falls. The downtown Strong Museum is a wondrous place full of more than 300,000 objects collected by Margaret Woodbury Strong. Children love the toys, dolls, and the children's history section. In the evening, see a play at the GeVa Theatre or enjoy a symphony at the Eastman Theatre.

ORIENTATION

Rochester has an excellent expressway system that forms an inner and outer loop. The inner loop circles downtown and the color-coded sign system leads visitors to area attractions. East Avenue starts at Main Street and is home to several of the city's premier attractions. A car allows for the easiest access to all areas of the region—nothing is more than 20 to 25 minutes away. Regional Transit System buses are also convenient to many attractions.

SIGHTSEEING HIGHLIGHTS

★★★★ **GEORGE EASTMAN HOUSE INTERNATIONAL MUSEUM OF PHOTOGRAPHY AND FILM**
900 East Ave., Rochester, 716/271-3361, www.eastman.org
This is two museums in one: the 50-room grand mansion of George Eastman, founder of Eastman Kodak, and the world's leading museum

SIGHTS

- Ⓐ Campbell-Whittlesey House Museum
- Ⓑ Center at High Falls
- Ⓒ Charlotte-Genesee Lighthouse
- Ⓓ Genesee Country Museum
- Ⓔ George Eastman House International Museum of Photography and Film
- Ⓕ Highland Park
- Ⓖ Memorial Art Gallery
- Ⓗ Rochester Museum and Science Center/Strasenburgh Planetarium
- Ⓘ *Sam Patch* Tour Boat
- Ⓙ Strong Museum
- Ⓚ Susan B. Anthony House

ROCHESTER'S NATIVE ROOTS

The area around Rochester first belonged to the Iroquois. The five tribes of the Iroquois Nation formed a confederacy to promote peace among themselves and to present a united front to outsiders. The Senecas of the Genesee Valley were the largest of these tribes. Outside Rochester in Victor is the **State Historic Site at Ganondagan**, 1488 Victor-Bloomfield Rd., 716/924-5848, the capital of the Senecas from 1650 to 1687. This is the only state historic site dedicated to Native Americans. Illustrated signs mark trails where visitors can learn about the Senecas. There's a replica of a seventeenth-century Seneca longhouse.

of photography and film. The Eastman home, a National Historic Landmark, has been renovated and is beautifully connected to the adjoining $7.8 million photography archive building. Eastman never married, but he loved to entertain in his elegant and comfortable home. He had a passion for flowers, and his extensive gardens have been lovingly restored. A second-floor exhibit traces Eastman's life from his early years at his mother's kitchen table—where he developed the photographic process that started Eastman Kodak—to his suicide in 1932 at age 77.

The International Museum of Photography and Film houses one of the world's largest collections of photographs, films, photo technology, and literature, including half a million fine works of art, historical prints, and the works of eight thousand international photographers from 1839 to the present. The Dryden and Curtis theaters present evening film programs.

Details: *Open Tue–Sat 10–4:30, Sun 1–4:30. $6.50 adults, $5 seniors and students, $2.50 children. (2 hours)*

★★★★ **STRONG MUSEUM**
One Manhattan Sq., Rochester, 716/263-2700
www.strongmuseum.org
Margaret Woodbury Strong, the largest single Kodak stockholder when she died in 1969, directed that her $77 million estate be used to create

this museum to hold her amazing collection of more than 300,000 objects. The museum is regarded as the nation's leading collection of cultural history and popular taste from 1820 to 1930. Special exhibits are held regularly. History Place, a special children's section, is a big hit with the three- to seven-year-old set. There are dolls to dress and undress, an attic filled with old clothes, games, toys, and puppets, a kitchen with child-sized implements, a replica steam train, and books. The glass atrium addition features an operating 1956 stainless-steel diner and a fully restored and operating 1918 carousel. The museum now boasts the first three-dimensional museum exhibit on Sesame Street, where kids can come face to face with characters from the famous neighborhood. Kids can also pilot a giant helicopter and board a whaling ship in Kid to Kid, an exhibit on communications. Wheelchair accessible.

Details: Open Mon–Thu 10–5, Fri 10–8, Sat 10–5, Sun noon–5. $6 adults, $5 seniors and college students, $4 children. (3 hours)

★★★ CENTER AT HIGH FALLS
60 Brown's Race, Rochester, 716/325-2030
vhalstea@mcls.rochester.liv.ny.us

At High Falls visitors can watch the Genesee River rush over a 96-foot waterfall; walk through Rochester's past, including actual 1816 factory ruins at Triphammer Forge and ruins of the old Granite Flour Mill; step across footbridges and look beneath the street at a replicated 240-foot section of the original raceway used to power mill wheels; walk over the Genesee River Gorge on the 858-foot-long Pont De Rennes Bridge; and enjoy fireworks, a laser light show, and music. A restaurant and picnic tables await diners. The 30-minute River of Light laser show is projected onto a 500-foot section of the gorge. It relates the story of a Seneca Indian spirit, Jonesho, who tells the history of the river and of Rochester to Chester, a young bear whose great-great-great-great-grandfather jumped over the falls with daredevil Sam Patch in 1829. (The bear lived but Patch did not.) Wheelchair accessible.

Details: Call for laser show schedule mid-May–mid-Oct. Open Tue–Sat 10–4, Sun noon–4. Suggested donation $1 adults, 50¢ children. (2 hours)

★★★ GENESEE COUNTRY MUSEUM
Flint Hill Rd., Mumford, 716/538-5822, www.gcv.org

Spend the day in the nineteenth century, strolling through a reconstructed village of 57 buildings that were gathered from 13 counties of the Genesee Valley and represent various stages in the development of the frontier. Costumed guides and craftspeople add to the atmosphere. The museum displays artifacts of an entire century and strives to show how the average person engaged in everyday activities of the period. Authentic nineteenth-century flower, vegetable, and herb gardens are scattered throughout the grounds. Throughout the season, special events designed to give an in-depth look at various aspects of nineteenth-century life are staged. The museum also features a 175-acre nature center with five miles of hiking trails. The **John L. Wehle Gallery of Sporting Art** displays one of the world's largest collections of sporting and wildlife art.

Details: *Open mid-May–Oct Tue–Sun 10–4. $11 adults, $9.50 seniors and students, $6.50 children. (4 hours)*

★★★ **MEMORIAL ART GALLERY**
500 University Ave., Rochester, 716/473-7720
www.rochester.edu/MAG
George Eastman donated his collection of Old Masters to this museum that houses art spanning more than 50 centuries. Notable artists of the last century on display here include Mary Cassatt, Henry Moore, Paul Cézanne, Winslow Homer, Henri Matisse, and Claude Monet. Wheelchair accessible.

Details: *Open Tue noon–9, Wed–Fri 10–4, Sat 10–5, Sun noon–5. $5 adults, $4 seniors and college students, $3 students. (2 hours)*

★★★ **ROCHESTER MUSEUM AND SCIENCE CENTER AND THE STRASENBURGH PLANETARIUM**
657 East Ave., Rochester, 716/271-4320, www.rmsc.org
This museum of natural science, history, and anthropology focuses on the cultural and natural heritage of the region. Permanent exhibits include colorful dioramas of area flora and fauna, the City of Rochester in 1838, fossil seas from 300 million years ago, and an Iroquois village. The permanent exhibit, *At the Western Door*, displays the finest examples of the museum's internationally acclaimed Seneca Iroquois collection. Full-length star shows and seasonal sky minishows are projected on the great domed ceiling of the star theater in the Strasenburgh Planetarium. Wheelchair accessible.

Details: *Open Mon–Sat 9–5, Sun noon–5. Star shows Wed–Sat 8 p.m., Sat 11, 2, and 3:30, Sun 2 and 3:30. $6 adults, $5 seniors, $3 students. (2 hours)*

SIX FLAGS DARIEN LAKE

New York's largest combination theme park, entertainment, and recreational resort, Six Flags Darien Lake is halfway between Rochester and Buffalo in Darien Center, 716/599-4641, www.sixflags.com/darienlake. It is open late May through September. There are more than one hundred rides, live shows, and attractions, including the tallest roller coaster east of the Mississippi. The state's coaster capital includes five world-class coasters, a giant waterpark, a 163-room hotel with swimming pool, a two-thousand-site campground and RV center, restaurants, and a 20,000-capacity Performing Arts Center, showcasing national acts. It has recently undergone $20 million in improvements, including the $12 million steel roller coaster, Superman—Ride of Steel.

★★ CAMPBELL-WHITTLESEY HOUSE MUSEUM
123 S. Fitzhugh St., Rochester, 716/546-7029

One of the finest examples of Greek Revival architecture in the country, this is the restored home of Benjamin Campbell, a prosperous merchant and miller. The museum represents the prosperity the Erie Canal brought to the city during the boom years of 1835 to 1850. A visitor can listen to melodies made by musical glasses, see dolls and children's toys of the period, and get a glimpse into the private life of a wealthy nineteenth-century family.

Details: *Open Fri–Sun noon–4. $2 adults, 25¢ children. (1 hour)*

★★ HIGHLAND PARK
Highland Ave., Rochester, 716/248-6280

Designed in 1888 by Frederick Law Olmsted, Highland Park features the world's largest collection of lilacs, an outdoor amphitheater used for summer concerts, an ice-skating pond, a sledding hill, and a warming shelter. The ten-day Lilac Festival is held in the park every May. The park's 1,200 lilac bushes feature more than 500 varieties, from the deepest purple to the purest white. The lilac collection was started by horticulturist John Dunbar in 1892 with 20 varieties, some descending from slips carried to the New World by colonists. Today lilacs cover 22 of the park's 155 acres. The **Lamberton Conservatory** on the park grounds was designed in 1911 along the lines of a Victorian greenhouse. During the Lilac Festival there are parades, concerts, tours, and other special events.

Details: Park open daily 10–11. Conservatory open May–Oct Wed–Sun 10–6; rest of year 10–4. Free. (2 hours)

★★ *SAM PATCH* TOUR BOAT
250 Exchange Blvd., Rochester, 716/262-5661
The 54-foot *Sam Patch* is operated by the Corn Hill Waterfront & Navigation Foundation on the upper Genesee River and the Erie Canal. The authentic canal boat was named after the daredevil waterfall jumper who lost his life jumping from High Falls in Rochester in 1829.

Details: Open May–Oct Tue–Sun. Excursions include afternoon river or canal cruises, lunch, dinner, and Sun brunch. Evening cruises on Fri and Sat. One-hour cruise $10 adults, $8 seniors, $5 children. Dinner cruises $37.95 adults; lunch cruises $16.95 adults. (2 hours)

★★ SUSAN B. ANTHONY HOUSE
17 Madison St., Rochester, 716/235-6124
www.susanbanthonyhouse.org
This National Historic Landmark was the residence of the famous advocate of women's rights. Here she met with Frederick Douglass, Elizabeth Cady Stanton, and other influential reformers. This Victorian home was the site of her arrest for daring to vote. On the third floor of the restored home, which is furnished in the style of the mid-1800s, Anthony wrote *The History of Woman Suffrage.* Next door is the new Education and Visitor Center, which is part of the tour.

ROOMS FOR JELL-O
The nearby town of LeRoy was the headquarters of Jell-O, and the LeRoy House, a museum, that boasts the Jell-O Gallery with memorabilia devoted to Jell-O; 23 E. Main St., 716/768-7433.

Details: Open Memorial Day–Labor Day Tue–Sun 11–5; Labor Day–Memorial Day Wed–Sun 11–4. $6 adults, $4.50 seniors, $3 students, $2 children. (1 hour)

★ **CHARLOTTE-GENESEE LIGHTHOUSE**
70 Lighthouse Rd., Rochester, 716/621-6179
This 1822 lighthouse-turned-museum is one mile south of Ontario Beach Park, so you can combine beachcombing or swimming with a visit to the lighthouse, one of the Great Lakes' oldest. The museum traces the history of lighthouses, the port, lake transportation, and Ontario Beach Park, once considered the Coney Island of the West. *Details*: Open mid-May–mid-Oct Sat and Sun 1–5. Free. (1 hour)

FITNESS AND RECREATION

The Rochester area enjoys a multitude of parks for hiking, walking, golf, cross-country skiing, and communing with nature. Durand-Eastman Park has two miles of frontage on Lake Ontario as well as an 18-hole golf course. Genesee Valley Park, on the Genesee River, has two 18-hole golf courses, tennis courts, an ice rink, canoeing, and swimming. Mendon Ponds Park is a 550-acre nature preserve with several self-guiding trails. The Cumming Nature Center, in Naples, is part of the Rochester Museum and Science Center. It is a 900-acre environmental education center with nature trails and cross-country skiing and snowshoeing in winter. Hiking and biking are popular along the Barge Canal Trail recreation area.

FOOD

The Rochester area has a wide array of dining establishments, many of them housed in historic buildings. Downtown in the historic Academy Building is **Edwards Restaurant**, 13 S. Fitzhugh, 716/423-0140, considered one of the city's best. Lunch weekdays, dinner Monday through Saturday. Across from the Eastman Theatre is the **Brasserie Restaurant**, 387 E. Main St., 716/232-3350, which offers fine food and outdoor dining in good weather. Lunch weekdays and dinner daily. The **Water Street Grill**, 175 N. Water St., 716/546-4980, on restored Water Street, serves American regional cuisine including beef and fresh seafood. Lunch weekdays and dinner daily. The **City Grill of Rochester**, 75 Marshall St., 716/232-1920, welcomes diners to this home in historic Wadsworth Square for steaks, seafood, and their famous chocolate fondue. Dinner Wednesday through Saturday. For Greek

ROCHESTER

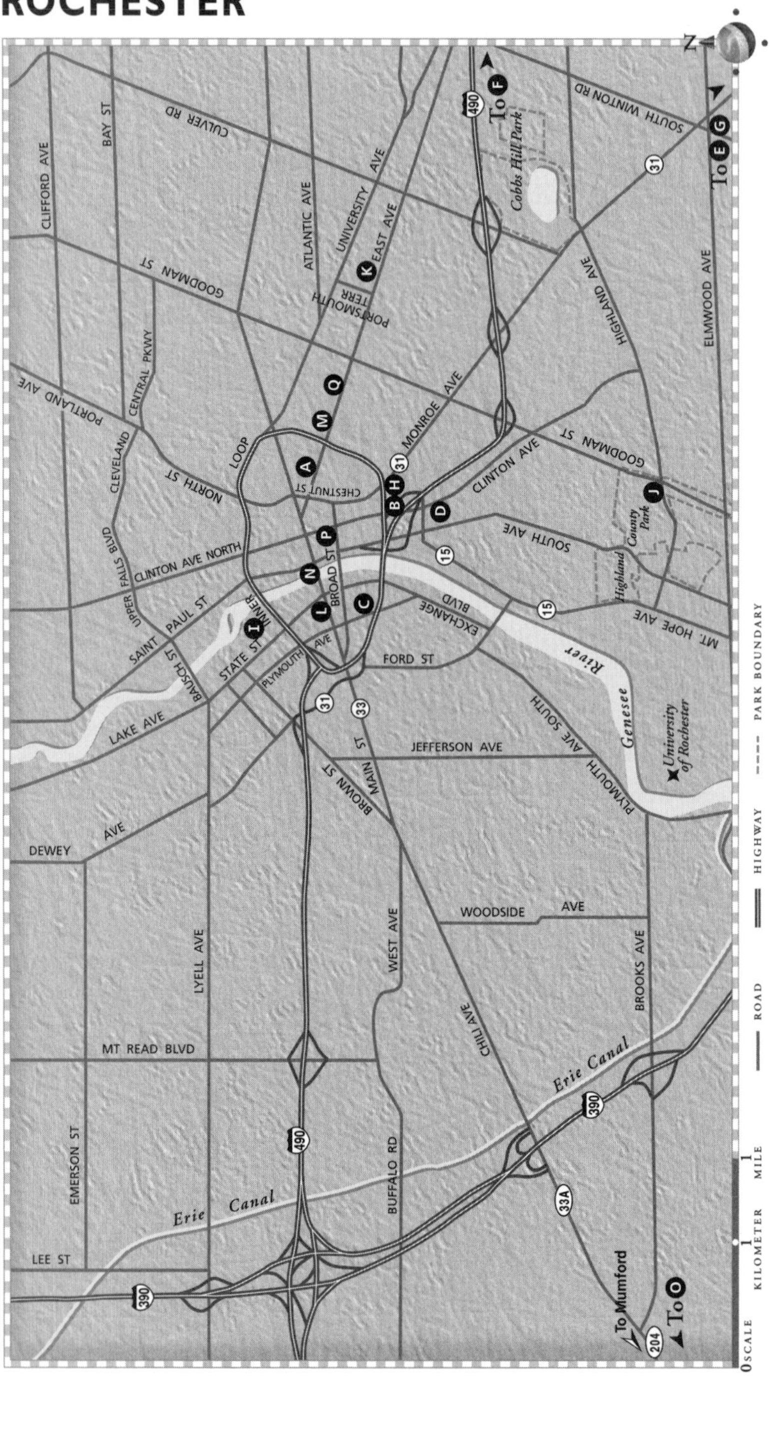

Cobbs Hill Park

Highland County Park

University of Rochester

Genesee River

Erie Canal

Erie Canal

Streets and roads:
CLIFFORD AVE, BAY ST, CULVER RD, ATLANTIC AVE, UNIVERSITY AVE, EAST AVE, SOUTH WINTON RD, GOODMAN ST, PORTSMOUTH TERR, HIGHLAND AVE, ELMWOOD AVE, PORTLAND AVE, CENTRAL PKWY, CLEVELAND ST, NORTH ST, LOOP, CHESTNUT ST, MONROE AVE, CLINTON AVE, GOODMAN ST, UPPER FALLS BLVD, CLINTON AVE NORTH, BROAD ST, SOUTH AVE, SAINT PAUL ST, PLYMOUTH AVE, INNER LOOP, STATE ST, FORD ST, EXCHANGE BLVD, MT HOPE AVE, BAUSCH ST, LAKE AVE, DEWEY AVE, JEFFERSON AVE, PLYMOUTH AVE SOUTH, BROWN ST, MANN ST, WEST AVE, WOODSIDE AVE, BROOKS AVE, LYELL AVE, CHILI AVE, MT READ BLVD, EMERSON ST, BUFFALO RD, LEE ST, To Mumford

Labeled points: F, E, G, K, Q, M, A, B H, D, I, P, N, C, L, T, O

Route markers: 490, 31, 15, 33, 390, 33A, 204

Legend:
HIGHWAY — — — PARK BOUNDARY
ROAD — — — ROAD

SCALE
0 ─── 1 KILOMETER
0 ─── 1 MILE

N

specialties, the place to be is the **Olive Tree**, 165 Monroe Ave., 716/454-3510, in a restored 1864 brick storefront. Lunch weekdays, dinner Monday through Saturday. **Mario's Via Abruzzi**, 2740 Monroe Ave., 716/271-1111, is the place for Italian-food lovers. Dinner daily. The **Spring House**, 3001 Monroe Ave., 716/586-2300, a National Landmark, is a former 1822 Erie Canal inn that offers moderately priced lunches and dinners daily in an elegant setting. **Richardson's Canal House**, 1474 Marsh Rd., Pittsford, 716/248-5000, is a restored 1818 Erie Canal tavern serving French country and American regional dinners Monday through Saturday. The **Highland Park Diner**, 960 South Clinton Ave., 716/461-5040, invites diners to enjoy the nostalgia of the city's last classic diner at breakfast, lunch, and dinner daily. It lives up to its motto: "Real food, served real well, at real prices."

LODGING

In the downtown area, the **Hyatt Regency Rochester**, 125 E. Main St., 716/546-1234, www.hyatt.com/pages/r/rochea.html, is the city's newest hotel, with 337 rooms, an indoor pool, and skyway connections to the convention center and shopping mall. The top floors of the neighboring **Four Points by Sheraton Rochester Riverside**, 120 E. Main St., 716/546-6400 or 888/596-6400, have good views of the river and the falls. Also overlooking the river downtown is the **Crowne Plaza Rochester**, 70 State St., 716/546-3450. **Days Inn Downtown**, 384 East Ave., 716/325-5010 or 800/329-7466, is just outside downtown in the Preservation District within walking distance of East Avenue attractions. The elegant European-style 150-suite **Strathallan**, 550 East Ave., 716/461-5010, is in the heart of the city's museum district. **428 Mt. Vernon**, 428 Mt. Vernon, 716/271-0792 or 800/836-3159, is a charming country inn in the city adjacent to Highland Park.

FOOD
- **Ⓐ** Brasserie Restaurant
- **Ⓑ** City Grill of Rochester
- **Ⓒ** Edwards Restaurant
- **Ⓓ** Highland Park Diner
- **Ⓔ** Mario's Via Abruzzi
- **Ⓕ** Richardson's Canal House
- **Ⓖ** Spring House
- **Ⓗ** Olive Tree
- **Ⓘ** Water Street Grill

LODGING
- **Ⓙ** 428 Mt. Vernon
- **Ⓚ** Bed of Roses Inn
- **Ⓛ** Crowne Plaza Rochester
- **Ⓜ** Days Inn Downtown
- **Ⓝ** Four Points by Sheraton Rochester Riverside
- **Ⓞ** Genesee Country Inn
- **Ⓟ** Hyatt Regency Rochester
- **Ⓠ** Strathallan

Bed of Roses Inn, 20 Portsmouth Terrace, 716/271-4980, is an elegant 1894 Victorian inn next to the George Eastman House that has seven luxury suites with fireplaces. Its Web site is www.bedofrosesinn.com. Down the road from the Genesee Country Museum is the **Genesee Country Inn**, 948 George St., Mumford, 716/538-2500 or 800/NYSTAYS, a lovely bed-and-breakfast with nine guest rooms, created from an 1833 stone mill.

NIGHTLIFE

In Rochester, EZ Rider Shuttle, 716/426-3520, makes it easy to go out on the town; the shuttle offers free transportation between hotels, restaurants, night spots, and entertainment venues Monday through Thursday from 5:30 p.m. to 11 p.m. and Friday and Saturday from 5:30 p.m. to 1 a.m. The Rochester Philharmonic Orchestra plays in the magnificent Eastman School of Music's Eastman Theatre, 26 Gibbs St., Rochester, 716/454-2620, from October to May. Frequent performances by talented students attending the University of Rochester's world-renowned Eastman School of Music are open to the public. GeVa Theatre, 75 Woodbury Blvd., Rochester, 716/232-GEVA, is the city's only professional resident theater. The Downstairs Cabaret Theatre, 151 St. Paul St., Rochester, 716/325-4370, is a professional theater that produces popular comedies and musicals. Little Theatre, 240 East Ave., Rochester, 716/258-0444, is one of the country's oldest and largest art-movie houses. The theater, which opened in 1929, is on the National Register of Historic Places.

SIDE TRIP: LETCHWORTH STATE PARK

Letchworth State Park, about one hour south of Rochester, has been dubbed the "Grand Canyon of the East." It is here that the Genesee River runs fast and deep between towering rock walls, forming a 17-mile gorge with three waterfalls. The park is named after nineteenth-century Buffalo industrialist William Pryor Letchworth, who rescued and preserved the area. Nearly every species of North American tree grows here, thanks to Letchworth. The park's creator was also determined to preserve the nation's rich Indian lore. In 1871 he relocated the last remaining Genesee Valley Seneca council house near his home, Glen Iris.

Nearby is a statue of Mary Jamison, the famed "White Woman of the Genesee." The Senecas called her Deh-ge-wa-nus. Born at sea in 1743, Mary spent her childhood as a pioneer in Pennsylvania. At 15, she and her family were taken prisoner by French and Shawnee raiders. Her family was killed, but Mary was spared and later adopted by the Indians she grew to love and respect. Mary came to the Genesee Valley before the Revolutionary War with her husband and children. The war brought destruction to the Seneca villages and Mary moved to Gardeau Flats in what is now Letchworth Park in 1779. Mary eventually moved to the Buffalo Reservation, where she died on September 19, 1833. She was originally laid to rest on the reservation, but was returned to her beautiful valley by William Pryor Letchworth in 1874.

*In 1906 Letchworth deeded his land and home to the state. The history of the lands and of Letchworth is told in the William Pryor Letchworth Museum in the park. The park now comprises 14,350 acres of magnificent scenery that encompasses dramatic cliffs along the Genesee, three waterfalls (one 107 feet high), lush forests, cabins and campsites, a swimming pool, a fishing pond, and guided nature programs. The **Glen Iris Inn**, 716/493-2622, overlooks the Middle Falls and offers fine dining, comfortable rooms, and a wonderful porch with rocking chairs. It is open April through November. For an extraordinary view of the park and countryside, take a hot-air balloon ride with **Balloons over Letchworth**, 716/237-2660, www.virtualtech.com/balloonsoverletchworth. For park information call 716/493-2611, or 800/456-CAMP for campsite reservations.*

11
NIAGARA FALLS

The first recorded tourist to witness the wonder of mighty Niagara Falls was the Reverend Louis Hennepin, who reported seeing the "incredible Cataract or Waterfall, which has no equal." Ever since that cold December day in 1678, Niagara Falls has been one of North America's greatest tourist attractions. More than 12 million visitors come each year to look upon the relentless waters. They drink in the vista from every conceivable angle: they line the promenade opposite the Falls, gape from the deck of a boat below, peer out from the caves behind, gaze from towers high, and ogle from helicopters above.

Writers have long struggled to capture the immensity of the Falls. Charles Dickens gushed, "I seemed to be lifted from the earth and to be looking into Heaven." Mark Twain wrote simply, "Niagara Falls is one of the finest structures in the known world." The Falls is indeed an awesome spectacle: a sprawling 182-foot-high cataract of thundering water surrounded by towering clouds of mist and spray. There are taller cataracts elsewhere, but the sheer size—more than one-half mile wide—and tremendous volume of Niagara are unsurpassed. The Falls drain four Great Lakes—Superior, Michigan, Huron, and Erie—into a fifth, Ontario, at a rate of 700,000 gallons per second in the summer.

The Falls border the United States and Canada. The American and Bridal Veil Falls are in the United States, and the Horseshoe Falls is on the Canadian side. Bridges make border crossings easy, but be sure to bring proof of citizenship.

A PERFECT DAY AT NIAGARA FALLS

As many times as you visit the Falls, you'll never tire of a ride on the *Maid of the Mist*, always an exciting experience. A walk through the Niagara Reservation State Park allows close-up views of the brink of the Falls. Flower lovers will enjoy the meticulously maintained formal gardens along the Niagara Parkway on the Canadian side. While on the Canadian side, stop at the Butterfly Conservatory and marvel at hundreds of amazing butterflies. At night, under the glow of multicolor floodlights, the Falls are even more magical.

SIGHTSEEING HIGHLIGHTS

★★★★ GOAT ISLAND
Niagara Falls, 716/285-3891, www.nysparks.com
This island, part of the Niagara Reservation State Park, offers the closest possible views of the American Falls and the upper rapids. Niagara Viewmobile sightseeing trains can be boarded at several locations on both Goat Island and Prospect Point. Terrapin Point on Goat Island provides a great viewing area for the Horseshoe Falls.
Details: *Open daily. Free. (1 hour)*

★★★★ *MAID OF THE MIST*
151 Buffalo Ave., Niagara Falls, 716/284-8897
www.maidofthemist.com
President Theodore Roosevelt called a ride on the *Maid of the Mist* boat "the only way fully to realize the Grandeur of the Great Falls of Niagara." Boat rides have been offered since 1846, and four *Maid of the Mist* boats can be boarded on either side of the Falls for a 30-minute ride past the Bridal Veil and American Falls and into the thunderous deluge of the Horseshoe Falls. The powerful engines fight the raging currents, and for a moment it seems as if the world is coming to a watery end. Of course, it's all perfectly safe. Disposable blue raincoats are provided, and you can count on getting wet. Wheelchair accessible.
Details: *Open mid-May–Oct 24 daily (opening depends on the breakup of the ice in the river); third week of June–Labor Day 9:30–8; spring and fall Mon–Fri 10–5, Sat and Sun 10–6. $8.50 adults plus 50¢ for the elevator, $4.80 children. (1 hour)*

NIAGARA FALLS

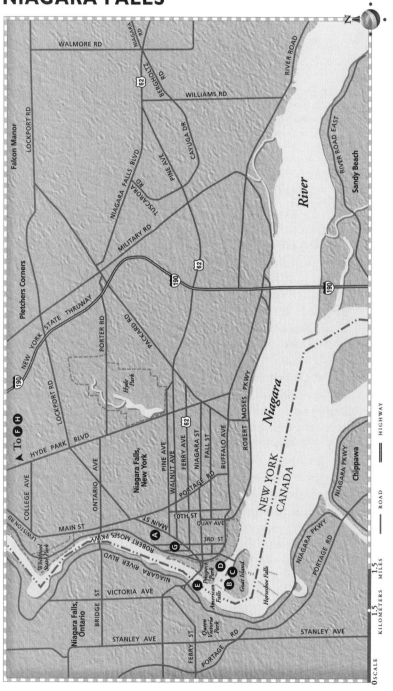

N

WALMORE RD

NIAGARA RD

62

BERGHOLTZ RD

WILLIAMS RD

RIVER ROAD

LOCKPORT RD

Falcon Manor

CAYUGA DR

PINE AVE

NIAGARA FALLS BLVD

TUSCARORA RD

River

RIVER ROAD EAST

Sandy Beach

MILITARY RD

Pletchers Corners

62

190

190

NEW YORK STATE THRUWAY

PORTER RD

PACKARD RD

190

LOCKPORT RD

Hyde Park

ROBERT MOSES PKWY

Niagara

To F H

HYDE PARK BLVD

COLLEGE AVE

ONTARIO AVE

WALNUT AVE

PINE AVE

FERRY AVE

62

NIAGARA ST

FALL ST

BUFFALO AVE

Niagara Falls, New York

PORTAGE RD

NEW YORK
CANADA

Niagara

LEWISTON RD

MAIN ST

MAIN ST

10TH ST

QUAY AVE

3RD ST

A

G

ROBERT MOSES PKWY

NIAGARA PKWY

Chippawa

Whirlpool State Park

NIAGARA RIVER BLVD

Prospect Park

D

C

B

Goat Island

Horseshoe Falls

NIAGARA PKWY RD

VICTORIA AVE

E

American Falls

NIAGARA PKWY

PORTAGE RD

BRIDGE ST

Niagara Falls, Ontario

STANLEY AVE

Queen Victoria Park

FERRY ST

PORTAGE RD

STANLEY AVE

0 SCALE

1.5
KILOMETERS

1.5
MILES

ROAD

HIGHWAY

★★★★ NIAGARA RESERVATION STATE PARK
Prospect Park, Niagara Falls, 716/278-1770
www.nysparks.com

Opened in 1885, this is the country's first state park, and it offers close-up views of the Falls as well as the Great Lakes Garden. Thousands of flowers, trees, shrubs, and ornamentals make up this colorful garden, which includes a scaled replica of the Great Lakes region—a living map that makes geography fun for kids. The visitors center houses a restaurant, displays, and hourly showings of *Niagara Wonders*, a fanciful, fun, 20-minute virtual-reality film projected on a giant 40-by-60-foot curved screen.

> **Details**: *Open daily. Free. Parking $4; film $2 adults, $1 children. (2 hours)*

★★★ CAVE OF THE WINDS
Goat Island, Niagara Reservation State Park
Niagara Falls, 716/278-1730, www.nysparks.com

A guide takes your group, attired in yellow rain slickers, through a tunnel in the rock behind the Falls. A web of catwalks and staircases leads to numerous points with astounding views. Rainbows abound here. The last stop, Hurricane Deck, is just 25 feet from the Bridal Veil Falls. Spray and mist are ever-present.

> **Details**: *Open mid-May–mid-Oct daily 9–7 (opening depends on ice conditions in the river). $6 adults, $5.50 children. (1 hour)*

★★★ NEW YORK STATE PARK OBSERVATION TOWER
Prospect Park, Niagara Falls, 716/285-3891
www.nysparks.com

An elevator takes visitors to the base of the Falls for the *Maid of the Mist* boat ride. There's also an elevator to the top and an open deck that offers a panoramic view of all three falls.

SIGHTS

Ⓐ Aquarium of Niagara Falls
Ⓑ Cave of the Winds
Ⓒ Goat Island
Ⓓ *Maid of the Mist*
Ⓔ New York State Park
 Observation Tower

Ⓕ Niagara Power Project Visitor's
 Center
Ⓖ Niagara Reservation State Park
Ⓖ Schoellkopf Geological Museum
Ⓗ Whirlpool Jet Boat Tours

***Details**: Open July–Aug daily 9–11; fall, winter, and spring 9–4:30. 50¢. (30 minutes)*

★★★ WHIRLPOOL JET BOAT TOURS
115 S. Water St., Lewiston, 888/438-4444 or 905/468-4800
www.whirlpooljet.com

Lewiston is one of the home ports of Whirlpool Jet Boat Tours (the other is in Niagara-on-the-Lake, Ontario, across the river). Boats depart May through October from the dock at the Riverside Inn, the village's award-winning classic American steak house. Jet boat and lunch or dinner packages are available.

The jet boats offer breathtaking rides into previously inaccessible areas of the lower Niagara River. The minimum age for the rides is six, and people well into their eighties have enjoyed the ride. Everyone is issued yellow raincoats but you will likely get wet, so it's a good idea to bring along towels and a change of clothes if you're planning a ride.

The boats are comfortable 40-seat jet boats that whisk passengers through the stone-walled Niagara Gorge. The boat stops just short of the Whirlpool Rapids, but it does blast through the rapids at Devil's Hole, where everyone gets soaked. It's an exciting ride that can be enjoyed by the whole family. Wheelchair accessible.

***Details**: Open May 1–third week in Oct daily; 10–7 during Jun–Aug; 10–5 May, Sept–Oct. $36 adults, $30 children. (2 hours)*

WHEN TO GO TO THE FALLS

July and August are the peak season at Niagara Falls. If you can plan your trip for May or September, you'll still be able to enjoy all the attractions and warm weather but with fewer crowds. Beginning the Saturday before Thanksgiving and continuing through early January, the **International Festival of Lights** bills itself as "Niagara's Gift to the World." The festival includes thousands of lights, big-name entertainment, animated displays, fireworks, and a dazzling New Year's Eve celebration on both sides of the border. Be sure to bring a photo I.D. and proof of citizenship if you plan to cross the border into Canada.

LOCKPORT CAVE AND UNDERGROUND BOAT RIDE

The Lockport Cave on the historic Erie Canal was blasted out of dolomite rock over a three-year period beginning in 1859. It was used as a water power tunnel to supply the Holly Manufacturing Co. and several other canal-side industries.

Hear the story behind the building of the canal and the nineteenth century industries. Walk down the steps near Locks 34 and 35. Inside the cave, board a flat-bottom boat designed to take visitors further underground. Cave temperatures remain at a cool 55 degrees Fahrenheit—refreshing on a hot summer day. Tours start at the Lockview Plaza, 21 Main St. at Pine in Lockport, at 10 and run hourly until 6. Tours operate daily from Memorial Day weekend to September 19. For more information call 716/438-0174 or visit www.lockportcave.com. Admission is $7.50 for adults and $5.25 for children.

★★ AQUARIUM OF NIAGARA FALLS
701 Whirlpool St., Niagara Falls, 716/285-3575
www.niagaranet.com/niagara/aquarium.html

This attraction, befitting the watery theme of Niagara Falls, showcases marine mammals and sea lions as well as fish and other aquatic creatures who make their homes in the Great Lakes region. Wheelchair accessible.

Details: *Open daily 9–5. $6.50 adults, $4.50 children. (2 hours)*

★★ NIAGARA POWER PROJECT VISITOR'S CENTER
5777 Lewiston Rd., Lewiston, 716/285-3211

This is one of the largest hydroelectric power projects in the world. Displays, computer games, paintings, and more explain the history of electricity. The observation deck offers a great view of the Niagara Gorge below the Falls. The Niagara River is world-renowned for salmon, trout, and steelhead fishing; the fishing platform and fish-cleaning station are helpful for successful anglers. Wheelchair accessible.

Details: *Open daily 10–5. Free. (1 hour, unless the fish are biting)*

NIAGARA FALLS

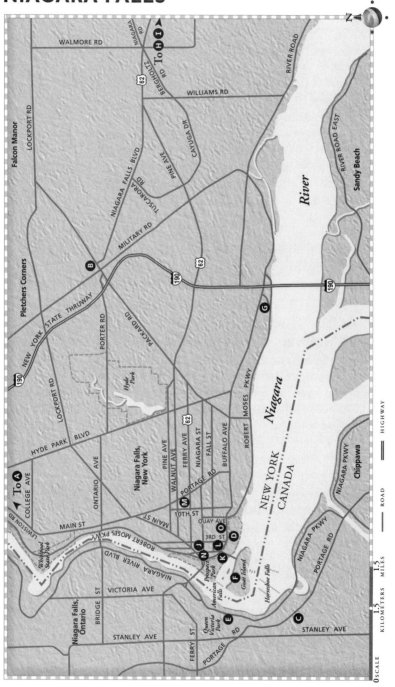

WALMORE RD

To H I

NIAGARA RD

BERGHOLTZ RD

62

WILLIAMS RD

RIVER ROAD

River

CAYUGA DR

PINE AVE

TUSCARORA RD

NIAGARA FALLS BLVD

RIVER ROAD EAST

Sandy Beach

Falton Manor

LOCKPORT RD

Pletchers Corners

MILITARY RD

NEW YORK STATE THRUWAY

190

62

B

190

PORTER RD

PACKARD RD

190

G

190

LOCKPORT RD

Hyde Park

ROBERT MOSES PKWY

Niagara

HYDE PARK BLVD

ONTARIO AVE

PINE AVE

WALNUT AVE

FERRY AVE

62

NIAGARA ST

FALL ST

BUFFALO AVE

Niagara Falls,
New York

PORTAGE RD

NEW YORK
CANADA

To A

COLLEGE AVE

LEWISTON RD

MAIN ST

10TH ST

M

MAIN ST

QUAY AVE

3RD ST

D

N J

L O

K

NIAGARA PKWY

Chippawa

ROBERT MOSES PKWY

NIAGARA RIVER BLVD

Whirlpool
State Park

Prospect
Park

American
Falls

Goat Island

F

Horseshoe Falls

NIAGARA PKWY

PORTAGE RD

VICTORIA AVE

BRIDGE ST

Niagara Falls,
Ontario

STANLEY AVE

Queen
Victoria
Park

E

FERRY ST

PORTAGE RD

STANLEY AVE

C

0 SCALE

1.5
KILOMETERS

1.5
MILES

ROAD

HIGHWAY

★★ SCHOELLKOPF GEOLOGICAL MUSEUM
Robert Moses Pkwy., Niagara Falls, 716/278-1780
www.nyparks.com
Although often overlooked by visitors to the Falls, this museum tells
the 435-million-year geologic history of the Niagara Gorge and the
12,000 years of the Falls' recession. The museum hosts park interpretive walks and programs that enhance your visit. Wheelchair accessible.
Details: *Take first exit on Robert Moses Pkwy. going north. Open
Memorial Day–Labor Day daily 9–7; Apr–day before Memorial Day and
day after Labor Day–Oct 31 9–5. $1, free to children 6 and under. (1 hour)*

FITNESS AND RECREATION
The Robert Moses Parkway and the Niagara Reservation State Park offer
some of the most spectacular venues for joggers anywhere. On the Canadian
side the Niagara Parkway extends from Fort Erie just across the river from
Buffalo 35 miles north to Niagara-on-the-Lake. There are jogging and bike
paths in Niagara-on-the-Lake, Ontario. Bikes can be rented from Niagara
Sportswear, 92 Picton St., Niagara-on-the-Lake, 905/468-0004.

FOOD
John's Flaming Hearth Restaurant, 1965 Military Rd., Niagara Falls,
716/297-1414, across from the Factory Outlet Mall, is a longtime favorite of
residents and visitors alike. Its fine steaks are most popular for dinner daily.
For one of the best views of the Falls while dining, try the revolving dining

---

FOOD
Ⓐ Clarkson House
Ⓑ John's Flaming Hearth Restaurant
Ⓒ Pinnacle Restaurant
Ⓓ Red Coach Inn
Ⓔ Skylon Tower
Ⓕ Top of the Falls Restaurant

LODGING
Ⓖ Best Western Inn on the River
Ⓗ Best Western Summit Motor Inn

LODGING (continued)
Ⓘ Budget Inn/Americana
Ⓙ Clarion Hotel Niagara Falls
Ⓚ Comfort Inn—The Pointe
Ⓛ Four Points Sheraton Hotel
Ⓛ Holiday Inn at the Falls
Ⓜ Hosteling International Niagara Falls
Ⓝ Quality Inn at the Falls
Ⓞ Ramada Inn by the Falls
Ⓓ Red Coach Inn

Note: Items with the same letter are located in the same area.

---

room for breakfast, lunch, and dinner daily at the **Skylon Tower**, on the Canadian side, 5200 Robinson St., Niagara Falls, Ontario, 905/356-2651. The **Pinnacle Restaurant** offers more great views from the Canadian side in the Minolta Tower Centre, 6732 Oakes Dr., Niagara Falls, Ontario, 905/356-1501 or 800/461-2492. Lunch and dinner daily. On the U.S. side the closest restaurant to the Falls is the **Top of the Falls Restaurant**, Goat Island in the state park, 716/278-0337 or 716/278-0340, open mid-May through Labor Day for lunch and dinner daily. The **Red Coach Inn**, 2 Buffalo Ave., Niagara Falls, 716/282-1459, is a popular dining spot overlooking the Upper Rapids. **Clarkson House**, 810 Center St., Lewiston, 716/754-4544, in an 1818 landmark building, is especially popular during the Artpark summer theater season. It has served such dinner favorites as steak and lobster for more than 50 years.

LODGING

The price of accommodations varies with the season and the proximity to the Falls. Summer is the high season, and, typically, the closer to the Falls the more expensive the hotel. If you are driving, you can stay farther afield and still enjoy the Falls. Buffalo is only a 20-minute drive away.

The closest hotel to the Falls is the **Comfort Inn—The Pointe**, One Prospect Pointe, 716/284-6835 or 800/284-6835. Breakfast is included. The **Clarion Hotel Niagara Falls**, 300 Third St., the largest city hotel, is just a block from the Falls and across from the Convention Center, 716/285-3361 or 800/95FALLS. There's an indoor pool. Other close-by hotels include the **Quality Inn at the Falls**, 443 Main St., 716/284-8801; **Holiday Inn at the Falls**, 231 Third St., 716/282-2211 or 800/HOLIDAY; and **Four Points Sheraton Hotel**, 114 Buffalo Ave., 716/285-2521 or 800/325-3535. **Best Western Inn on the River**, 7001 Buffalo Ave., 716/283-7612 or 800/245-

PICNIC AT THE SHRINE

The National Shrine Basilica of Our Lady of Fatima, 716/754-7489, outside Lewiston, is an outdoor cathedral with more than 100 life-size statues, a giant rosary, and a translucent domed chapel that has an observation deck on top. Picnicking is permitted.

7612, is three miles above the Falls on the Niagara River. The **Ramada Inn by the Falls**, 219 Fourth St., 716/282-1734 or 800/333-2557, has an indoor pool and is one block from the Falls. The small, Tudor-style **Red Coach Inn**, 2 Buffalo Ave., 716/282-1459 or 800/282-1459, overlooks the Upper Rapids and has suites with fireplaces.

Less expensive motels on Niagara Falls Blvd. in Niagara Falls include the **Budget Inn/Americana**, 9401 Niagara Falls Blvd., 716/297-2660, and **Best Western Summit Motor Inn**, 9500 Niagara Falls Blvd., 716/297-5050. The **International Bed & Breakfast Club Reservation Service**, 7009 Plaza Dr., handles bed-and-breakfast reservations; call 800/723-4262. **Hosteling International Niagara Falls**, 1101 Ferry Ave., Niagara Falls, 716/282-3700, www.hiayh.org, offers dormitories and rooms for families with a communal kitchen and lounge.

CAMPING

There are many good campgrounds in the Niagara Falls area. Four Mile Creek State Campgrounds, SR 18, Youngstown, 716/745-3802, and Golden Hill State Park Campgrounds, 9691 Lower Lake Rd., Barker, 716/795-3885, are both state parks; reserve your campsite by calling 800/456-CAMP. Closer to the falls is the Niagara Falls Campground, 2405 Niagara Falls Blvd., Niagara Falls, 716/731-3434. On Lake Ontario in the picturesque community of Olcott is the Harbor Inn & Campground, 5764 W. Lake Rd., 716/778-5190. On Grand Island, south of the Falls, is the Niagara Falls KOA, 2570 Grand Island Blvd., 716/773-7583. The Niagara Falls North KOA, 1250 Pletcher Rd., 716/754-8013, is in Lewiston.

SHOPPING

Factory outlet shopping is popular in Niagara Falls. The Niagara Factory Outlet Mall, 1900 Military Rd., 716/297-2022, is one of the country's largest, with more than 150 stores. The Rainbow Centre Factory Outlet Mall, 302 Rainbow Blvd., 716/285-9758, is just a short walk from the State Park and Falls. Hours for both malls are 10 to 10 Monday through Saturday and noon to 5 on Sunday. Nearby is Artisans Alley, 10 Rainbow Blvd., 716/282-0196, with a shop representing more than six hundred American craftspeople.

NIGHTLIFE

The dazzling Casino Niagara, 5705 Falls Ave., 905/374-3598, located just across the Rainbow Bridge in Niagara Falls, Ontario, is operated by the

Canadian government. The casino, Canada's largest, opened in December 1996 to large crowds and is open 'round the clock, seven days a week. It is one of the world's most successful casinos. Another hot spot is the Hard Rock Cafe, 333 Prospect St., Niagara Falls, 905/356-7625, open 11 a.m. to midnight daily. Fans have been flocking to the bar-restaurant since its opening in the summer of 1996. The Falls themselves are a major nightlife attraction. The lights stay on until midnight during the summer months, making them even more romantic and magical.

Scenic Route: Seaway Trail

From Niagara Falls, travel north along the Robert Moses Parkway. This route follows the river and the Seaway Trail, which hugs lakes Erie and Ontario and the Niagara and St. Lawrence rivers. In 1996 the Seaway Trail was named one of the top 20 scenic highways in the country by the U.S. Department of Transportation. Stop at **Devil's Hole State Park** or **Whirlpool State Park** to enjoy a picnic, hiking and nature trails, and fishing.

The first village you'll come to is Lewiston, where Niagara Falls had its origins 12,000 years ago. In 1974 **Artpark**, 800/659-7275, www.artpark.net, the only state park in the United States devoted to the visual and performing arts, was opened on two hundred acres overlooking the river. In the summer, musical and theatrical performances are held in the Artpark Theater, with lawn seating and spectacular views of the Niagara River Gorge, especially at sunset. The park is wheelchair accessible. Fishing enthusiasts flock to the fishing dock, which provides access to world-famous Niagara River fishing.

For many years the **Frontier House**, built in 1824, welcomed weary travelers.

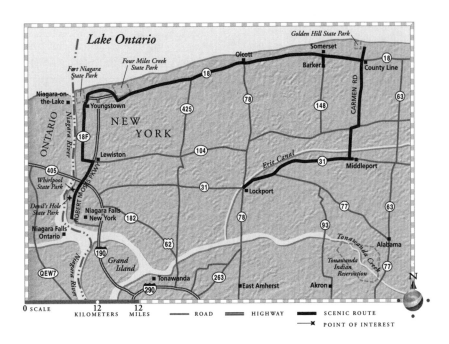

It now serves Big Macs as the country's only McDonald's in a registered National Landmark.

Continue north on SR 18F to Youngstown, home to **Fort Niagara State Park** and **Old Fort Niagara**. Located at the mouth of the Niagara River and overlooking Lake Ontario, the fort has a commanding view of the river and lake; on a clear day you can see across Lake Ontario 40 miles to Toronto and its futuristic skyline. Occupied at various times by the French, British, and Americans, the fort's original stone buildings have been preserved in their pre-Revolutionary state. Built in 1726, **French Castle** is the oldest building in the Great Lakes area, and it schedules military reenactments, battles, grand reviews, tent camps, fife-and-drum concerts, and archaeological digs. The fort's proudest possession is a flag captured by the British at Fort Niagara on December 19, 1813. The flag, one of the oldest in the country, was returned by Great Britain in 1994.

From Youngstown, continue on SR 18, along the shore of Lake Ontario. Stop in Olcott Beach, a pleasant lakeside village with many fishing charters. From there, go to Barker, home to the **Thirty Mile Point Lighthouse** at Golden Hill State Park. This 1875 lighthouse, built of hand-carved stone, provides a great view of Lake Ontario. Campsites are available. The lighthouse was honored in 1995 with its own U.S. postage stamp.

From Barker, take Carmen Road, designated the Niagara Historic Trail, south to Middleport, an historic village on the Erie Canal. There are more cobblestone buildings in this area than anywhere else in the world. This unique form of regional architecture owes its existence to the Erie Canal: After the canal was completed, the English stonemasons who had built the canal needed work and convinced local residents to face their homes with water-rounded stones.

The last stop is Lockport, named for the canal locks in town. The best way to experience the locks is to hop on board a canal boat operated by **Lockport Locks & Canal Tours**, 210 Market St., Lockport, 800/378-0352, which offers cruises from May through October seven days a week: three times daily in the spring and fall, and four a day in the summer. The boat travels through Locks 34 and 35—rising nearly 50 feet to overcome the difference in elevation of the Niagara Escarpment. The boat passes by Lockport's original locks and under the widest bridge in the country. As guests motor along, old canal songs play on the boat's sound system:

I've got an old mule and her name is Sal
Fifteen miles on the Erie Canal.
She's a good ol' worker and a good ol' pal
Fifteen miles on the Erie Canal.

12
BUFFALO

Although it's the second-largest city in the state, Buffalo still manages to convey the feeling of an overgrown small town. It is well situated as a port city at the head of the Niagara River, where Lake Erie empties into the river. The city's fortunes changed forever in 1825 when the Erie Canal opened, linking the city and Lake Erie with the Atlantic Ocean. From its early days it was an outpost of the east and a gateway to the west.

Buffalo has the dubious distinction of being "Blizzard City," but much of the snow falls south of the city in the ski country (Syracuse actually beats Buffalo in the snow Olympics). Strong ethnic neighborhoods and identities define Buffalo. This is also a city of taverns and churches, although the taverns are now sedate compared to their character in the nineteenth century, when the two-block-long Canal Street on the waterfront buzzed with 93 saloons and 15 dance halls.

The city has received worldwide recognition for its rich architectural treasures, including five Frank Lloyd Wright homes and a grand downtown office building designed by Louis Sullivan. Allentown, just north of downtown, is one of the nation's largest historic preservation districts. The area also has a strong cultural heritage, with a revitalized theater district.

Buffalo is well-known for its enthusiastic—some would say fanatic—sports fans. Though one of the smallest markets in the nation, the region is one of the leaders in the National Football League in football attendance, and baseball

BUFFALO

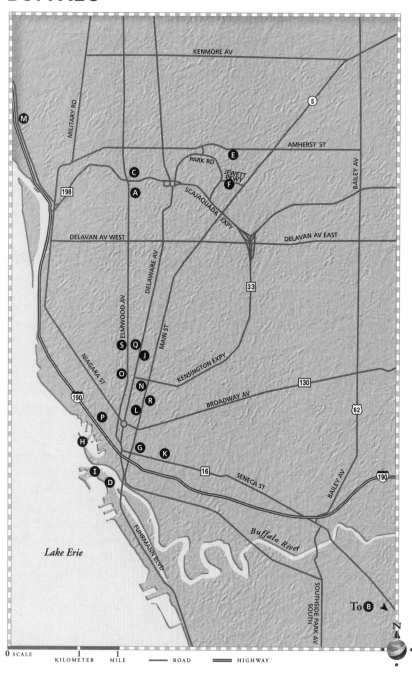

KENMORE AV

MILITARY RD

5

M

AMHERST ST

PARK RD

E

C

JEWETT PKWY

F

198

A

SCAJAQUADA EXPY

BAILEY AV

DELAVAN AV WEST

DELAVAN AV EAST

DELAWARE AV

33

ELMWOOD AV

MAIN ST

S Q

J

KENSINGTON EXPY

O

NIAGARA ST

N

BROADWAY AV

130

R

190

L

62

P

H

G

K

190

I

16

SENECA ST

BAILEY AV

D

FUHRMANN BLVD

Lake Erie

Buffalo River

SOUTHSIDE PARK AV SOUTH

To B

N

0 SCALE   1   1
KILOMETER MILE   ROAD   HIGHWAY

fans regularly set attendance records in the classic downtown baseball field. Hockey fans enjoy one of the nation's most dazzling venues at the new Marine Midland Arena.

A PERFECT DAY IN BUFFALO

Spend the morning at the Albright-Knox Art Gallery, known worldwide for its superb collection of modern art. If it's a pleasant day, eat lunch at a table in the outdoor Sculpture Court. The food is great and the ambiance can't be beat. Visit the world-famous Frank Lloyd Wright–designed Darwin Martin House. It's a short distance to the Erie Basin Marina, one of the city's loveliest spots, with a dramatic view of the skyline and gorgeous gardens. Then take a ride aboard *Miss Buffalo*, which cruises the Niagara River and the Black Rock Canal. Spend the evening in the city's theater district.

ORIENTATION

It's been said that nothing is more than 20 minutes away in the Buffalo area. It's just 15 minutes from the Buffalo Niagara International Airport to downtown Buffalo along the Kensington Expressway. The major streets branch off from the central business district in a radial pattern. Because Lake Erie borders the city's southwest side, most roads begin downtown and branch to the

SIGHTS
- **A** Albright-Knox Art Gallery
- **B** Buffalo and Erie County Botanical Gardens
- **C** Buffalo and Erie County Historical Society
- **D** Buffalo and Erie County Naval and Military Park
- **E** Buffalo Zoological Gardens
- **F** Darwin Martin House
- **G** Dunn Tire Park
- **H** Erie Basin Marina
- **I** *Miss Buffalo* and *Niagara Clipper* Cruise Boats
- **J** Theodore Roosevelt Inaugural National Historic Site

FOOD
- **K** Chef's Restaurant
- **L** E. B. Green's Steakhouse
- **M** Harry's Harbour Place Grille
- **N** Rue Franklin Restaurant
- **O** Towne Restaurant

LODGING
- **P** Adam's Mark Buffalo Hotel
- **Q** Holiday Inn Downtown
- **R** Hostel Downtown Buffalo
- **S** Hotel Lenox
- **T** Hyatt Regency Buffalo
- **R** Radisson Suites Downtown

Note: Items with the same letter are located in the same area.

north and east. Niagara Square is the primary downtown intersection. From the square, Delaware Avenue runs north and south. Driving is the best way to get around. The major Metro bus routes operate in the city and the suburbs. A lightrail rapid-transit system runs from the foot of Main Street through the theater district, ending at the North Buffalo campus of the State University of New York at Buffalo.

BUFFALO SIGHTSEEING HIGHLIGHTS

★★★★ ALBRIGHT-KNOX ART GALLERY
1285 Elmwood Ave., Buffalo, 716/882-8700
www.albrightknox.org
Though the art in this museum spans the centuries, the modern art collection is considered one of the nation's finest, with magnificent works by the masters of that period. There are masterpieces by Van Gogh, Derain, Monet, Renoir, and Warhol. This was the first U.S. museum to buy works by Picasso and Matisse. It is especially rich in American and European art of the past 50 years. There's an entire room devoted to the massive works of Clyfford Still, who gave the gallery 31 pieces. Overlooking Hoyt Lake, the museum also has a lovely restaurant with tables in the outdoor **Sculpture Court** and a gift shop. Wheelchair accessible.
Details: *Open Tue–Sat 11–5, Sun noon–5. $4 adults, $3 seniors and students, free to children. Free Sat 11–1. (2 hours)*

★★★★ ERIE BASIN MARINA
329 Erie St., Buffalo, 716/842-4141
One of the crown jewels on Buffalo's waterfront, the marina is a popular spot for boaters, water lovers, joggers, and anyone who simply enjoys relaxing and watching boats and the Buffalo skyline. The delightful grounds include lovely rose gardens and test gardens for new flowers. There are restaurants here, and it's a great spot for a picnic.
Details: *Open May–Oct. Free. (2 hours)*

★★★ BUFFALO AND ERIE COUNTY HISTORICAL SOCIETY
25 Nottingham Ct., Buffalo, 716/873-9644
http://intotem.buffnet.net/bechs
Housed in the only building left from the Pan-American Exposition

THE BIRTH OF BUFFALO CHICKEN WINGS

Buffalo is famous as the birthplace of Buffalo chicken wings, now served in restaurants 'round the globe. It was 1964 when Teressa Bellissimo had a brainstorm. Half of the Frank and Teressa team at Frank and Teressa's Anchor Bar, she needed to feed a crowd of her son's friends. She had been about to put some plump wings into a pot of soup when she decided to put them in the deep fryer instead. Teressa served them with special sauce (which now comes in mild, medium, or hot), celery, and blue-cheese dressing, and the rest is history. Wings are now shipped around the country to former Buffaloians and anyone who craves the real thing. Presidents and visiting celebrities have enjoyed them. The Anchor Bar is on the outskirts of downtown Buffalo at 1047 Main Street, 716/886-8920, www.anchorbar.com.

of 1901, this museum offers a look into the history of the area. Bflo. Made! features more than seven hundred products and inventions created in Buffalo, including Cheerios, the pacemaker, Keri lotion, mentholatum, and kazoos.

Details: *Open Tue–Sat 10–5, Sun noon–5. $3.50 adults, $2 seniors, $1.50 children, $7.50 family. (2 hours)*

★★★ **BUFFALO AND ERIE COUNTY NAVAL AND MILITARY PARK**
One Naval Park Cove, Buffalo, 716/847-1773
npark@ci.buffalo.ny.us
Located next to the Erie Basin Marina, this is the largest inland naval park in the country. Climb aboard the USS *Sullivans*, named in honor of the five Sullivan brothers who lost their lives together in World War II. Tour the decks of the USS *Little Rock*, a guided missile cruiser, and the USS *Croaker*, a battle-decorated submarine from World War II, where it definitely paid to be small. There's also a military museum.

Details: *Open Apr–Oct daily 10–5; Nov weekends only, weather permitting. $6 adults, $3.50 seniors and children. (2 hours)*

★★★ DARWIN MARTIN HOUSE
125 Jewett Pkwy., Buffalo, 716/856-3858
www.darwinmartinhouse.org

After years of neglect, this monumental Frank Lloyd Wright masterpiece is undergoing a massive, multimillion-dollar renovation that is expected to be complete by 2001. However, weekend tours are offered now at this complex in the heart of Buffalo's Central Park area just a block from the Buffalo Zoo. Darwin Martin was an executive of the Larkin Soap Company whose brother William had Wright design his house in Chicago. Greatly impressed, Darwin Martin decided he wanted a Wright house himself. He first had Wright design the Barton House on the property for his brother-in-law. After the Barton House was successfully completed in 1903, the Martin House was built in 1904–06. Tours include both houses. The Martin House is considered one of the finest examples of Wright's "Prairie" style.

Details: Tours by reservation only, until renovations are complete. Sat at 10, Sun at 1. $10 adults, $8 students. Children under 10 not allowed. (1 1/2 hours)

THE BROADWAY MARKET

Since 1888 there has been a public food market at 999 Broadway in the heart of Buffalo's Polish community. The Broadway Market, www.broadwaymarket.com, is open year-round, but the best time to capture the unique flavor of the market is the week before Easter. There are more than 40 restaurants, food stores, and bakeries. Many old-time food vendors and bakeries prepare their special foods in front of hungry visitors. This is the place to go for butter lambs, pussy willows (a necessity for celebrating Dyngus Day—the day after Easter), fresh horseradish, freshly baked *chrusciki* (a buttery pastry sprinkled with sugar), and chocolate sponge candies. At the Redlinski and Sons stand, workers make more than 14 miles of special sausage just for the Easter season. Nearby at Bentkowski Poultry, the cooks make pounds and pounds of pierogi, a noodle filled with farmers cheese fried in butter.

★★★ DUNN TIRE PARK
275 Washington St., Buffalo, 716/846-2000
www.bisons.com
Home to International League champion Triple "A" Buffalo Bison Baseball, this ballpark has received national recognition for its design, and it regularly breaks season attendance records. Many games are happenings, with pre- and post-game parties, fireworks, and concerts. It's an affordable, fun way for families to attend a baseball game. Wheelchair accessible.
Details: Open Apr–Sept. $3.25–$8.75. (4 hours)

★★★ *MISS BUFFALO* AND *NIAGARA CLIPPER* CRUISE BOATS
79 Marine Dr., Buffalo, 716/856-6696
www.missbuffalo.com
The perfect way to learn about the role of Lake Erie and the Niagara River in the development of this port city is to take a cruise on *Miss Buffalo* or *Niagara Clipper*. The boats pass through the historic Black Rock Lock and Canal, by the 1833 lighthouse, Old Fort Erie, and the Peace Bridge, one of the world's busiest international bridges.
Details: July and Aug Tue–Sun 12:30 and 3, Fri and Sat 8 p.m.; June and Sept weekends only 3 p.m. $10 adults, $7 children; evening cruises $16. Lunch and dinner cruises available on Niagara Clipper. *(2 hours)*

★★ BUFFALO AND ERIE COUNTY BOTANICAL GARDENS
2655 S. Park Ave. at McKinley Pkwy., Buffalo, 716/696-3555
http://intotem.buffnet.net/gardens/welcome.html
Flower lovers flock to these gardens year-round, but they're especially wonderful during winter when everything is white outside. The glass conservatory is listed on the State and National Register of Historic Places.
Details: Open Mon–Fri 9–4, Sat and Sun 9–5. Free. (1 hour)

★★ BUFFALO ZOOLOGICAL GARDENS
300 Parkside Ave., Buffalo, 716/837-3900
www.buffalozoo.org
Though limited in size compared to some of the country's more expansive zoos, this is the nation's third-oldest zoo and home to more

BUFFALO AND THE UNDERGROUND RAILROAD
In pre–Civil War America, the Underground Railroad offered slaves a route to freedom. Neither underground nor a railroad, the route consisted of homes and other structures where slaves could seek shelter. Buffalo, on the Canadian border, was an important stop on the route to freedom and contained many stations of the Underground Railroad. Unfortunately, all except the **Michigan Avenue Baptist Church**, 511 Michigan Avenue, have been torn down. The church was completed in 1849 and contains hiding places still visible under the staircase.

than one thousand animals. Many are housed in settings that simulate their natural environments. The zoo contains a children's zoo, gift shop, and picnic area.

Details: Open spring and summer daily 10–5, fall and winter 10–4:30. $7 adults, $3 seniors, $3.50 children. (3 hours)

★★ **THEODORE ROOSEVELT INAUGURAL NATIONAL HISTORIC SITE**
641 Delaware Ave., Buffalo, 716/884-0095, www.nps.gov/thri
If you're a Teddy Roosevelt fan, you'll enjoy a visit to this home in the heart of the elegant and historic Delaware Avenue neighborhood. Theodore Roosevelt was inaugurated here as the 26th president on September 14, 1901, following the assassination of President William McKinley. The Teddy Bear Picnic is held here in August, and the Victorian Christmas celebration is in December.

Details: Open Mon–Fri 9–5, Sat and Sun noon–5. $3 adults, $2 seniors, $1 children, $6.50 family. (1 hour)

BUFFALO REGION SIGHTSEEING HIGHLIGHTS

★★★ **RALPH WILSON STADIUM**
One Bills Drive, Orchard Park, 716/649-0015
www.buffalobills.com

A must-see for football fans, this stadium is where the greatest come-back in the history of the National Football League was staged, by the Buffalo Bills under the leadership of backup quarterback Frank Reich. In 1993 the Bills were down 35–3 in a playoff game against the Houston Oilers. Many fans left the stadium in despair and disgust. The Bills came back to win 41–38 in an overtime victory. Of course, it was also here that running back O. J. Simpson ran into the history books and earned a place in the Football Hall of Fame.

Parking lots start filling early because tailgating has become as much a part of the festivities as the game itself. Some tailgaters even bring elaborate menus. There's music, touch-football games, and area radio stations broadcasting live from the lots. Wheelchair accessible.

Details: *Sun and occasional Mon nights Aug–Dec. $30–$37. (4 hours)*

★★ DR. VICTOR REINSTEIN WOODS NATURE PRESERVE
77 Honorine Dr., Depew, 716/683-5959

It's thanks to Dr. Reinstein, a land developer, that this 290-acre preserve exists at all. Located in one of the area's most developed suburbs, there are 65 acres of primeval forest within the preserve that existed before the first European settlement of the area in the 1820s. Visitors are allowed only on guided walks, where they will likely spot deer, great blue herons, and other birds.

Details: *May–Aug guided walks on Wed and Sat (except the first Sat of the month) at 9 and 1; rest of year walks at 9 only. Free. (1 hour)*

★★ HERSCHELL CAROUSEL FACTORY MUSEUM
180 Thompson St., N. Tonawanda, 716/693-1885

Allan Herschell was the best-known carousel maker in the United States. This museum showcasing his work is filled with hand-carved wooden carousel figures. Children delight in riding the 1916 hand-carved wooden carousel.

Details: *Open mid-June–Labor Day daily 1–5; Apr–mid-June and day after Labor Day–Dec 30 Wed–Sun 1–5. $3 adults, $1.50 children, 25¢ per extra carousel ride. (2 hours)*

FITNESS AND RECREATION

In warmer weather, the Erie Basin Marina is a favorite place for joggers. The Frederick Law Olmsted–designed Delaware Park is another popular jogging

BUFFALO REGION

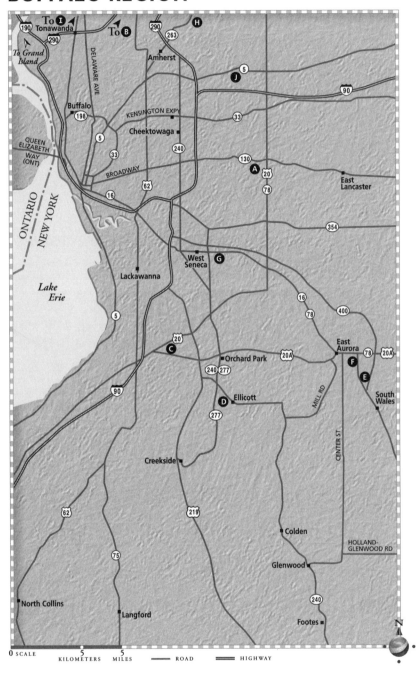

To **I** Tonawanda
To **B**
H
190
290
To Grand Island
263
290
Amherst
DELAWARE AVE
5
J
Buffalo
198
KENSINGTON EXPY
90
QUEEN ELIZABETH WAY (ONT)
5
Cheektowaga
33
33
240
130
A
20
East Lancaster
78
ONTARIO
NEW YORK
33
BROADWAY
16
62
354
Lake Erie
5
West Seneca
G
Lackawanna
16
78
400
20
East Aurora
F
78
20A
C
Orchard Park
20A
240 277
E
South Wales
D
Ellicott
277
MILL RD
CENTER ST
Creekside
62
219
HOLLAND-GLENWOOD RD
75
Colden
Glenwood
North Collins
240
Langford
Footes
N

0 SCALE   5   5
KILOMETERS   MILES   ROAD   HIGHWAY

area. The park boasts one of the country's more authentic Japanese gardens and a lush rose garden. The Riverwalk, which follows the river from downtown Buffalo north, is another good jogging route. Chestnut Ridge Park, in Orchard Park, offers wonderful walking and jogging trails and a great view of Buffalo and Lake Erie.

FOOD

Buffalo is well-known for local and ethnic specialties, including Buffalo chicken wings and "beef on weck" sandwiches (thinly sliced beef on a fresh kimmelweck roll with a dash of horseradish). **Eckl's Beef on Weck Restaurant**, 4936 Ellicott Rd., Orchard Park, 716/662-2262, and **Schwabl's Restaurant** (in business since 1837), 789 Center Rd., West Seneca, 716/674-9821, are well known for this beef dish. For the best in steak, try **E. B. Green's Steakhouse**, 2 Fountain Plaza, Buffalo, 716/855-4870. **Chef's Restaurant**, 291 Seneca St., Buffalo, 716/856-9187, is a longtime favorite for Italian food and is located within a few blocks of both the baseball park and the hockey arena. For a wonderful view of the Niagara River and Canadian sunsets and fine American fare, try **Harry's Harbour Place Grille**, 2191 Niagara St., 716/874-5400, which serves dinners nightly and lunches Monday through Saturday.

Visit the **Roycroft Inn**, 40 S. Grove St., East Aurora, 716/652-5552, to see the beautiful $8 million restoration and enjoy a fine meal. Lunch and dinner daily. Nearby is the **Old Orchard Inn**, 2095 Blakeley Rd., East Aurora, 716/652-4664, offering beautiful home-in-the-country ambiance. Dinner daily. For a romantic French dinner, try **Rue Franklin Restaurant**, 341 Franklin St., Buffalo, 716/852-4416. The **Towne Restaurant**, 186 Allen St., Buffalo, 716/884-5128, in the heart of historic Allentown, offers plentiful Greek food at reasonable prices. Open 23 hours daily.

SIGHTS
- Ⓐ Dr. Victor Reinstein Woods Nature Preserve
- Ⓑ Herschell Carousel Factory Museum
- Ⓒ Ralph Wilson Stadium

FOOD
- Ⓓ Eckl's Beef on Weck Restaurant
- Ⓔ Old Orchard Inn
- Ⓕ Roycroft Inn
- Ⓖ Schwabl's Restaurant

LODGING
- Ⓗ Buffalo/Niagara Marriott
- Ⓘ Holiday Inn Grand Island Resort
- Ⓙ Radisson Hotel and Suites
- Ⓕ Roycroft Inn

Note: Items with the same letter are located in the same area.

SIDE TRIP: WYOMING, THE GASLIGHT VILLAGE

Wyoming, also known as the Gaslight Village, 800/338-XMAS or 716/495-6637, is halfway between Buffalo and Rochester off SR 20. It is still lit by original gaslights and boasts more than 70 homes listed on the National Register of Historic Places. Back in the nineteenth century the rich and famous journeyed to Wyoming and visited the Hillside Inn, an 1851 estate built as a mineral spa and set on 48 acres of woods. After the heyday of the inn, not much attracted folks to Wyoming.

The village's revival began in 1987 when Pam and Brock Yates turned the village's old fire hall into the **Gaslight Christmas & Holiday Shoppe**, a store overflowing with ornaments, lights, and Santas. The couple had moved to the village eight years earlier. Brock Yates, a screenwriter, had just finished filming his Cannonball Run, starring Burt Reynolds. From this beginning, new shops and restaurants opened, including the **Cannonball Run Pub**, stuffed with auto racing and movie memorabilia.

Wyoming is so small that it takes up a mere two-and-a-half pages in the phone book. Everyone's number starts with the same exchange, and most villagers don't bother with the first three digits when they give out their numbers. A fun place to visit any time of the year, Wyoming really comes alive during the Christmas shopping season.

The Hillside Inn, 890 East Bethany Rd., 716/495-6800 or 800/544-2249, has been restored and is again a gracious country inn with 14 elegant bedrooms that feature fireplaces, sitting rooms, and balconies. A lovely restaurant is open to inn guests and the public.

LODGING

Buffalo-area hotels are mostly centered downtown, around the airport, and in the rapidly growing suburb of Amherst, home to the State University of New York at Buffalo. Many offer special weekend and other package plans, so be sure to ask for the best rates.

Downtown, the major hotels include **Adam's Mark Buffalo Hotel**, 120 Church St., 716/845-5100 or 800/444-ADAM, www.adamsmark.com, which features many rooms with good views of the lake and river. Nearby is the **Hyatt Regency Buffalo**, 2 Fountain Plaza, 716/856-1234 or 800/233-1234, www.hyatt.com, which began life as the E. B. Green–designed Genesee Building and retains much of the early architectural charm. Down the street is the **Radisson Suites Downtown**, 601 Main St., 716/854-5500 or 800/333-3333, www.radisson.com. The suites are popular with business travelers and families. It's in the heart of the theater district. **Holiday Inn Downtown**, 620 Delaware Ave., 716/886-2121 or 800-HOLIDAY, www.harthotels.com/Buffalo_Downtown, offers large rooms and includes breakfast. Around the corner is the old-fashioned **Hotel Lenox**, 140 North St., 716/884-1700, popular with visitors on extended stays. Many rooms have kitchenettes. Also downtown is the **Hostel Downtown Buffalo**, 667 Main St., 716/852-5222 or 800/909-4776, www.hiayh.org. Guests share a communal kitchen, laundry room, and lounges in this historic renovated building.

The **Roycroft Inn**, 40 S. Grove St., East Aurora, 716/652-5552 or 800/267-0525, www.someplacesdifferent.com/roycroft.htm, reopened in 1995 after an award-winning $8 million restoration that remained true to its founder, Elbert Hubbard. This National Landmark boasts modern comforts and the Arts and Crafts ambiance of a century-old building. Across the street from the airport, **Radisson Hotel and Suites**, 4243 Genesee St., Cheektowaga, 716/634-2300 or 800/333-3333, www.radisson.com, offers an award-winning restaurant and airport convenience. The **Holiday Inn Grand Island Resort**, 100 Whitehaven Rd., Grand Island, 716/773-1111 or 800/HOLIDAY, www.holiday-inn.com, has a golf course, pools, boat dock, and a grand location on the Niagara River. In Amherst, the **Buffalo/Niagara Marriott**, 1340 Millersport Hwy., Amherst, 716/689-6900 or 800/228-9290, is a longtime favorite with a popular indoor-outdoor pool; it's close to the state university.

CAMPING

Colden Lakes Resort, 9504 Heath Rd., Colden, 716/941-5530, is open May through October. Evangola State Park, on the shores of Lake Erie, Shaw Rd., Irving, 716/549-1760 or 800/456-CAMP, is open May 15 through October 15. Three Valley Campground, Rt. 16, Holland, 716/537-2372, is open May 1 through October 15. Sprague Brook Park, 9674 Foote Rd., Glenwood, 716/592-2804, is open year-round. Point Breeze Campground and Marina, also on Lake Erie, 9456 Lake Shore Rd., Angola, 716/549-3768, is open April 15 through October 15.

NIGHTLIFE

Buffalo's downtown theater district is thriving. Shea's Performing Arts Center, 646 Main St., 716/847-0850, was built in 1926 and is one of the finest movie palaces of its period. It recently reopened after a $14.8 million expansion and renovation. It presents the best of the big Broadway touring shows, concerts, operas, dance, and children's shows. Studio Arena Theatre, 710 Main St., 716/856-5650 or 800/77-STAGE, is the only professional regional theater company and has served as a showcase for many of America's stage stars. Pfeifer Theatre, 681 Main St., 716/847-6461, stages performances in the intimate theater. The Irish Classical Theater, 625 Main St., 716/853-4282, performs Irish classics on an intimate stage. Marquee at the Tralf, 100 Theatre Place, 716/852-0522, is a first-class nightclub in the heart of the district. Nearby is the acoustically perfect Kleinhans Music Hall, 71 Symphony Circle, 716/885-5000, home to the renowned Buffalo Philharmonic Orchestra. During the summer, Shakespeare in the Park offers free performances next to the Rose Gardens in Delaware Park.

13
CHAUTAUQUA COUNTY

Chautauqua County takes its name from its largest lake, called "Jad-dah-gwah" by the Native Americans. The county follows the shores of Lake Erie south of Buffalo to the border of Pennsylvania.

The area's focal point for many visitors is the Chautauqua Institution. Established in 1874 as a training center for Sunday-school teachers, the Institution rapidly grew into a summer-long cultural camp. The center for arts, education, religion, and recreation boasts a full complement of schools and day camps, a lecture series, and top-name performances in its five-thousand-seat amphitheater. President Clinton chose Chautauqua as a weekend retreat to prepare for his presidential debates with Senator Robert Dole. President Teddy Roosevelt, who visited five times and enjoyed muskie fishing, called it "the most American place in America." In keeping with the nineteenth-century atmosphere, a paddlewheeler, the *Chautauqua Belle*, offers cruises around the lake.

At nearby Cassadaga Lake is the Lily Dale Assembly, the country's largest spiritualist center, which began in 1879. Other regional highlights include the Amish community in the Conewango Valley; the Chautauqua Wine Trail; Westfield, the self-proclaimed Grape Juice Capital of the world; and historic Fredonia, the one-time seed capital of the United States. Jamestown, home-town of actress and comedienne Lucille Ball, houses the Lucille Ball–Desi Arnaz Center and hosts the Lucille Ball Festival of New Comedy.

CHAUTAUQUA COUNTY

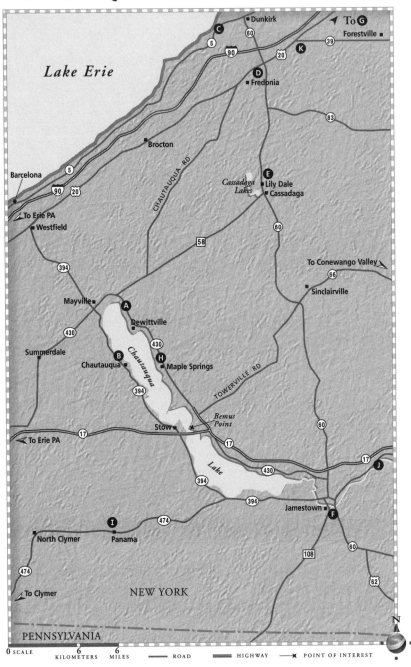

Dunkirk

To G

Forestville

Lake Erie

Fredonia

Brocton

Barcelona

To Erie PA

Westfield

CHAUTAUQUA RD

Cassadaga Lakes

Lily Dale

Cassadaga

To Conewango Valley

Sinclairville

Mayville

Dewittville

Summerdale

Chautauqua

Maple Springs

Chautauqua

TOWERVILLE RD

Bemus Point

Stow

To Erie PA

Lake

Jamestown

North Clymer

Panama

To Clymer

NEW YORK

PENNSYLVANIA

0 SCALE   6   6
       KILOMETERS   MILES   ROAD   HIGHWAY   POINT OF INTEREST

N

A PERFECT DAY IN CHAUTAUQUA

Get an early start to try to catch the wily muskie or lake trout on Chautauqua Lake. There are many choices for classes and activities if you are staying at the Chautauqua Institution, but the morning lectures at the amphitheater are usually thought-provoking. The *Chautauqua Belle* offers an ideal way to see the lake. Afterward, there's time for a swim before dinner. The dining room at the Athenaeum Hotel is a longtime favorite. Ordering two desserts is standard, perfect for someone with a sweet tooth. The rocking chairs on the hotel porch provide an ideal way to relax and watch the lake before an evening concert in the amphitheater.

SIGHTSEEING HIGHLIGHTS

★★★★ **CHAUTAUQUA INSTITUTION**
SR 394, Chautauqua, 716/357-6200 or 800/836-ARTS
www.chautauqua-inst.org
Many people spend the entire nine-week summer season on the grounds of this unique center for the arts, religion, sports, and education. But visitors are also welcome for a day, evening, weekend, or week. Admission is by gate ticket, and, in keeping with the Institution's religious heritage, Sundays are free. The 750-acre Victorian village is a National Historic Landmark and has been welcoming visitors interested in a learning vacation on the shore of Chautauqua Lake since 1874.

The season is filled with classes, concerts, opera, plays, and big-name entertainers. The five-thousand-seat amphitheater overflows on Sundays for the morning religious services, during the day for lectures, and in the evening for concerts. The Institution is also home to the oldest book club in America, and the grounds offer golf, tennis, sailing, hiking, swimming, and fishing. Some hotels and the bookstore

---

SIGHTS

- Ⓐ *Chautauqua Belle*
- Ⓑ Chautauqua Institution
- Ⓒ Dunkirk Lighthouse and Veteran's Park Museum
- Ⓓ Fredonia Opera House
- Ⓔ Lily Dale Assembly
- Ⓕ Lucille Ball–Desi Arnaz Museum
- Ⓖ Merritt Estate Winery
- Ⓗ Midway Park
- Ⓘ Panama Rocks
- Ⓙ Roger Tory Peterson Institute
- Ⓚ Woodbury Vineyards

---

are open during the off-season, and it's a popular spot for cross-country skiing. On weekends in January and February there are horse-drawn carriage rides.

Details: *Open daily nine-week summer season late June–late Aug. No tickets are required for children 12 and under or for anyone 90 and over. The ticket covers admission to the grounds and most events. There are one-day, weekend, one-week, and season tickets available. A one-day ticket is $33–40 for an adult depending on entertainment. These charges are not included in fees for accommodations, except in vacation packages. Tickets for opera and theater must be purchased separately, but no gate ticket is required. Free on Sun. Free during off-season. (1 day)*

★★★ CHAUTAUQUA BELLE
15 Water St., Mayville, 716/753-2403 or 800/753-2506

The *Chautauqua Belle* is one of only three genuine steam-powered boats east of the Mississippi River. In the 1880s and 1890s, the steamboats, called the "Great White Fleet," could each carry as many as three thousand passengers up and down 16-mile-long Chautauqua Lake. The *Chautauqua Belle*, a much smaller version of the nineteenth-century behemoths, comfortably accommodates 120 passengers. It's painted a festive blue and white with an enormous red paddlewheel powered by steam, which sends the wheel around 18 times per minute.

Details: *Jun–Sept departs daily from Mayville at 11, 1:15, and 3. $12 adults, $6 children. (2 hours)*

★★★ MIDWAY PARK
SR 430, Maple Springs, 716/386-3165

If you like amusement parks, you'll love Midway Park, a throwback to another era. It opened in the summer of 1898. Admission is free, unlike just about every other park in the country. Visitors enjoy miniature golf, a roller rink, bumper boats, an arcade, a beach, and docking facilities (you can come by boat).

Details: *Late May–late June open weekends; late June–Labor Day open Tues–Sun. Closed Mon, except holidays. Free entrance; charges on a per-ride basis. (4 hours)*

★★ DUNKIRK HISTORIC LIGHTHOUSE AND VETERAN'S PARK MUSEUM
One Lighthouse Point Dr., Dunkirk, 716/366-5050

ABOARD THE OLDEST U.S. FERRY

Since 1811, the *Bemus Point & Stow* ferry, 716/753-2403, has been carrying people and vehicles across Chautauqua Lake. It is now the oldest continuously operating ferry in the United States. In the early days when Thomas Bemus operated the ferry, it was a log raft that carried vehicles, people, and animals across the thousand-foot narrows. It's a pleasant alternative to the modern bridge that also spans the lake at Bemus Point. The ferry is open weekends from Memorial Day through July 1 and the day after Labor Day through Columbus Day, and daily from July 2 to Labor Day, 9 to 9.

This lighthouse on the shores of Lake Erie offers a great view of the lake and surrounding countryside. The museum has 11 rooms of displays on maritime history and military service.

Details: July–Aug daily 10–4; Apr–June and Sept–Nov daily except Wed. $4.50. (1 1/2 hours)

★★ FREDONIA OPERA HOUSE
9–11 Church St., Fredonia, 716/679-1891
www.fredopera.org

This beautifully restored nineteenth-century theater adds to the ambiance of this historic village. Recipient of a New York State Historic Preservation Award, the region's only year-round performing arts center offers live performances, a cinema series, guided tours, and professional summer theater.

Details: Open Mon–Fri 10–5, evenings for performances. $2 for tours. (1 hour)

★★ LILY DALE ASSEMBLY
5 Melrose Pk., Lily Dale, 716/595-8721

This is the world's largest Spiritualist community, formed in 1879 as an annual meeting place for members of the "Religious Society of Free Thinkers." Visitors can have their fortune told, their palms read, or attend daily clairvoyance demonstrations, lectures, or healing workshops. Over the years many famous people including Mahatma

Gandhi, Sir Arthur Conan Doyle, Susan B. Anthony, and Franklin and Eleanor Roosevelt have visited. Located on the shores of Cassadaga Lake, the Assembly features a bookstore, museum, library, and overnight accommodations.

Details: *Open daily late June–early Sept. $6. (3 hours)*

★★ LUCILLE BALL–DESI ARNAZ MUSEUM
212 Pine St., Jamestown, 716/484-7070
www.lucy-desi.com

Named in honor of the Jamestown native, this center has received strong support from Lucille Ball's family. The museum is filled with interactive displays and Lucy memorabilia donated by her family. Each Memorial Day weekend the community sponsors the Festival of New Comedy, with films and new comedy acts.

Details: *Open Mon–Fri noon–5, Sat 11–5, Sun 1–5. $5 adults, $3.50 seniors and students, $15 family. The comedy festival is held at the Reg Lenna Civic Center, 116 E. Third St., Jamestown, 716/484-7070. Admission varies for festival programs. (2 hours)*

★★ MERRITT ESTATE WINERY
2264 King Rd., Forestville, 716/965-4800

This winery hosts a variety of special events and festivals throughout the year, including strawberry and fall festivals. It hosts free tours and tastings.

Details: *Open Mon–Sat 10–5, Sun 1–5. Free. (1 hour)*

★★ PANAMA ROCKS
11 Rock Hill Rd., Panama, 716/782-2845, www.pana-marocks.com

It's always cool in this park filled with towering rocks, crevice passageways, and deep cavernous dens. Walk along the hiking path through lush forests. Native Americans used these rocks and caves for shelter long before the arrival of French explorers in the mid-1600s. Local legend has it that a gold shipment is buried somewhere here, hidden and then lost by robbers of a nearby bank. Special programs include a Folk Fair and Fall Foliagefest.

Details: *Open May–Oct 20, 10–5. $3 adults, $2 children. (3 hours)*

★★ ROGER TORY PETERSON INSTITUTE
311 Curtis St., Jamestown, 716/665-2473, www.rtpi.org

Named in honor of the late Roger Tory Peterson, who grew up in this area and published his first *Field Guild to the Birds* in 1934, this institute sponsors nature workshops and programs. The fieldstone exterior and rough-sawn siding on the building, as well as the use of wood interiors, complement the meadows and woods that surround it. The area retains the rural character that Dr. Peterson knew as a boy, with woods and fields to roam in search of birds, butterflies, and moths. Regular exhibits include wildlife photography and paintings. Roger Tory Peterson served as the honorary chairman of the board until his death in 1996.

Details: Open Tues–Sat 10–4, Sun and most holidays 1–5. Admission varies with exhibits but it's usually $3 adults, $2 seniors, $1 students and children. (2 hours)

★ **WOODBURY VINEYARDS**
3230 S. Roberts Rd., Fredonia, 716/679-9463 or 888/NYS-WINE
This Fredonia winery produces award-winning wines. You can try out some of these vintages during free tours of the facility.

Details: Open Mon–Sat 10–5, Sun noon–5; summer hours Mon–Sat 9–8, Sun noon–8. Free. (1 hour)

FITNESS AND RECREATION

Early-morning walks at the Chautauqua Institution are delightful, and the mostly car-free 750-acre village makes an ideal spot for cross-country skiing in the winter or jogging. The 73-acre Thayer Road Overview Park escarpment is more than one thousand feet above Lake Erie. Hiking trails include a viewing station accessible to those with disabilities. On a clear day you can see the Buffalo skyline and Canadian shoreline. The French Creek Preserve is a nature preserve with easily accessible, self-guided trails. The Westside Overland Trail, a part of the National Trail System, begins just outside Mayville and extends 25.5 miles south into Panama.

FOOD

The **Athenaeum Hotel**, South Lake Dr., Chautauqua, 716/357-4444 or 800/821-1881, on the grounds of the Chautauqua Institution, welcomes the public to its old-fashioned, elegant dining room that overlooks the lake. No alcohol is served, but two desserts are standard. Breakfast, lunch, and dinner

CHAUTAUQUA COUNTY

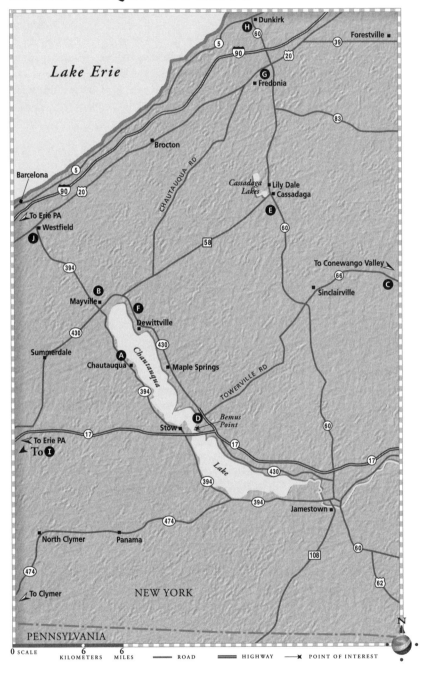

Lake Erie

Dunkirk

Forestville

Fredonia

Brocton

Barcelona

To Erie PA

Westfield

Cassadaga Lakes

Lily Dale

Cassadaga

To Conewango Valley

Sinclairville

Mayville

Dewittville

Summerdale

Chautauqua

Maple Springs

TOWERVILLE RD

CHAUTAUQUA RD

Chautauqua

Bemus Point

Stow

To Erie PA

To

Lake

Jamestown

North Clymer

Panama

To Clymer

NEW YORK

PENNSYLVANIA

0 SCALE   6   6
    KILOMETERS   MILES   ROAD   HIGHWAY   POINT OF INTEREST

N

served daily in season. In Bemus Point, both the **Italian Fisherman**, 61 Lakeside Dr., 716/386-7000, and **Ye Hare 'n Hounds Inn**, 64 Lakeside Dr., 716/386-2181, overlook the lake and are popular dining spots for lunch and dinner. **Webb's Captain's Table**, West Lake Rd., Mayville, 716/753-3960, overlooks the lake and offers several dining rooms, including an outdoor deck. It's open for breakfast, lunch, and dinner daily. **Giambrone's Seafood House**, 7 Water St., Mayville, 716/753-2525, is another popular Mayville eatery serving lunch and dinner daily with an emphasis on seafood, of course.

Lazzaroni's Lakeside Espresso Bar & Restaurant, 282 Dale Dr., Cassadaga, 716/595-2557, offers fine dining on Cassadaga Lakes. Nearby is the **White Horse Inn**, Rt. 60, Cassadaga, 716/595-3523, with good food in a friendly setting. A welcome idea: optional smaller portions at reduced prices for all ages. The **White Inn**, 52 E. Main St., Fredonia, 716/672-2103, has a reputation for fine dining, local wines, and a delectable chocolate mousse cake. Lunch and dinner daily. Close to Amish country and across from Cockaigne Ski Area is the **Grainery Restaurant**, 1494 County Rt. 66, Cherry Creek, 716/287-3500, with fresh food from the area served in a century-old converted barn.

LODGING

The grounds of the Chautauqua Institution have a wide variety of accommodations, including hotels, inns, guest houses, rooms, condominiums, apartments, private homes, and denominational houses operated by various Protestant denominations. Many are open only during the nine-week summer

FOOD
- **A** Athenaeum Hotel
- **B** Giambrone's Seafood House
- **C** Grainery Restaurant
- **D** Italian Fisherman
- **E** Lazzaroni's Lakeside Expresso Bar & Restaurant
- **F** Webb's Captain's Table
- **E** White Horse Inn
- **G** White Inn
- **D** Ye Hare 'n Hounds Inn

LODGING
- **A** Athenaeum Hotel
- **H** Four Points Sheraton Harbourfront Hotel
- **D** Hotel Lenhart
- **I** Peek 'n Peak Resort and Conference Center
- **A** Plumbush
- **A** The Spencer
- **A** We Wan Chu Cottages
- **F** Webb's
- **G** White Inn
- **J** William Seward Inn

Note: Items with the same letter are located in the same area.

season, although some condos and hotels are open year-round. Call 800/836-ARTS or 716/357-6200 for information and a directory. **Chautauqua Lake Vacation Rentals**, 716/789-2600 or 800/344-2198, lists more than 125 homes, condos, cottages, and townhouses for rent. Many are on the Institution grounds. Everyone staying on the Institution grounds must purchase a gate ticket (except children under 12 and adults 90 and over).

The venerable **Athenaeum Hotel**, South Lake Dr., Chautauqua, 716/357-4444 or 800/821-1881, www.athenaeum-hotel.com, is the grande dame of Chautauqua Institution hotels, wired for electricity by Thomas Alva Edison himself, son-in-law of one of the founders. It welcomes guests on the American Plan only—breakfast, lunch, and dinner, with two desserts at lunch and dinner, of course. **The Spencer**, 25 Palestine Ave., Chautauqua, 716/357-3785, www.thespencer.com, is a 27-room Victorian hotel on the Institution grounds and has a loyal following. **Plumbush**, 4542 Chautauqua-Stedman Rd., Chautauqua, 716/789-3093, www.chautauquainfo.com/plumbush.html, is a charming bed-and-breakfast just one mile from the Institution gates and adjacent to the golf course. **We Wan Chu Cottages**, SR 394, Chautauqua, 716/789-3383, is one mile from the Institution and on the lake. All cottages have kitchens. Weekly rates only during summer and minimum two nights otherwise.

In Bemus Point, on Chautauqua Lake, the **Hotel Lenhart**, 20–22 Lakeside Dr., 716/386-2715, has a long history dating back to 1881 and wonderful rocking chairs on the porch painted in primary colors. Breakfast and dinner are included. At the other end of the lake is **Webb's**, 115 W. Lake Rd., Mayville, 716/753-2161, www.usontheweb.com/webbscandies/webbsyearround.htm. Rates vary with the season and there are accommodations overlooking the lake; a boating, pool, and fitness center; and delicious goat-milk fudge in the candy shop. **Four Points Sheraton Harbourfront Hotel**, 30 Lakeshore Dr. E., Dunkirk, 716/366-8350 or 800/525-8350, overlooks the popular fishing harbor and has indoor and outdoor pools. The **White Inn**, 52 E. Main St., Fredonia, 716/672-2103 or 888/FREDONIA, www.whiteinn.com, has been beautifully restored and offers elegant rooms, some with fireplaces. The **William Seward Inn**, 6645 South Portage, Westfield, 716/326-4151 or 800/338-4151; visit www.williamsewardinn.com, was the one-time home of Seward, secretary of state under President Lincoln who was credited with buying Alaska. The rooms are both historic (some date back to the 1830s) and comfortable. **Peek 'n Peak Resort & Conference Center**, 1405 Olde Rd., Clymer, 716/355-4141, www.pknpk.com, offers a hotel and condos, a ski resort, golf course, and conference facilities.

SIDE TRIP: THE VILLAGE OF WESTFIELD

The Village of Westfield, on the shores of Lake Erie, has a place in the nation's history despite its diminutive size. **Barcelona Harbor** was once home to the largest whitefish fleet in North America and continues to offer smoked whitefish at the fishery. It was here that **Welch's Foods** was founded and the pasteurization process for grape juice was invented by Charles Edgar Welch, who declared that "God did not mean for the grape to be fermented."

The village is in the midst of vineyards and orchards. **The Sugar Shack**, 716/326-3351 or 888/563-4324, on SR 5 on the bluffs above Lake Erie, is a must for those with a sweet tooth. This 100-acre farm boasts a special gift shop. The owner, Gail Black, makes more than 25 different flavors of fruit syrups. Free samples are offered and pancake meals are served on weekends by reservation in the adjoining Pancake House.

A couple of miles away is the **Cross Roads Farm & Craft Market** on County Route 21. Open Saturdays from May through December, it offers Amish crafts, antiques, collectibles, books, toys, local foods, wines, and clothing. The village is also the antique capital of the county with more than 20 antique shops—many on SR 20.

Westfield is the hometown of Grace Bedell, who, at the age of 11, is credited with transforming Abraham Lincoln's appearance. During the presidential campaign of 1860, Grace wrote to smooth-shaven Lincoln that she thought he would be much better-looking with whiskers. On February 15, 1861, when Lincoln's train stopped in the village on his way to Washington and his inauguration, he greeted the crowd and told them the story of Grace and his new beard. He called for her to come forward, kissed her, pointed to his whiskers, and said, "You see, I have followed your advice." That historic meeting is commemorated in a larger-than-life bronze statue of Lincoln and Grace that the citizens of the village erected in the summer of 1999.

There's another Lincoln connection in the village: William Seward, Lincoln's secretary of state, who negotiated the purchase of Alaska, lived here in the late 1830s when he was an agent for the Holland Land Co. His home was moved to a hill with a lake view, renovated, and expanded, and is now open to all as the **William Seward Inn**— a most comfortable and welcoming inn.

CAMPING

Camping is popular in the Chautauqua area. Most campgrounds are open mid-April through October. Camp Chautauqua is on Chautauqua Lake, in Stow, 716/789-3435. Blue Water Beach Campground, 7364 E. Lake Rd., Westfield, 716/326-3540, is also on the lake. Nearby is the Westfield-Lake Erie KOA, 8001 Rte. 5, Westfield, 716/326-3573. Chautauqua Heights Campground, 5652 Thumb Rd., Dewittville, 716/386-3804, isn't on the lake but does have a pool.

NIGHTLIFE

There are concerts, operas, ballets, plays, and other programs every evening during the nine-week season at the Chautauqua Institution; call 716/357-6200 or 800/836-ARTS for reservations or program information. In keeping with its Methodist origins, no alcohol is sold on the grounds, although people may partake in their rooms or homes. The absence of alcohol adds to the genteel atmosphere of the Institution. The 1891 Fredonia Opera House, 716/679-1891, offers a year-round schedule of concerts, films, plays, and professional theater.

14
CATTARAUGUS COUNTY

The name "Cattaraugus" traces its roots to the Native Americans who still live in the area. The county is home to the only city in the nation on Native American lands, and the Seneca Indian Nation, a branch of the Iroquois, has a proud history, which is chronicled at the Seneca-Iroquois National Museum.

Allegany State Park, New York's largest state park, annually attracts hundreds of thousands of visitors who come to camp, hike the trails, swim in the two lakes, fish in the streams, ponds, and lakes, snowmobile, cross-country ski, hunt, ride horses, and just take in nature's bountiful beauty. Adjoining the park is the Allegany Reservoir, which spans the New York–Pennsylvania border. Holiday Valley, in the historic and picturesque village of Ellicottville, is a thriving year-round resort, with such activities as golf, swimming, and mountain biking. But it really comes alive during the winter, when skiers flock to the state's largest ski center.

Artists have long been drawn to the peace and serenity of the area. Griffis Sculpture Park is a private park that welcomes visitors to picnic and hike amidst more than two hundred colossal sculptures. Surprisingly, one of the country's major herds of buffalo grazes on a ranch just outside Ellicottville. The state's largest community of old-order Amish live here, forsaking all modern conveniences. Many sell their unique furniture, quilts, and baked goods from their homes.

CATTARAUGUS COUNTY

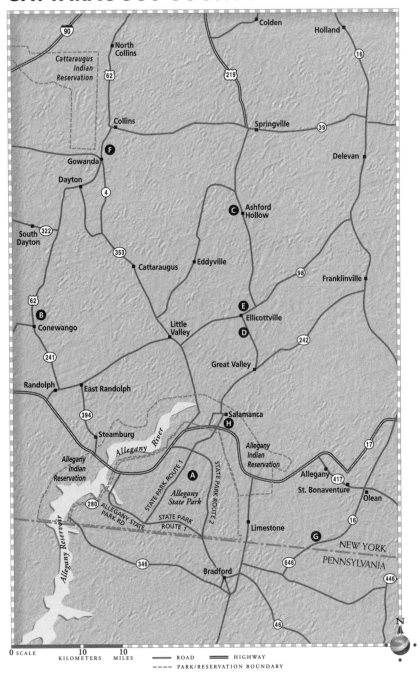

Colden

Holland

90

North
Collins

16

Cattaraugus
Indian
Reservation

62

219

Collins

Springville

39

F

Delevan

Gowanda

Dayton

4

C Ashford
Hollow

South
Dayton

322

353

Cattaraugus

Eddyville

98

Franklinville

62

E

B

Ellicottville

Conewango

Little
Valley

D

241

242

Great Valley

Randolph

East Randolph

394

Salamanca

Steamburg

H

Allegany
River

Allegany
Indian
Reservation

17

Allegany
Indian
Reservation

STATE PARK ROUTE 1

A

STATE PARK ROUTE 2

Allegany
Allegany

417

St. Bonaventure

Olean

280

ALLEGANY STATE
PARK RD

STATE PARK
ROUTE 1

Allegany
State Park

Limestone

16

Allegany Reservoir

G NEW YORK
PENNSYLVANIA

346

646

446

Bradford

46

N

0 SCALE

10
KILOMETERS

10
MILES

ROAD   HIGHWAY

- - - - PARK/RESERVATION BOUNDARY

A PERFECT DAY IN CATTARAUGUS COUNTY

Though this area is blessed with a bountiful snowfall and winter is a favorite season for many, it's hard to match a fine fall day, when the hillsides are ablaze with color. There's no better place for a brisk morning hike than Allegany State Park. Park rangers lead guided nature walks. Stop at the Red House administrative building for a trail map and pick a route. Afterward, take a drive through Amish country, in the western section of the county. Largely undiscovered by tourists, the Amish area has road signs illustrated with a buggy, warning motorists that they now share the roads with horse-drawn vehicles. In the evening head to Ellicottville, a historic village that has been called "the Aspen of the East," filled with restaurants, inns, shops, and boutiques. It's the perfect spot for dinner and after-dinner drinks in one of the many nightspots, always busy on weekends.

SIGHTSEEING HIGHLIGHTS

★★★★ ALLEGANY STATE PARK
Off SR 17, Salamanca, 716/354-2535 or 800/456-CAMP
www.nysparks.com

New York's largest state park has more than 65,000 acres along the Pennsylvania border. The park is surrounded on three sides by the Allegany Indian Reservation. It's a beautiful and wild land with mountains, streams, and lakes. The Erie and Seneca Indian Nations once lived here; Allegany is an Indian word meaning "beautiful waters." Despite Allegany's popularity, it's possible to find solitude here. Wildlife you might spot include deer, wild turkey, pheasant, raccoon, and even bear. Red House and Quaker are the two main recreational areas.

SIGHTS

- Ⓐ Allegany State Park
- Ⓑ Amish Community
- Ⓒ Griffis Sculpture Park
- Ⓓ Holiday Valley Resort
- Ⓔ Nannen Arboretum
- Ⓕ New York and Lake Erie Railroad
- Ⓖ Rock City Park
- Ⓗ Salamanca Rail Museum
- Ⓗ Seneca-Iroquois National Museum

Note: Items with the same letter are located in the same area.

The park has two one-hundred-acre lakes with sand beaches and lifeguards, 80 miles of hiking trails, and cross-country skiing and snowmobile trails. Nearly 400 cabins (130 of which are winterized) are available, as well as three restaurants; a camp store; and bicycles, rowboats, and paddleboats for rent. Various seasonal programs attract visitors to the park. During January the highlight is the **Trappers Special Sled Dog Races**, and in February the **Winter Funfest** welcomes snowmobilers and anyone interested in taking a ride. Snowmobile trails connect with Pennsylvania trails. Be sure your snowmobile is registered in both states if you are crossing the border.

Details: *Open year-round. $4 per car during summer (late June–Labor Day), otherwise free. (5 hours)*

★★★★ **HOLIDAY VALLEY RESORT**
Holiday Valley Rd. off SR 219, Ellicottville, 716/699-2345
www.holidayvalley.com

This is the state's largest ski resort, with 52 slopes and 12 lifts, including the Mardi Gras Express High-Speed Quad. The resort has grown tremendously since it opened in 1957. An average 210 inches of snowfall, supplemented by a snowmaking system, cover the slopes and trails, ensuring skiers a long ski season. During the winter of 1995–96, the resort opened on November 16 and stayed open until April 14, a record 151 days of skiing. The resort encompasses a snowboard park, cross-country ski trails, a complete ski school for adults and children, and a licensed childcare center. Condos and townhouses built on the slopes allow guests the freedom to ski in and out their front door. When the season is over, visitors enjoy an 18-hole golf course, a three-pool complex, and hiking and mountain-bike trails.

Details: *Open daily 8:30–10:30. $21 to $35 for lift ticket depending on day of week and time of day. Special prices for juniors and seniors; weekend and three-, four-, and five-day lift-ticket packages available, as well as season passes and various packages with lodging included. (1 day)*

★★★ **AMISH COMMUNITY**
Western region of county between Randolph and South Dayton

This is the largest community of old-order Amish people in the state. They began coming to the area from Ohio in 1949, seeking farmland. Primarily farmers and carpenters, they live much as their ancestors

THE VILLAGE OF ELLICOTTVILLE

Seventy buildings in Ellicottville (www.ellicottville.com) are listed on the National Register of Historic Places. The most historic of all is a white frame house in the center of the village that was built in 1817 and served as a tavern, trading post, post office, and home. The tiny village's first wedding was held here. Probably most remarkable in today's fast-changing world, the house has been occupied continuously by the same family for more than 180 years.

The house is next to **St. John's Episcopal Church**, built in 1838 on land donated by the Holland Land Co. Regular services are still held in the unique Gothic Revival structure. The bell in its tower was cast in Malaga, Spain, in 1708. The monastery where it originally hung was sacked during a religious war and the bell sold as ballast to a New York sea captain. It was brought to Buffalo on the Erie Canal and then by ox team to Ellicottville.

Best known as a ski town, Ellicottville hosts a variety of summer events ranging from a symphony on the slopes to art shows to a rodeo. The **Ellicottville Fall Festival** attracts thousands and is held every October when the leaves are at their peak of color.

did, without modern conveniences such as cars, tractors, electricity, telephones, television, or radio. The Amish live in the western region of the county between Randolph and South Dayton. You'll know you're in the Amish community when you see simple wooden homes without electric wires, and road signs illustrated with horse-drawn buggies. The Amish sell their leather work, quilts, furniture, and baked goods from their homes. All are of the finest handmade quality. Remember, no photographs, and no business conducted on Sundays.

Details: *No business on Sundays. (3 hours)*

★★★ GRIFFIS SCULPTURE PARK
Ahrens Rd. off SR 219, Ashford Hollow, 716/257-9344

This unique private park is a four-hundred-acre nature preserve with 10 miles of hiking trails. It is also filled with two hundred colossal abstract and representational sculptures, so you can commune with nature and enjoy art at the same time. Tours are available by appointment, but visitors are also free to walk, hike, and picnic amidst the sculptures. Concerts and special programs are held in the summer and fall.

Details: *Open May–Oct daily 9–9; closed Nov–Apr. Free. (2 hours)*

★★★ NEW YORK AND LAKE ERIE RAILROAD
50 Commercial St., Gowanda, 716/532-5716

This excursion train offers a step back in time. One route provides a two-hour ride through the countryside with a stop at the South Dayton depot, where scenes from the movies *The Natural*, starring Robert Redford, and *Planes, Trains and Automobiles*, starring Steve Martin and John Candy, were filmed. In South Dayton, there's time to shop in quilt and antique stores or enjoy an ice cream soda.

Details: *20-mile round trip mid-June–last weekend in Oct Sat and Sun at 1; July and Aug Wed at noon; special excursions rest of year including Santa Claus Express in Dec, Dinner Train, and Murder Mystery Dinner Train. $9 adults, $8 seniors, $4 children, $25 family fares (two adults and up to four children). (2 hours)*

★★★ SENECA-IROQUOIS NATIONAL MUSEUM
794–814 Broad St. Extension, Salamanca, 716/945-1738

The Senecas were known as the Keepers of the Western Door of the Iroquois Confederacy. They still live in the area, and this museum located on Seneca lands is devoted to the history of their culture. The Senecas are one of the original five native nations of the Haudenosaunee, or "People of the Longhouse." At one time their territory spread from northern Canada to South Carolina and from the Hudson River to the Mississippi.

JOHNNY APPLESEED

Johnny Appleseed, who carried apple seeds throughout the country, was from Olean, and he is celebrated every September in his hometown. Push's Cider Mill, SR 98 in Great Valley, is open daily from mid-September through October.

Details: Open Apr–Sept daily 9–5; Oct–Mar Mon–Fri 9–5. Closed Jan. $4 adults, $2 children. (2 hours)

★★ **ROCK CITY PARK**
505 Rock City Rd., Olean, 716/372-7790
Once an Indian fortress and signal station, this park is filled with gigantic rock formations, one in the shape of a teepee. Some of the rocks tower 80 feet high. Once the bottom of a prehistoric ocean, this area contains the largest deposit of cemented quartz conglomerate irregular rock formation. Rock fans can buy rocks in the rock shop. There's also a museum and black-light room to see more rocks.
Details: Open May, June, Sept, and Oct daily 9–6; open July and Aug daily 9–8. $4. (2 hours)

★★ **SALAMANCA RAIL MUSEUM**
170 Main St., Salamanca, 716/945-3133
This Buffalo, Rochester, and Pittsburgh depot was built in 1912 and has been beautifully restored to house this museum of railroad history. Railroad buffs will especially enjoy the train memorabilia, including an authentic rail car to explore.
Details: May–Sept Mon–Sat 10–5, Sun noon–5; Apr and Oct–Dec closed Mon. Closed Jan–Mar. Donation. (1 hour)

★ **NANNEN ARBORETUM**
28 Parkside Dr., Ellicottville, 716/699-2377
This peaceful and lovely spot in the heart of Ellicottville has perennial gardens, more than 260 species of trees, the Lowe Herb Garden, the Ryoanji Temple Stone Garden—an abstract garden of stone and sand created to encourage contemplation—and the Amano-Hashidate Bridge, or "Japanese Bridge to Heaven." The Chapman Nature Sanctuary contains park benches, formal plantings of Kentucky coffee trees, and a stone altar in case you want to get married here or hold other special celebrations.
Details: Open daily. Free. (1 hour)

FITNESS AND RECREATION
Allegany State Park is one of the most popular spots in the region for recreation of all kinds, including hiking, cross-country skiing, and snowmobiling in the winter. There are six golf courses in the area. Holiday Valley boasts 52

CATTARAUGUS COUNTY

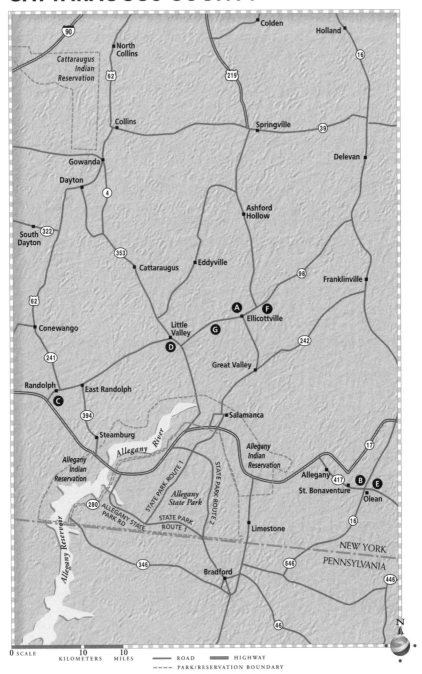

Colden
Holland
90
North Collins
Cattaraugus Indian Reservation
62
16
219
Collins
Springville
39
Gowanda
Delevan
Dayton
4
Ashford Hollow
South Dayton
322
353
Cattaraugus
Eddyville
98
Franklinville
62
A
F
Conewango
Little Valley
G
Ellicottville
241
D
242
Randolph
East Randolph
Great Valley
C
394
Steamburg
Salamanca
Allegany Indian Reservation
17
Allegany River
Allegany Indian Reservation
Allegany
417
B
E
St. Bonaventure
Olean
Allegany Reservoir
STATE PARK ROUTE 1
STATE PARK ROUTE 2
280
ALLEGANY STATE PARK RD
Allegany State Park
STATE PARK ROUTE 7
16
Limestone
NEW YORK
346
PENNSYLVANIA
Bradford
646
446
46

0 SCALE   10   10
KILOMETERS   MILES   ROAD   HIGHWAY
PARK/RESERVATION BOUNDARY

N

slopes and 12 lifts for skiing enthusiasts. During the summer and fall, the resort welcomes hikers and mountain-bike fans.

The Zoar Valley is a wilderness area surrounding deep gorges carved over the millennia by the Cattaraugus Creek. Two whitewater-rafting outfitters offer guided trips for excursions through the gorges: Adventure Calls Rafting, S. Water St., Gowanda, 716/343-4710, and Zoar Valley Canoe & Rafting, 21 S. Water St., Gowanda, 716/679-7238 or 800/724-0696. Spring rafting is by appointment, fall rafting if there is enough water. Cost: $33 for both outfitters. Deer Lick Nature Sanctuary, 716/546-8030, a preserve in Gowanda, offers trails to hike ranging from easy walking to more difficult terrain.

FOOD

Though Cattaraugus County is largely a rural area, a wide range of restaurants offer everything from casual to sophisticated dining. Because of the number of second homes and condos in the area and the influx of visitors who come for the ski season, Ellicottville has more restaurants than might be expected in a small town. (The village has a population of just five hundred year-round residents.) **Ellicottville Brewing Co.**, 28A Monroe St., Ellicottville, 716/699-ALES, is a popular microbrewery and grill house. The **Barn Restaurant**, 7 Monroe St., Ellicottville, 716/699-4600, is another longtime favorite serving lunch and dinner daily, housed in a converted one-hundred-year-old barn. **Fenton's**, 10 Washington St., Ellicottville, 716/699-2373, is in the Ellicottville Inn and is a favorite with skiers. The **Silver Fox Restaurant**, 23 Hughey Alley, Ellicottville, 716/699-4672, offers fine food and a warm welcome. **Dina's**, 15 Washington St., Ellicottville, 716/699-5330, is a popular village eatery. The **Old Library Restaurant**, 120 S. Union St., Olean, 716/373-6662, on the Register of National Historic Sites, is an award-winner and a favorite with locals and visitors for lunch and dinner daily.

FOOD
- Ⓐ Barn Restaurant
- Ⓐ Dina's
- Ⓐ Ellicottville Brewing Co.
- Ⓐ Fenton's
- Ⓑ Old Library Restaurant
- Ⓒ R & M Restaurant
- Ⓐ Silver Fox Restaurant

LODGING
- Ⓓ Bush Bed & Breakfast
- Ⓔ Castle Inn
- Ⓐ Ellicottville Inn
- Ⓕ Ilex Inn
- Ⓖ Inn at Holiday Valley
- Ⓐ Jefferson Inn

Note: Items with the same letter are located in the same area.

R & M Restaurant, 265 Main St., Randolph, 716/358-5141, is in the heart of Amish country and serves family-style meals at reasonable prices. Breakfast, lunch, and dinner daily.

LODGING

Many overnight accommodations are available in the Ellicottville area because of the ski resort. Most Ellicottville lodgings have higher rates on weekends and during the winter. **Ye Olde Towne & Country Realty**, 30 Washington St., Ellicottville, 716/99-2456 or 800/680-0863, handles rentals for chalets, condos, townhouses, and private homes. The **Inn at Holiday Valley**, SR 219, Ellicottville, 716/699-2345, www.holidayvalley.com, is an award-winning inn with an indoor-outdoor pool and easy access to the slopes. It adjoins a golf course and promotes its year-round recreational features. The **Ellicottville Inn**, 4–10 Washington St., Ellicottville, 716/699-2373, is in the heart of the village in a restored, century-old building. Also in the middle of the village is the **Jefferson Inn**, 3 Jefferson St., Ellicottville, 716/699-5869, a lovely Victorian bed-and-breakfast. The **Ilex Inn**, SR 219, Ellicottville, 716/699-2002 or 800/496-6307, www.ilexinn.com, is another elegant bed-and-breakfast with a hot-tub whirlpool spa. Outside Ellicottville, **Bush Bed & Breakfast**, SR 353, Little Valley, 716/938-6106, is a nearly century-old home updated for today's guests. The **Castle Inn**, 3220 W. State St., Olean, 716/372-1050 or 800/422-7853, is just across from St. Bonaventure University and is a complete resort with a golf course, pool, and ski packages.

CAMPING

Naturally, Allegany State Park contains the most popular and biggest campground, with nearly four hundred sites (including 130 winterized cabins) and a full year-round park program. It is located off SR 17, Salamanca; call 716/354-2535 or 800/456-CAMP for reservations. J.J.'s Pope Haven, Pope Rd., SR 241, Randolph, 716/358-4900, is in the heart of Amish country. Highbanks Campground, operated by the Seneca Nation of Indians, is on the Allegany Reservoir, SR 394, Steamburg, 716/354-4855 or 888/341-8890. Triple R Campground, 3491 Bryant Hill Rd., Franklinville, 716/676-3856, is a full-service RV facility with a tent area.

15
CORNING AND ELMIRA

Glass, Mark Twain, and soaring help to define the Corning and Elmira area, which anchors the Finger Lakes region near the Pennsylvania border. Corning is the hometown of Corning Glass Works. Bulbs for Thomas Edison's incandescent lamps were one of the company's early products; today, Steuben Glass creations are often given as gifts by American presidents to foreign heads of state. The Corning Glass Center opened in 1951 to mark the one hundredth birthday of Corning Glass Works and is now one of the top tourist attractions in the state. Housing the world's largest collection of glass objects, the Corning Museum of Glass has objects ranging from weapons chipped from volcanic glass by prehistoric people to exquisite handblown pieces by contemporary artists.

Nearby Elmira is known as "Mark Twain Country." Samuel Clemens, a.k.a. Mark Twain, called the area "a garden of Eden." He married an Elmira native, Olivia Langdon, and the family spent 20 summers at the home of Olivia's sister and brother-in-law atop East Hill. In his beloved Octagon Study, he brought to life Huck Finn, Tom Sawyer, the Connecticut Yankee, and many other characters.

Since 1930, when a national soaring contest was held on a mountaintop south of the city, Elmira has also been called the Soaring Capital of America. The National Soaring Museum tells the story of soaring; just outside, sailplanes and pilots stand by to take visitors into the air on a motorless flight. In the

CORNING AND ELMIRA REGION

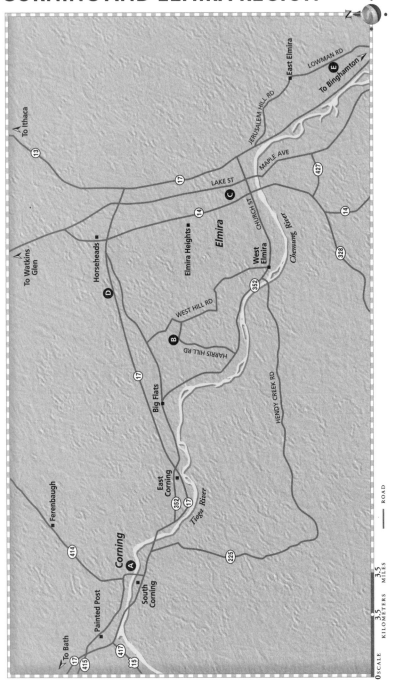

N

To Ithaca

13

To Watkins Glen

17

Horseheads

LAKE ST

14

Elmira Heights

Elmira

JERUSALEM HILL RD

East Elmira

LOWMAN RD

To Binghamton

E

MAPLE AVE

CHURCH ST

CHURCH ST

427

14

328

Chemung River

West Elmira

352

D

WEST HILL RD

B

HARRIS HILL RD

HENDY CREEK RD

17

Big Flats

Tioga River

East Corning

352

17

225

Ferenbaugh

414

Corning

A

South Corning

Painted Post

417

To Bath

17

415

15

SCALE

0   3.5
KILOMETERS

0   3.5
MILES

ROAD

summer of 1998 the National Warplane Museum moved nearby, so aviation fans now have a wealth of area attractions. The Near Westside Historic District in Elmira, listed on the National Register of Historic Places, contains the largest number of Victorian-style buildings in the state.

A PERFECT DAY IN CORNING AND ELMIRA

The Corning Glass Center is always a fascinating place. Watch talented craftspeople in the magical act of glass blowing at the Steuben Glass Factory. After a morning at the center, hop on a free bus that operates in the summer and ride to Market Street (it's a short walk if the buses aren't running). Stop at the Ice Cream Works, in the middle of the historic Market Street District, for lunch and ice cream. Take time to stroll through the district and admire the nineteenth-century architecture. Mark Twain called the area "a foretaste of heaven." It's easy to accept his assessment from a sailplane more than three thousand feet in the air. Soaring is exhilarating, pure, and simple. Top off the day with dinner at Pierce's 1894 Restaurant in Elmira, complete with a glass of fine Finger Lakes wine.

SIGHTSEEING HIGHLIGHTS

★★★★ **CORNING GLASS CENTER**
One Corning Glass Center off SR 17, Corning, 607/974-8271 or 800/732-6845, www.corningglasscenter.com
Housed in a spectacular Gunnar Birkerts building, this complex is constructed, appropriately enough, mostly of glass. The Glass Center is currently undergoing a multimillion-dollar renovation, scheduled for completion by 2001, in commemoration of the company's 150th anniversary and the 50th anniversary of the opening

---

SIGHTS

- **A** Benjamin Patterson Inn
- **A** Corning Glass Center
- **B** Harris Hill Soaring Corp.
- **C** Mark Twain Octagon Study
- **A** Market Street

- **B** National Soaring Museum
- **D** National Warplane Museum
- **E** Newtown Battlefield Reservation
- **A** Rockwell Museum

Note: Items with the same letter are located in the same area.

of the Glass Center and the **Corning Museum of Glass**. Begin your museum tour in the new 80-seat theater, where you can view a film that introduces you to the nature of glass. The museum displays the world's greatest collection of glass—more than 30,000 objects in all—dating from 1400 B.C. through the twentieth century. Visitors may gently touch a bottle found in a two-thousand-year-old Roman tomb. Methods of making and decorating glass are described and shown in short movies. Four new galleries have been added: a gallery for twentieth-century glass sculpture, a gallery on the history of the glassmaking industry in Corning, a study gallery, and a gallery for special temporary exhibits.

The **Glass Innovation Center** has three galleries that tell the stories of glass innovations that have dramatically shaped our world. In the Optics Gallery, visitors follow the scientist's quest to control light with glass.

A popular stop is the daily **Hot Glass Show**, a narrated demonstration of glassblowing. Visitors are seated theater-style with cameras to facilitate viewing every action—even within the furnace (called a glory hole). Temperatures in the glory hole reach 2,350 degrees Fahrenheit. Suspended above the hot-glass stage area, a series of video monitors display magnified images of the live presentation.

*Corning makes an ideal stop for travelers who are driving across the state. It is on SR 17, a popular southern route for motorists, and there's enough to see and do for a day or more. Even if there isn't time for sightseeing, a visit to the **Ice Cream Works** on Market Street offers a step back in time, wonderful ice cream, and a pleasant break from driving.*

The final stop is the **Steuben Factory**, the only place in the world where Steuben glass artisans create crystal masterpieces from molten glass. Visitors are invited to sit in the tiered gallery to watch the process. Visitors can also enjoy close-up views of the artisans using rotating copper wheels to engrave intricate designs in the crystal. If the result is not perfect—if it does not meet exacting Steuben standards—it is destroyed and recycled. There are no seconds in the Steuben world. The Steuben showroom has $150 paperweights and art objects selling for $5,000 or more. The center's gift shops sell all manner of glass objects, including Corningware and Pyrex cookware. Wheelchair accessible.

MARK TWAIN OCTAGON STUDY

© NYS Department of Economic Development

Details: *Open daily 9–5; Jul–Aug 9–8. $6 adults, $5 seniors, $4 children, $16 family maximum. (4 hours)*

★★★★ HARRIS HILL SOARING CORP.
63 Soaring Hill Dr., Elmira, 607/739-7899 (office) or 607/734-0641 (field)

This soaring club in Harris Hill Park sits next to the National Soaring Museum. Many people enjoy coming to the park just to watch the sailplanes take off and land—scenes reminiscent of the old barnstorming days. If you are willing to accept that these fragile-looking planes can transport you into the sky and then safely back to earth, then the club is ready to indulge your fantasy. It offers rides daily (weather permitting) during the summer and on weekends the rest of the year, or by special arrangement. Some 3,500 feet above the earth, it is incredibly quiet and peaceful. In today's noisy world it's harder and harder to find quiet, but here there are no engines, just the soft rush of the wind outside. The Wright brothers once were asked why they kept flying sailplanes after they invented powered flight. Their answer: "Everyone knows sailplanes are more fun." Most everyone who has experienced a sailplane ride would agree.

Details: *Open daily 10–6 during the summer; weekends rest of year. $45 for a ride in a sailplane trainer, $60 for a ride in a high-performance sailplane. Free if you just want to watch, of course. (1 hour)*

★★★ MARK TWAIN OCTAGON STUDY
Elmira College campus, Elmira, 607/735-1941
www.elmira.edu

Mark Twain spent 20 summers in Elmira. It was at his wife's sister and brother-in-law's farm that he wrote some of his classics, including *The Adventures of Huckleberry Finn*. Twain loved his study at the farm: "It is the loveliest study you ever saw. It is octagonal, with a peaked roof, each face filled with a spacious window . . . . It is a cozy nest and just room in it for a sofa, table and three or four chairs . . . imagine the luxury of it." The study has been moved from Quarry Farm to the campus of Elmira College, where there is also an exhibit of photographs and memorabilia relating to Twain's connection with Elmira. The exhibit displays a typewriter similar to the one Twain used—he was one of the first authors to submit a typewritten manuscript to his publisher.

Details: *Open daily late June–Aug 10–5 or by appointment. Free. (1 hour)*

★★★ MARKET STREET
Corning, 607/936-4686, www.corning-chamber.org

Brick sidewalks lead pedestrians down Market Street, Corning's commercial center, which has thrived for a century and a half. Now a National Historic District, the area's buildings have been beautifully restored. During the summer, shuttle buses stop along Market Street and at the Glass Center. Rides are free. This street is ideal for window shoppers and browsers, with more than one hundred antique shops, bookstores, clothing shops, glass studios, outlets, and restaurants. Benches and outdoor tables and chairs offer places to relax and dine in warmer weather. Shops are wheelchair accessible.

Details: *(2 hours)*

★★★ NATIONAL SOARING MUSEUM
51 Soaring Hill Dr., Elmira, 607/734-3128
www.soaringmuseum.org

Anyone with an interest in flying will enjoy this museum. It boasts the world's largest collection of sailplanes, along with the only full-scale

replica of the Wright Glider No. 5. This was the glider in which Orville Wright started the world soaring movement in 1911 with his then record-breaking flight of 9 minutes, 45 seconds. The flight simulator is open to anyone who wants to climb in and imagine what it's like to fly off into the wild blue yonder. The museum includes a restoration area and exhibits sprinkled with quotes from the town's most famous summer resident, Mark Twain. Wheelchair accessible.
Details: *Open daily 10–5. $3. (1 hour)*

★★★ NATIONAL WARPLANE MUSEUM
Elmira-Corning Regional Airport, off SR 17, Horseheads
607/739-8200, www.warplane.org
This museum moved here from Geneseo in the summer of 1998. It restores and maintains in flying condition World War II, Korean War, and Vietnam War–era aircraft. The highlight of the museum's collection is the "Fuddy Duddy," a B-17 Flying Fortress. The B-17 was one of the most dramatic symbols of U.S. air strength during World War II. Of the 12,731 B-17s built during the war, only 11 remain in flying condition, including the museum's "Fuddy Duddy." The museum's collection also includes a TBM Avenger (the type of aircraft flown by George Bush in World War II), an F-14 Tomcat (of *Top Gun* fame), a PBY Catalina, a PT-17 Stearman, and an R4D (the Navy version of the famous DC-3).
Details: *Open Mon–Sat 9–5, Sun 11–5. $5 adults, $4 seniors, $3 children, $13 family. The museum offers sightseeing rides on the B-17 for $300. In mid-Sept the Wings of Eagles Air Show features more than one hundred vintage and modern military aircraft. (1 hour)*

GLASSBLOWING CLASSES
Have you always wanted to learn glassblowing or beadmaking? The Studio of the Corning Museum of Glass, 607/974-6467, e-mail TheStudio@cmog.org, offers one-day, weekend, and one- and two-week courses in glassblowing, beadmaking, paperweights, marble making, and various other glassmaking techniques. One-day sessions are designed for the entire family, including children 10 and older.

CORNING AND ELMIRA REGION

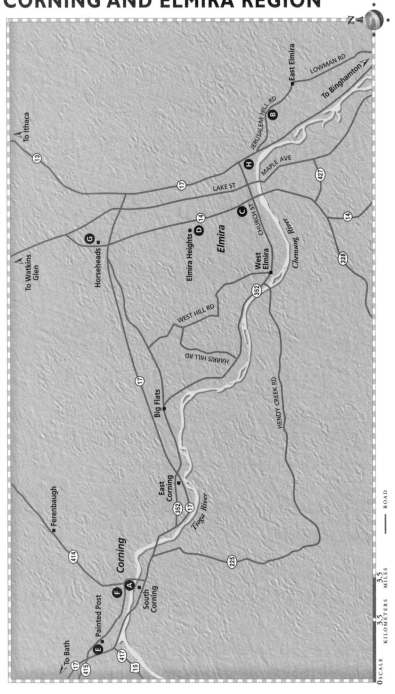

N

To Binghamton

LOWMAN RD

East Elmira

JERUSALEM HILL RD

B

To Ithaca

13

427

H

MAPLE AVE

17

LAKE ST

14

CHURCH ST

D

14

C

Elmira

Chemung River

328

To Watkins Glen

G

Horseheads

Elmira Heights

West Elmira

352

WEST HILL RD

HARRIS HILL RD

17

Big Flats

HENDY CREEK RD

Ferenbaugh

East Corning

352

17

Tioga River

114

Corning

225

A

F

South Corning

E

Painted Post

To Bath

17

414

17

15

0 SCALE 3.5 KILOMETERS 3.5 MILES

——— ROAD

★★★ ROCKWELL MUSEUM
111 Cedar St., Corning, 607/937-5386
www.stny.lrun.com/RockwellMuseum

This museum is filled with the eclectic collection of art and objects amassed by the Robert F. Rockwell Jr. family, whose fortune came from a small chain of department stores in the Corning area. It is located in the heart of town in a huge Romanesque building that once housed the city hall and jail. Rockwell was a friend of Frederick Carder, founder of Steuben Glass, who spent 80 of his 100 years designing and making glass in town. More than two thousand pieces of Carder glass are on display. The museum also houses an outstanding collection of Western art—the largest such collection east of the Mississippi—including paintings and sculptures by Frederic Remington and Charles M. Russell, the most famous cowboy artists of all. The wonderful collection of antique toys appeals to the child in all of us. Wheelchair accessible.

Details: *Open daily 10–5, Sun noon–5. $5 adults, $4 seniors, $2.50 children. (2 hours)*

★★ BENJAMIN PATTERSON INN
59 W. Pulteney St., Corning, 607/937-5281

This inn re-creates what life was like for the area's early settlers. The original inn was constructed in 1796 and has been carefully restored. The grounds also display the 1784 DeMonstoy Log Cabin, an 1878 one-room schoolhouse, a blacksmith shop, and a barn.

Details: *Open Mon–Sat 10–4; closed major holidays. $3 adults, $1 children ages 6–18. (2 hours)*

FOOD
Ⓐ Boomers
Ⓑ Hill Top Inn
Ⓐ Ice Cream Works
Ⓐ London Underground Café
Ⓒ Moretti's Restaurant
Ⓓ Pierce's 1894 Restaurant
Ⓐ Sorge's Restaurant
Ⓐ Taste of China

LODGING
Ⓔ Best Western Lodge on the Green
Ⓕ Days Inn of Corning
Ⓖ EconoLodge
Ⓗ Holiday Inn Riverview
Ⓐ Radisson Hotel Corning
Ⓕ Rosewood Inn

Note: Items with the same letter are located in the same area.

★ **NEWTOWN BATTLEFIELD RESERVATION**
455 Oneida St. off SR 17, Elmira, 607/732-6067
This is the site of General Sullivan's famous Revolutionary War battle. Sullivan, under the command of George Washington, destroyed 41 settlements in the area. The reservation marks a decisive victory for Sullivan over a large force of Indians and Tories. Not far from the actual battlefield is Sullivan's Monument, which commemorates this confrontation on August 29, 1779. Today the reservation is part of a 330-acre park with facilities for camping, hiking, and picnicking. **Details:** *Open daily. Free. (2 hours)*

FITNESS AND RECREATION

Harris Hill Park, 599 Harris Hill Rd., Big Flats, 607/737-2907, offers a chance to watch planes landing and taking off, and to gaze at hang gliders and the lovely Chemung River Valley below. There are trails for walking or hiking, a pool, an amusement park, and picnic facilities. During the winter there are cross-country ski trails, slopes for toboggans and sleds, and a frozen pond for skating. The Tanglewood Nature Center, West Hill Rd., Elmira, 607/732-6060, has marked trails through flora and fauna. Visitors can hang glide, cross-country ski, hike, picnic, and enjoy panoramic views at Mossy Bank Park, off County Route 10, Bath, 607/776-3811.

FOOD

Pierce's 1894 Restaurant, 228 Oakwood Ave., Elmira Heights, 607/734-2022, is an award-winning family-owned restaurant in a rambling brick building with Victorian parlors; the wine list features New York State wines. Dinner Monday through Saturday. **Hill Top Inn**, 171 Jerusalem Hill, Elmira, 607/732-6728, offers outstanding views from atop the hill and indoor and outdoor dining. Dinner Monday through Saturday. **Moretti's Restaurant**, 800 Hatch St., Elmira, 607/734-1535, is a popular restaurant that has welcomed diners for dinner nightly since 1917.

Sorge's Restaurant, 66–68 Market St., Corning, 607/937-5422, is a popular Italian-food establishment. Lunch and dinner daily. **Taste of China**, 84 E. Market St., Corning, 607/962-6176, features an extensive Cantonese and Szechuan menu. Lunch and dinner daily. **Ice Cream Works**, W. Market St. and Centerway Sq., Corning, 607/962-8481, offers light meals and a big selection of ice-cream creations in a restored 1880s ice cream parlor. The **London Underground Café**, 69 E. Market St., Corning, 607/962-2345, has fine dining in a three-level setting. Lunch and dinner daily. **Boomers**, 35 E. Market St., Corning, 607/962-6800, is a good choice for families and offers 99-cent kids' meals. Lunch and dinner daily.

LODGING

The **Radisson Hotel Corning**, 125 Denison Parkway E., Corning, 607/962-5000 or 800/333-3333, www.radisson.com, anchors the Market Street Historic District. Also well located is the **Days Inn of Corning**, 52 Ferris St., Corning, 607/936-9370 or 800/DAYS-INN. A few miles outside Corning is the **Best Western Lodge on the Green**, SR 15 and 417, Painted Post, 607/962-2456. The **Rosewood Inn**, 134 E. First St., Corning, 607/962-3253, www.bbchannel.com, is a charming bed-and-breakfast inn just two blocks from Market Street. Each of the antique-filled rooms is named after a famous Corning-area resident. **Holiday Inn Riverview**, 760 E. Water St., Elmira, 607/734-4211 or 800/HOLIDAY, www.holiday-inn.com, is right on the Chemung River in the heart of downtown Elmira. The **EconoLodge**, 871 County Rt. 64, Elmira, 607/739-2000, is just five miles from Harris Hill.

CAMPING

In Corning, the Ferenbaugh Campsite, 4121 SR 414, 607/962-6193, has 140 campsites as well as swimming and fishing; it is open from April 15 to October 15. The Newtown Battlefield Reservation, 599 Harris Hill Rd., Elmira, 607/737-2907, is a small campground in an historic setting, with 19 sites; it is open from May 12 to October 9.

SHOPPING

A large store at the Corning Glass Center stocks all manner of Corning glass, jewelry, kitchenware, and other items. Bargains can be had here on seconds and discontinued items. The Steuben Glass Store in the Glass Center carries lovely glass art works but no bargains or seconds (if a Steuben piece is not perfect, it is destroyed). Along Market Street there are more stores with glass objects and studios where artists create glass works of art in front of shoppers. There are also several factory outlets along the historic street. Call 607/936-4686 for information on Market Street shopping.

16
THE FINGER LAKES

Cayuga, Canandaigua, Keuka, Hemlock, Honeoye, Otisco, Owasco, Canadice, Conesus, Skaneateles, and Seneca—these names sound like a roll call for the Indians of the Iroquois Confederacy, who dominated this area in the middle of the state for more than two centuries. But they are also the names of the Finger Lakes. Iroquois legend has it that the Finger Lakes region was formed when the Great Spirit placed his hand in blessing on this favored land. Geologists have a more prosaic explanation: the lakes were created when Ice Age glaciers retreated about one million years ago. The intense pressure of those ice masses created the long narrow lakes lying side by side, the deep gorges with rushing falls, and the wide, fertile valleys that extend south for miles. These features are found nowhere else in the world.

The Finger Lakes region is the land of dreamers—dreamers who founded a religion, began the women's rights movement, pioneered the motion-picture industry, and founded prestigious schools and universities. Viticulture is another of the region's many offerings. Not only did the retreating glaciers create the lakes, but they also created ideal conditions for grape growing by depositing a shallow layer of topsoil on sloping shale beds above the lakes. The deep lakes also provide protection from the climate by moderating temperatures along their shores.

"The land of silly names," political scientist Francis Lieber called the region in the 1830s. There are towns named Ovid and Homer, Etna and Ulysses,

Marathon and Virgil, Hector and Hemlock. Museums abound and they are devoted to such varied subjects as agriculture, auto racing, aviation, dolls, electronics, the Erie Canal, Indians, salt, soaring, and winemaking.

A PERFECT DAY AT THE FINGER LAKES

Begin the day with a hike along the Gorge Trail in Taughannock Falls State Park. At 215 feet, this is the highest vertical waterfall in the East. The flat, easy walk heads through a rugged canyon and quiet woods, along a peaceful stream to the falls. Take a tour of one of the nearby wineries. A longtime favorite is Wagner Vineyards, home to the Ginny Lee Café, overlooking the vineyards and deep blue Seneca Lake. During the warmer months it's the perfect spot to enjoy lunch and a glass of wine. Ithaca, home to Cornell University, is a beautiful and cosmopolitan small city with a wide array of dining choices. Finish your day at Watkins Glen State Park for the production of *Timespell*, a sound and light show set against the spectacular natural stage of the gorge.

SIGHTSEEING HIGHLIGHTS

★★★★ WATKINS GLEN STATE PARK
Franklin St., Watkins Glen, 607/535-4511, www.nysparks.com

This is the most famous of the many parks in the region. The best way to experience the beauty of the glen is to hike the gorge trail. This trail and others are accessible from the main, south, and upper entrances. Most visitors walk uphill from the main entrance and return. Others take a shuttle bus to the upper entrance and walk the one-and-one-half miles back down to the main entrance. The trail has more than eight hundred stone steps. It's not a difficult walk, but the footing can get slippery, so be sure to wear suitable footwear. The park encompasses 19 waterfalls, which bear such names as Rainbow, Diamond, and Pluto, plus a series of grottoes, caves, and cataracts. You'll pass over and under bridges and through handcut tunnels—the "narrows," with a microclimate almost like that of a rain forest.

Some 302 campsites are available here, divided into villages named for the Native Americans who lived in the area. At dusk, witness *Timespell*, where the haunting voice of the narrator explains the creation of Watkins Glen as vivid laser lights dance off waterfalls and cliffs and sounds convey erupting volcanoes, crackling ice, and the

THE FINGER LAKES

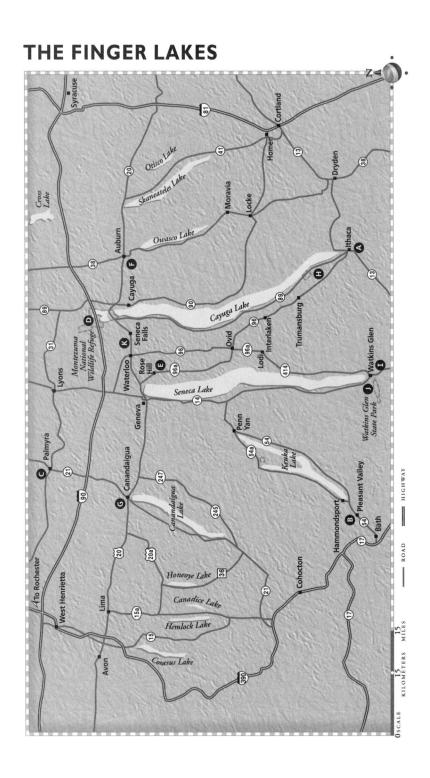

rhythmic beating of the Senecas' drums. It's a stirring performance set against a spectacular stage—the gorge of the park.

Amenities at the park include a main swimming pool, a children's pool, a recreation building, a picnic area, a playground, playing fields, and other hiking trails. The main entrance is on SR 14 in the village of Watkins Glen, at the southern tip of Seneca Lake.

Details: *Open daily year-round, but the camping area and gorge trail are open only mid-May–Columbus Day. Summer $5 per car, otherwise free. Timespell $5.25 adults, $4.75 seniors and children. (3 hours)*

★★★ HILL CUMORAH VISITOR CENTER
603 SR 21, Palmyra, 315/597-5851
www.canaltown.net/hillcumorah

This is the site of the founding of the Mormon Church and is believed to be where Joseph Smith received a history of ancient American people on gold plates, which became the Book of Mormon. The Hill Cumorah Pageant, held here during the second week of July, is America's largest outdoor drama, attracting more than 100,000 annually. The pageant, which is free, features high technology, magnificent music, and a costumed cast of six hundred. It has been presented by the Church of Jesus Christ of Latter-day Saints since 1935. Joseph Smith's home, built in 1820, has been restored and is open for touring.

Details: *Open daily 9–6. Free. (1 hour for tour)*

★★★ MONTEZUMA NATIONAL WILDLIFE REFUGE
3395 SR 5 and 20 E., Seneca Falls, 315/568-5987
www.fws.gov/r5mnwr

This refuge, at the north end of Cayuga Lake, was established in 1938 as a breeding ground for migratory birds and other wildlife as a unit

---

SIGHTS

- **O** Cornell University Plantations
- **B** Glenn H. Curtiss Museum
- **A** Herbert F. Johnson Museum of Art
- **C** Hill Cumorah Visitor Center
- **D** Montezuma National Wildlife Refuge
- **E** Rose Hill Mansion
- **A** Sciencenter

- **F** Seward House
- **G** Sonnenberg Gardens
- **H** Taughannock Falls State Park
- **I** Watkins Glen International Track
- **J** Watkins Glen State Park
- **K** Women's Rights National Historical Park

Note: Items with the same letter are located in the same area.

---

of the Atlantic Flyway. Motorists crossing the state via the New York Thruway pass through it, but it's hard to see much at highway speed. The refuge is worth a stop, especially for bird lovers. A total of 315 species of birds have been identified here. While birds are in abundance year-round, it's best to time your visit for the fall or spring migration seasons to see hundreds of Canada geese, ducks, and snow geese. Stop first at the visitors center, where rangers are on duty to answer questions and provide up-to-date information on the latest sightings. The observation deck and tower provide excellent opportunities to see wildlife. During our recent visit the highlight was the sight (through a telescope) of a bald eagle sitting on her nest. Wheelchair accessible.

Stewart Park, off SR 13 on the shores of Cayuga Lake, was the site of the early movie industry of 1912–20. During this era Pearl White, Lionel Barrymore, and Irene Castle were featured in films made in Ithaca. Today, it's the perfect picnic spot, and young and old enjoy the restored historic carousel.

Details: *Open daily during daylight hours. Visitors center staffed on weekends, most Tuesdays, and holidays. Free. (2 hours)*

★★★ **SCIENCENTER**
601 First St., Ithaca, 607/272-0600, www.sciencenter.org
This hands-on museum adjoins an outdoor science park and is popular with families. More than 50 exhibits include a water raceway, a computer voyage through the galaxy, a you-build-it bridge, and a flume exhibit where visitors can control the speed and direction of the flowing water. Wheelchair accessible.

Details: *Open Tue–Sat 10–5, Sun noon–5. $3.75 adults, $2.75 children. (2 hours)*

★★★ **SONNENBERG GARDENS**
151 Charlotte St., Canandaigua, 716/924-5420
www.sonnenberg.org
A great bronze Buddha sits in the lotus position in the Japanese Garden, an oasis of serenity under sheltering trees and one of the 10 formal gardens here. Sonnenberg, meaning "sunny hill" in German, is a beautiful 50-acre turn-of-the-century garden estate the Smithsonian Institution called "one of the most magnificent late-Victorian gardens ever created in America." This was the summer

home of Frederick Ferry Thompson and his wife, Mary Clark Thompson. The home, completed in 1887, is on the National Register of Historic Places and has been beautifully restored. Tours of the gardens are offered daily, or you may stroll on your own.

Details: *Open May–Oct daily 9:30–5:30; open Dec for Festival of Lights. $7.50 adults grounds and mansion ($6.50 for grounds only), $6.50 seniors grounds and mansion ($5.50 grounds only), $3 children ($2.50 grounds only). (2 hours)*

★★★ TAUGHANNOCK FALLS STATE PARK
2221 Taughannock Park Rd., Trumansburg, 607/387-6739 or 800/456-CAMP, www.nysparks.com

Taughannock Falls, 215 feet high, is the highest vertical waterfall in the eastern United States. There are two falls lookout points: one from below at the end of the Gorge Trail, the other from above at the Falls Overlook on Taughannock Park Road. You can reach the base by walking along a gentle one-mile trail. Pick up a Gorge Trail brochure in the park office and follow the numbered markers, which correspond to those described in the brochure. The 783-acre park includes more than one mile of Cayuga Lake shore, 76 campsites, 16 cabins, a swimming beach, a boat launch, playgrounds, and playing fields; it hosts camper recreation programs and a summer music festival.

SAGAN PLANET WALK

Visitors to Ithaca can take a walk through the solar system by taking the Sagan Planet Walk. This outdoor model of the sun and planets, named in honor of the late astronomer Carl Sagan, who lived in Ithaca, stretches three-fourths of a mile from the Ithaca Commons to the Sciencenter. The sun and nine planets are each marked by a monument and accurately sized and spaced to scale. The monuments display fascinating facts and colorful images provided by NASA. The walk is free. For information call the Sciencenter at 607/272-0600.

Details: Open daily. Camping last weekend in March–mid-October. $5 per car during the summer season, otherwise free. (3 hours)

★★★ WOMEN'S RIGHTS NATIONAL HISTORICAL PARK
136 Fall St., Seneca Falls, 315/568-2991
www.rochester.edu/SBA/park.htm
The park includes a visitors center, the National Women's Hall of Fame, and the Elizabeth Cady Stanton home. Elizabeth Cady Stanton was one of the organizers of the first Women's Rights Convention, held in Seneca Falls on July 19 and 20, 1848, and was the author of the Declaration of Sentiments read at the convention. She became the major author, policymaker, and speechmaker for the women's rights movement. The house, at 32 Washington Street, has been restored to its 1848 appearance. The permanent exhibits of the Hall of Fame focus on the lives of women inducted through public nomination. Changing exhibits provide an interpretation of women's roles in society. Wheelchair accessible.
Details: Open daily 9–5. Free. (2 hours)

★★ CORNELL UNIVERSITY PLANTATIONS
One Plantation Rd., off SR 366, Ithaca, 607/255-3020
www.plantations.cornell.edu
From early spring until late fall, blooms can always be found at the 1,500-acre Cornell Plantations, a unit of Cornell University that includes the arboretum, botanical gardens, and natural acres of the university. The plantations were the dream of Liberty Hyde Bailey, often called "the dean of American plant scientists." One of the unique specialty gardens is the **Walter C. Muenscher Poisonous Plants Garden**, dedicated to the late Professor Muenscher, an eminent Cornell botanist and author of a classic text on poisonous plants. The **Robinson York State Herb Garden** has been designed to serve as a living reference library for herb study and research. There are more than eight hundred herbs to be seen, studied, and just enjoyed for their color, texture, or fragrance. The **International Crop Garden** displays the nine major crops that feed the world. The **Heritage Crop Garden** showcases old-time crops.
Details: Open daily 9–dusk. Free. (1 hour)

★★ GLENN H. CURTISS MUSEUM
8419 SR 54, Hammondsport, 607/569-2160

This museum displays the accomplishments of native son Curtiss, a pioneer in aviation, motorcycling, cycling, engineering, and other fields. The famous June Bug and Curtiss Jenny planes are on display. There's also an eclectic collection of antique toys, farm equipment, photographs, quilts, fire engines, and many other items that help to tell the story of life in the area during the late nineteenth and early twentieth centuries. Wheelchair accessible.

Details: Open May–Oct Mon–Sat 9–5, Sun 11–5; Apr, Nov–Dec Mon–Sat 10–4, Sun noon–5; Jan–Mar Thu–Sat 10–4, Sun noon–5. $5 adults, $3.50 seniors, $2.50 children. (1 hour)

★★ HERBERT F. JOHNSON MUSEUM OF ART
Cornell University, Ithaca, 607/255-6464
www.museum.cornell.edu

The building was designed by world-renowned architect I. M. Pei. Its collection is particularly strong in American, Asian, and contemporary art and graphics. The George and Mary Rockwell Galleries, on the fifth floor, offer panoramic views of Cornell, Ithaca, and Cayuga Lake. Wheelchair accessible.

Details: Open Tue–Sun 10–5. Free. (1 hour)

★★ ROSE HILL MANSION
SR 96A, Geneva, 315/789-3848

UP CLOSE AND ANIMAL

Have you always wanted to hold a little piglet? **Misty Meadow Farm**, 607/869-9243, a half-hour drive north of Ithaca along the west shore of Cayuga Lake in Romulus, raises 1,200 pigs every year and has lots of piglets to see and hold. In the summer the farm offers tours of the barn, a narrated hay-wagon ride, special Sunday programs, a sunflower maze, a hay jump, and hundreds of other animals to watch, touch, and hold, including ducks, calves, ponies, and turkeys. There's a restaurant with barbecue pork, fresh vegetables, hot dogs and hamburgers, pig-faced cookies, and delicious fresh raspberry pie.

Located just outside the lovely city of Geneva overlooking Seneca Lake, this mansion is a National Historic Landmark and considered one of the country's finest examples of Greek Revival architecture. Guided tours lead through 24 rooms decorated with wood and plaster moldings and furnished in the Empire style. The Jenny Lind bedroom contains the original bed in which the "Swedish Nightingale" slept when it was in a Connecticut home. During the nineteenth century, Robert Swan lived in the house and turned the property into one of the most productive farms in the state. The restored gardens are lovely when in bloom.

Details: Open May–Oct Mon–Sat 10–4, Sun 1–5. $3 adults, $2 seniors and children. (1 hour)

★★ SEWARD HOUSE
33 South St., Auburn, 315/252-1283

This was the home of William Henry Seward, New York governor, U.S. senator, and secretary of state under presidents Lincoln and Johnson. He was a leading figure in the founding of the Republican Party and in the Alaska purchase. At the time of its purchase, Alaska was referred to as "Seward's Ice-Box" and "Seward's Folly," but at two cents an acre it has to be regarded as one of the best bargains ever. The home was built in 1816 by Judge Elijah Miller, Seward's father-in-law, and the only residents have been four generations of the Seward family. The Federal-style mansion is a registered National Historic Landmark. Each room in the 30-room house is furnished only with original family pieces and gifts and memorabilia collected by Seward in his travels. Guests in the dining rooms have included U.S. presidents John Adams, Martin Van Buren, Andrew Johnson, and William McKinley.

Details: Open Apr–Dec Tue–Sat 1–4. $3 adults, $2 children. (1 hour)

★ WATKINS GLEN INTERNATIONAL TRACK
2790 County Rt. 16, Watkins Glen, 607/535-2486
www.theglen.com

The first auto race in Watkins Glen took place on October 2, 1948. It was run on a 6.6-mile course of backroads and highways east of Watkins Glen and through village streets. For safety reasons the races were moved to a 2.3-mile track outside of the village. Over the years the course has hosted Formula One, Can-Am, CART Indy, Formula 500, and TransAm races. There are usually five to eight events at the track each summer. On race weekends practice and qualifying runs are made on Thursday and Friday, and races are run on Saturday and Sunday. The track is approximately three miles outside of the village. Go south on ST 414 to the light and turn right on County Rt. 16 to the track. Wheelchair accessible. **Details**: *Open on race weekends during the summer. Camping permitted on grounds. $7 to $40; packages available. (4 hours)*

FITNESS AND RECREATION

A host of trails throughout the region are used for walking, hiking, and, in the winter, cross-country skiing. The Finger Lakes Trail consists of 785 miles of hiking trails and connects Canada's Bruce Trail with the Appalachian Trail. Finger Lakes National Forest, between Seneca and Cayuga lakes, four miles from Watkins Glen, is the state's only national forest and boasts more than 25 miles of connecting trails, including the 12-mile Interlaken National Recreation Trail and two miles of the Finger Lakes Trail. It also boasts five acres of blueberries, free for the picking in midsummer. Cumming Nature Center, in Naples, has six miles of walking trails. The state parks in the Ithaca area—Buttermilk Falls, Taughannock Falls, Robert H. Treman, and nearby Watkins Glen—all have well-marked hiking trails. The 6,100-acre High Tor Wildlife Management Area, in Naples, has miles of hiking trails. Bristol Mountain, in Canandaigua, is a popular ski resort.

FOOD

Because of Cornell University and Ithaca College, Ithaca offers the widest range of dining opportunities in the region. Popular spots include the **Station Restaurant**, W. Buffalo St., Ithaca, 607/272-2609, located in the restored Lehigh Railroad Station and three railroad cars. Dinner daily. The famous **Moosewood Restaurant**, 215 N. Cayuga St., 607/273-9610, is a vegetarian restaurant open for lunch and dinner daily. It is well known for its own best-selling cookbooks. Since 1932, **Joe's Restaurant**, 602 W. Buffalo St., Ithaca, 607/273-2693, has been a popular Italian eatery for dinner daily. **Oldport Harbour Restaurant**, 702 W. Buffalo St., Ithaca, 607/272-4868, offers waterfront dining and lunch and dinner daily. **Chef Yeppi Presents**, 919 Elmira Rd., Ithaca, 607/272-6484, located in a converted nineteenth-century mansion, is considered the grande dame of Ithaca and specializes in New York regional cooking and New York wines. **Thendara Inn & Restaurant**, 4356 E. Lake Rd., Canandaigua, 716/394-4868, offers fine dining and a wonderful view

THE FINGER LAKES

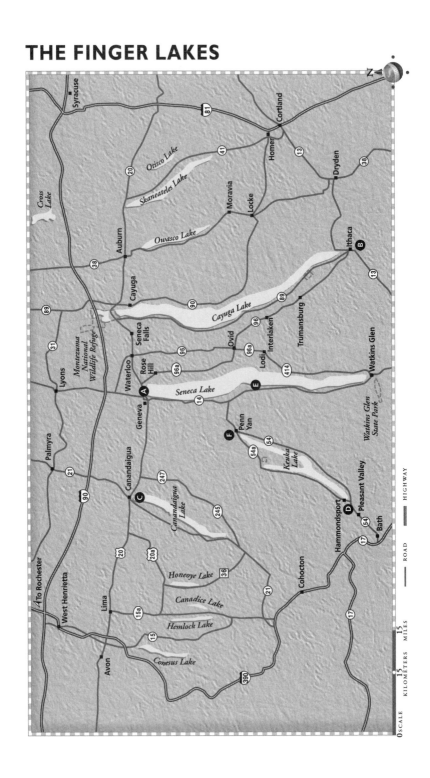

N

Syracuse

81

Cortland

Otisco Lake

20

41

Homer

13

Dryden

38

Cross Lake

Skaneateles Lake

Moravia

Locke

Ithaca B

Auburn

Owasco Lake

13

38

Cayuga

90

Cayuga Lake

89

Trumansburg

89

31

Lyons

Seneca Falls

96

Ovid

Interlaken

Watkins Glen

Montezuma National Wildlife Refuge

Waterloo

Rose Hill

96A

Lodi

98A

96

414

Watkins Glen State Park

Palmyra

Geneva A

Seneca Lake E

14

Penn Yan F

21

Canandaigua

247

54

Keuka Lake

54A

Pleasant Valley

90

To Rochester

Canandaigua Lake

245

Hammondsport D

54

Bath

West Henrietta

20

20B

Cohocton

17

Lima

Honeoye Lake

36

21

15B

Canadice Lake

17

Avon

15

Hemlock Lake

Conesus Lake

390

0 SCALE   15   15
KILOMETERS   MILES

ROAD ——— HIGHWAY

of Canandaigua Lake. Dinner daily. The **Belhurst Castle**, SR 14 S., Geneva, 315/781-0201, overlooks Seneca Lake and provides fine food for lunch and dinner daily in a magnificent setting. **Spinnakers on Seneca Lake**, 4375 W. Lake Rd., Geneva, 315/781-5323, serves lunch and dinner Tuesday through Sunday from April through December. In warm weather, sit outside looking out on the lake and enjoy alligator and other delicacies. For a wide selection of Finger Lakes wines, visit the **Village Tavern**, On the Square, Hammondsport, 607/569-2528, which offers casual dining and more than 140 Finger Lakes wines—including 20 selections by the glass. Lunch and dinner daily during the summer; Wednesday through Sunday the rest of the year.

LODGING

Some of the state's most unique accommodations are in this region. In many cases rates go up during the summer months. Geneva has two very special inns: Geneva-on-the-Lake and the Belhurst Castle, within a mile of each other on the shores of Seneca Lake. **Geneva-on-the-Lake**, 1001 Lochland Rd., SR 14 South, Geneva, 315/789-7190 or 800/3-GENEVA, is a 1911 Italianate villa modeled after Villa Lancellotti, a sixteenth-century villa near Rome. It has been a Capuchin monastery, an apartment complex, and, since 1981, a small, elegant resort with 30 luxurious suites. Its Web site is www.genevaonthelake.com. **Belhurst Castle & White Springs Manor**, Lochland Rd., SR 14 South., Geneva, 315/781-0201, www.genevany.com/biz/belhurst, with 12 guest rooms, was constructed from 1885 to 1889 in Richardson Romanesque style. There's a suite on the third floor in the former ballroom with a turret overlooking the lake and another with an 1810 four-poster bed that requires a stool to get in. The castle boasts a spigot on the second floor that dispenses

---

FOOD
- **A** Belhurst Castle
- **B** Chef Yeppi Presents
- **B** Joe's Restaurant
- **B** Moosewood Restaurant
- **B** Oldport Harbour Restaurant
- **A** Spinnakers on Seneca Lake
- **B** Station Restaurant
- **C** Thendara Inn & Restaurant
- **D** Village Tavern

LODGING
- **A** Belhurst Castle & White Springs Manor
- **B** Best Western University Inn–Ithaca
- **C** Canandaigua Inn on the Lake
- **A** Geneva-on-the-Lake
- **E** Rainbow Cove Motel
- **B** Rose Inn
- **B** Statler Hotel
- **F** Viking Resort

Note: Items with the same letter are located in the same area.

---

complimentary wine for guests. White Springs Manor, a mansion about a mile and a half from the castle, is operated by the castle owners and has eight renovated rooms. **Canandaigua Inn on the Lake**, 770 S. Main St., Canandaigua, 716/394-7800 or 800/228-2801, is a popular lakefront Canandaigua resort with 147 rooms—many have balconies and a lake view. On Keuka Lake, the **Viking Resort**, 680 E. Lake Rd., Penn Yan, 315/536-7061, boasts one thousand feet of lakeshore and a wide range of accommodations, including efficiency apartments and cabins ideal for families. The Viking is open May 15 to October 15 and also operates Viking Spirit Cruises. **Rainbow Cove Motel**, SR 14, Himrod, 607/243-7535, is on Seneca Lake, 14 miles north of Watkins Glen. The 150-room **Statler Hotel**, Cornell University campus, Ithaca, 607/257-2500 or 800/541-2501, http://hotelschool.cornell.edu/statler, is a Cornell landmark and serves as a training ground for students in the School of Hotel Administration. Ask for a lakeview room. Hotel guests may use the university's athletic facilities. **Best Western University Inn–Ithaca**, East Hill Plaza, Ithaca, 607/272-6100 or 800/528-1234, is adjacent to the Cornell University campus and has some rooms with fireplaces. **Rose Inn**, 813 Auburn Rd., Ithaca, 607/533-7905, www.roseinn.com, is an elegant inn with 15 rooms and suites in an 1850s Italianate mansion about 10 miles outside of town. The centerpiece of the mansion is the circular staircase made of polished mahogany that spirals up to the third floor.

CAMPING

Camping is popular in the Finger Lakes region, which has several top-rated state and private campgrounds. For reservations at state campgrounds, call 800/456-CAMP. Taughannock Falls State Park, SR 89, Trumansburg, near Ithaca, 607/387-6739, is on Cayuga Lake and has a small beach, boat launch site, and trails to the falls and beyond. Keuka Lake State Park, SR 54A, Bluff Point, 315/536-3666, has a prime location on the shores of Keuka Lake. Buttermilk Falls State Park, SR 13, Ithaca, 607/273-5761, was the site for the filming of *The Perils of Pauline* back in the 1920s. The waterfalls end in a wonderful swimming hole. Cayuga Lake State Park, 2678 Lower Lake Rd., Seneca Falls, 315/568-5163, is on Cayuga Lake and has 286 sites. Watkins Glen State Park, SR 14, Watkins Glen, 607/535-4511, has 305 sites, swimming, fishing, and a popular trail through the glen.

Scenic Route: The Finger Lakes Wine Region

Wineries galore grace the slopes of Keuka Lake and Seneca Lake. Hammondsport, on Keuka Lake, is the birthplace of grape culture in the Finger Lakes wine region. In 1829 Reverend William Bostwick transplanted Isabella and Catawba grapevines from the Hudson Valley to his garden at St. James Episcopal Church. The grapes flourished, and news of Bostwick's success spread rapidly among nearby farmers.

The 22-mile-long Keuka Lake, one of the loveliest in the region, is the only lake shaped like a "Y." Nineteenth-century settlers called it "Crooked Lake" and "the Lady of the Lakes." Even the wines taste better when you are within sight of the lake. For the best view of the lake and the vineyards along the hillsides, take a ride on the **Keuka Maid**, *which hosts lunch and dinner cruises from May to October.*

From the village take SR 76 north. Just one mile outside town are the famed **Bully Hill Winery** *and the* **Greyton H. Taylor Wine Museum**. *Walter S. Taylor named the museum in honor of his father, one of the sons of the founder of the Taylor Wine Company. Walter S. Taylor is known throughout the wine world for his court battles with the Coca-Cola Company (which owned Taylor Wine at the time) over the use of his name on Bully Hill Wines. Although Walter S. lost the court battles, he won public opinion. Free tours and tastings are offered at the winery.*

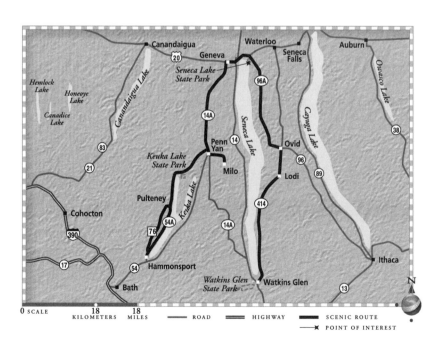

For other wineries follow the **Keuka Winery Route**, marked by red and white signs. Although SR 54A hugs the lake, the higher SR 76 offers some of the most scenic vantage points in the region, and most of the wineries can be reached from this route.

SR 54A continues into Penn Yan, the world's largest producer of buckwheat products. Tours of Birkett Mills are given during the annual **Buckwheat Harvest Festival**, held the last weekend in September. In 1987 the largest pancake ever made—28 feet 1 inch across—was made at the festival. If you are traveling on a Saturday between May and December, take a detour south from Penn Yan on State 14A to the **Windmill Farm & Craft Market**. More than 150 vendors offer farm-fresh foods, plants, crafts, antiques, quilts, cheeses, baked goods, Mennonite specialties, and more. Going north on SR 14A from Penn Yan, road signs are illustrated with a horse and buggy, indicating a Mennonite community in the area. You may spot a horse and buggy clip-clopping down the road.

Continue on to **Geneva**, named after the town on the shores of Lake Geneva in Switzerland. Geneva is on the northern tip of Seneca Lake, the self-proclaimed "Lake Trout Capital of the World." There is an air of elegance and solid permanence about Geneva, which was one of the earliest settlements in this part of the state. During the nineteenth century, the town prospered, becoming a place where many residents "enjoyed, rather than made, their fortune." The legacy of early Geneva resides in the variety and quality of its buildings. The city's South Main Street has been proclaimed "the most beautiful street in America."

Continue south on SR 96A along the east side of Seneca Lake and follow the signs for the Seneca Lake Wine Trail. The first stop and the perfect choice for lunch or dinner overlooking the lake and vineyards is **Wagner Vineyards**, in Lodi, home of the Ginny Lee Café. The next stop is Poplar Ridge Vineyards, and a few miles farther down is Hazlitt 1852 Vineyards. Continue south on SR 414 to Watkins Glen, best known for the gorge and the state park of the same name, on the southern end of the 38-mile-long Seneca Lake.

17
CENTRAL
LEATHERSTOCKING

The Leatherstocking area takes its name from James Fenimore Cooper's *Leatherstocking Tales*. It was the author's father, William, who bought up rights to a colonial land grant surrounding Lake Otsego and founded Cooperstown in 1786 in the wilds of upstate New York (about 70 miles from Albany and 200 miles from New York City). While most people know Cooperstown as the birthplace of America's favorite pastime, it would still be a classic without baseball. The village, population 2,300, looks as if it were created by Disney. Cooperstown sometimes describes itself as the "Village of Museums," but the well-preserved, prosperous, old-time village is itself a museum. The streets, lined with Victorian houses, have changed little since Abner Doubleday pitched the first ball. Baseball greats converge every summer for the Annual Induction Ceremonies and Hall of Fame Game at Doubleday Field.

Cooper dubbed Lake Otsego "Glimmerglass." He was prophetic when he wrote of his town that "the beauty of its situation, the lake, the purity of the air, and the other advantages seem destined to make it more peculiarly a place of resort." Visitors can tour the lake in a classic turn-of-the-century wooden boat, the *Chief Uncas*. The Otesaga Resort Hotel is a grand old summer hotel, built in 1909, that maintains an atmosphere of a genteel, simpler era. One of the country's most highly acclaimed opera houses is also here, overlooking the shimmering lake.

CENTRAL LEATHERSTOCKING

Great Sacandaga Lake

Mayfield

30

Amsterdam

To Albany

Rotterdam

443

N

Middleburgh

30

Howes Cave

D

20

Canajoharie

10

Ft. Plain

Mohawk River

80

Glimmerglass State Park

10

88

Milford

Richfield Springs

Springfield Center

Osego Lake

28

A

Cooperstown

Herkimer

C

28

Canadarago Lake

F

Oneonta

Bridgewater

To Rome

To B

49

Utica

E

8

80

90

5

Deansboro

12B

12

Sherburne

Norwich

Durhamville

20

12B

12

To Chenango Forks

To Syracuse

Chittenango

13

Cazenovia

G

26

80

De-Ruyter

80

26

SCALE 0   15   KILOMETERS
        0   15   MILES

ROAD —— HIGHWAY ═══ POINT OF INTEREST ★

Beyond the village lie a multitude of unexpected surprises: miles of country roads filled with antique shops; underground caverns; an Indian museum hosting storytellers; and the state's first casino.

A PERFECT DAY IN CENTRAL LEATHERSTOCKING

In Cooperstown, one is never far from lovely, nine-mile-long Otsego Lake. One of the best introductions to the lake is on board the *Chief Uncas*. After the cruise, stroll through the picturesque village before visiting the Fenimore House Museum, built on the site of the Cooper family farm overlooking the lake. The museum houses a wondrous collection of American Indian art as well as Cooper memorabilia. Across the road is the Farmers' Museum, which re-creates a nineteenth-century village. Almost everyone who visits Cooperstown pays homage to America's favorite pastime by visiting the National Baseball Hall of Fame. Even non–baseball fans find the museum fascinating. Cap off your day with an evening performance at the Glimmerglass Opera. Next door is the famed Doubleday Field where you can catch a game or practice most days during the summer. Dine at the historic Ostesaga Resort Hotel.

SIGHTS

- **A** Doubleday Field
- **B** Erie Canal Village
- **A** Farmer's Museum
- **A** Fenimore House Museum
- **C** Herkimer Diamond Mines
- **D** Howe Caverns
- **A** Hyde Hall
- **C** Iroquois Indian Museum
- **A** Lake Otsego Boat Tours
- **E** Munson-Williams-Proctor Institute
- **A** National Baseball Hall of Fame
- **F** National Soccer Hall of Fame

FOOD

- **G** Brae Loch Inn
- **D** Brooks House of Barbecue
- **O** Cathedral Farms
- **A** Gabriella's on the Square
- **A** Otesaga Resort Hotel
- **A** Pepper Mill
- **A** Red Sleigh Restaurant
- **O** Tunnicliff Inn

LODGING

- **G** Brae Loch Inn
- **G** Brewster Inn
- **O** Holiday Inn Oneonta
- **A** Inn at Cooperstown
- **A** Lake 'N Pines Motel
- **A** Lake View Motel & Cottages
- **G** Lincklaen House
- **A** Otesaga Resort Hotel

Note: Items with the same letter are located in the same area.

SIGHTSEEING HIGHLIGHTS

★★★★ **LAKE OTSEGO BOAT TOURS**
Foot of Fair St., Cooperstown, 607/547-5295
A boat tour offers the best way to experience Lake Otsego and learn a little history at the same time. The *Chief Uncas* is a 60-foot Honduran mahogany boat, built for the Anheuser-Busch family in 1912. The hour-long cruise begins at the foot of the lake, near the headwaters of the Susquehanna River. Next to the river is Council Rock, where Indians held tribal meetings. The boat passes the village's two historic golf courses as well as Fenimore House. From the vantage of this spring-fed glacial lake, it's easy to appreciate the wisdom of William Cooper, who established a community of land owners in the wilds of New York, and of Edward Clark, who bought up the lakefront to protect it from developers.

Details: Open Memorial Day–Columbus Day weekend. Daily one-hour tours available: Jul–Aug six tours offered per day; two tours per day rest of season. $8.50 adults, $5 children. (1 hour)

★★★★ **NATIONAL BASEBALL HALL OF FAME**
25 Main St., Cooperstown, 607/547-7200 or 888/425-5633
www.baseballhalloffame.org
The red-brick facility on Cooperstown's Main Street traces its beginnings to the discovery of a misshapen, homemade ball stuffed with cloth, believed to be the baseball used by Abner Doubleday in the first game. It was purchased by Stephen C. Clark, the grandson of one of the village's first families, and put on exhibit along with other baseball objects. The exhibit was so popular that the National Baseball Hall of Fame was created, officially opening in 1939, to commemorate the game's one-hundredth anniversary.

The Hall of Fame is really the Hall of Nostalgia, where grown men and women can return to the magical times of their youth. Even non–baseball fans will find themselves drawn into this wondrous museum with more than six thousand items on display. A two-hundred-seat grandstand theater is the setting for a fast-paced multimedia presentation that captures the spirit of the game. During the baseball season, the Game of the Week plays continuously on video screens. Tributes to Babe Ruth include his Yankee Stadium locker; the ball, bat, and uniform from his 60th home run; and photos galore. There's Ty Cobb's glove, the bat Ted Williams used when he slammed his

Cazenovia: Where the Yellow Perch Swim

Cazenovia on SR 20 is one of the region's prettiest villages. Indians called the land Owahgena, "where the yellow perch swim." "Situation superb, fine land" were the words of John Lincklaen, agent for the Holland Land Company, when he first viewed the land at the foot of Cazenovia Lake. His elegant Federal-style 1807 mansion, with 20 acres of lawns, formal gardens, and woods, is called Lorenzo. There's a collection of horse-drawn vehicles and a restored carriage house. The village became the summer retreat of wealthy East Coast families who discovered it after the Civil War. The lake remains the focal point of the town. The **Lorenzo Historic Site**, 315/655-3200, which is generally open mid-May through September, hosts a horse-drawn sleigh rally and candlelit Christmas tours in winter.

521st home run in his very last time at the plate, Shoeless Joe Jackson's shoes, and Mark McGwire's bat. Wheelchair accessible.

Details: *May–Sept daily 9–9; Oct–Apr daily 9–5. $9.50 adults, $8 seniors, $4 children 7–12. Cooperstown Discovery Pass available for reduced admission to three village museums. (3 hours)*

★★★ **DOUBLEDAY FIELD**
Main St., Cooperstown, 607/563-8970
This baseball field is a must-see for baseball fans. You can sit in the stands to absorb the atmosphere and watch a practice if one is going on. It is just down the street from the Baseball Hall of Fame. The annual Hall of Fame Game is played here every summer as part of the Hall of Fame induction ceremonies. The semi-professional Oneonta Macs play here on weekends from May through Labor Day.

Details: *Open daily for viewing. Games $2 adults, $1 children. (3 hours per game)*

★★★ **FARMERS' MUSEUM**
SR 80 one mile east of Cooperstown, 607/547-1400 or 888/547-1450, www.nysha.org
This living-history museum of New York's frontier period, 1790 to

Turning Stone Casino Resort

During the Revolutionary War, the Oneida Indians fought side by side with the colonists and helped George Washington's starving troops at Valley Forge. Over the years treaties were broken and the Oneida Nation lost most of its large land holdings in central New York. A casino is helping to reverse the fortunes of the Oneidas. The **Turning Stone Casino Resort**, 315/361-7711 or 800/771-7711, http://turning-stone.com, and its related development is now the area's largest private employer and the state's first casino. Located just off Thruway exit 33 at Verona between Syracuse and Utica, the casino operates 24 hours a day with casino games, high-stakes bingo, and Vegas-style revues. The Hotel at Turning Stone Casino is a 285-room luxury resort with a spa and fine dining. The Shoppes at Turning Stone are six retail boutiques in the hotel where no sales tax is collected. Just down the road is the 175-site RV village, the **Villages at Turning Stone**, with hiking trails, a swimming pool, and free shuttle service to the casino. Nearby is the Oneida Indian Nation Shako:Wi Cultural Center, a museum and cultural center.

1860, includes a collection of one dozen historic buildings assembled from a one-hundred-mile radius of Cooperstown. Sheep graze on the common and horse-drawn wagons travel through the village. Stop at the print shop to learn the latest news or visit the general store, where you can play a game of checkers and learn the latest gossip. Craftspeople give visitors a glimpse of nineteenth-century technologies at work. This is also the home of the Cardiff Giant, America's most famous hoax. The Leatherstocking Baseball Club plays here on the Village Crossroads from May to October. It is a scene reminiscent of Abner Doubleday's era. Wheelchair accessible.

Details: Open June–Sept daily 10–5; Apr–May Tue–Sun 10–4; Oct–Nov Tue–Sun 10–4. $9 adults, $8 seniors, $4 children. Discovery Pass available for reduced admission to three Cooperstown museums. (2 hours)

★★★ **FENIMORE HOUSE MUSEUM**
SR 80 one mile east of Cooperstown, 607/547-1400 or 888/547-1450, www.nysha.org

This museum is on an historic site—it was once the Cooper family farm. The magnificent house was built by Edward Clark, heir to the Singer Sewing Machine fortune. Its newest attraction is the most impressive $10 million American Indian Wing (donated by Jane Forbes Clark). It was built to house the Eugene and Clare Thaw Collection of American Indian Art, more than seven hundred objects that include masterworks of extraordinary quality and represent a broad range of cultures across North America, including Northwest Coast, Alaska, California, Southwest, Plains and Prairie, and Woodlands Indians. Highlights include a rare ledger book of drawings by Black Hawk, a rare and beautiful late-eighteenth-century Montagnais–Naskapi caribou-skin coat, and several Eskimo masks from the late 1800s.

James Fenimore Cooper, author of 32 novels including the *Leatherstocking Tales*, is the focus of the museum's Cooper Room. Portraits of his family include one of his mother sitting on the rocking chair that came with her from New Jersey. Tradition has it that Elizabeth Fenimore Cooper refused to leave New Jersey for the wilds of central New York, saying she "could not face the wilderness." After much pleading to no avail, her husband simply lifted the rocker with his wife in it and placed it in a wagon for the long trip. There's also a remarkable series of bronze life masks of such luminaries as John Adams, Thomas Jefferson, and James Madison. Wheelchair accessible.

Details: Open June–Sept daily 10–5; Apr–May Tue–Sun 10–4; Oct–Dec Tue–Sun 10–4. $9 adults, $8 seniors, $4 children. Discovery Pass available for reduced admission to three Cooperstown museums. (2 hours)

★★★ HOWE CAVERNS
RR 1, Howes Cave, 518/296-8990, www.howecaverns.com

Lester Howe discovered this cavern and named it after himself when he opened it to the public in 1842. It was soon heralded as a tourist attraction second only to Niagara Falls. Today an elevator lowers visitors 156 feet to a subterranean walkway. From there a guide leads explorers through the cavern, with stalactites and stalagmites well-lit by spotlights. It is always 52 degrees in the caverns. It doesn't seem to be the perfect setting for a wedding, but more than four hundred couples have tied the knot here, beginning with Howe's daughter, Elgiva, who was married here as an early marketing stunt. Legend has it that if you are single and looking, you will be married within the year if you step on the heart-shaped stone at the Bridal Altar. Two 22-passenger boats carry visitors across the Lake of Venus.

Details: *Take SR 7 to Caverns Rd. to RR 1. Open daily 9–6. $11.50 adults, $6 children. (1 hour)*

★★★ IROQUOIS INDIAN MUSEUM
Caverns Rd. off SR 7, Howes Cave, 518/296-8949
iroquois@telenet.net

This museum is designed in the shape of an Iroquois longhouse and is in the ancient territory of the Iroquois, whose confederacy includes the Mohawk, Oneida, Tuscarora, Onondaga, Cayuga, and Seneca. The children's museum on the lower level lets youngsters get a glimpse of the Iroquois way of life. They can play musical instruments, try on clothes, handle tools and furs, and make some beadwork to take home. An Onondaga storyteller is often on hand to tell traditional Iroquois tales, and there are musical and dance performances. The gallery shows works of contemporary Indian artists. The museum is set in a 45-acre nature preserve with marked trails and a picnic area. Wheelchair accessible.

Details: *Open July–Labor Day Mon–Sat 10–6, Sun noon–6; Apr–June and day after Labor Day–Dec Tue–Sat 10–5, Sun noon–5. $5.50 adults, $4.50 seniors and students 13–17, $2.50 children. (2 hours)*

★★ ERIE CANAL VILLAGE
5789 New London Rd., Rome, 315/337-3999 or
888/ERIECAN, www.eriecanalvillage.com

This re-created mid-1800s village along the Erie Canal is near the site where the first shovelful of dirt was turned in 1817 for the start of construction on the canal. A mule-drawn packet boat plies a section of the enlarged canal, giving visitors a taste of early-nineteenth-century water travel. A narrow-gauge railroad ride gives the experience of slightly later travel. The village is home to three museums: the Harden Carriage Museum, which houses a variety of horse-drawn vehicles from upstate New York; the New York State Museum of Cheese, housed in the former Merry and Weeks cheese factory; and the Canal Museum, which depicts the history and construction of and life along the Erie Canal. The village also contains Bennett's Tavern, a blacksmith shop, the Shull Victorian House, a canal general store, a print shop, the Crosby House (an early 1800s settler's house), the Maynard Methodist Church, and a one-room schoolhouse.

Details: Open May 23–Sept 7 daily 9:30–6; Sept 8–Columbus Day weekends only 9:30–5. $6 adults, $5 seniors, $4 children. Packet boat $3, train $3. (3 hours)

★★ HYDE HALL
Glimmerglass State Park, Cooperstown, 607/547-5098
www.hydehall.org

Hyde Hall, a National Historic Landmark and New York State Historic Site, is a restoration in progress. Hyde Hall was built for George Clarke, whose great-grandfather was a prominent figure in New York before the Revolutionary War. The house is considered the finest example of a neoclassic country mansion anywhere in America. The site was chosen for its commanding view of Otsego Lake and construction began in 1817. The four structures of the Hyde complex contain some 50 rooms and enclose an open, stone-paved courtyard. The house was a showplace, built to impress. It remained in the Clarke family until 1963 when New York State acquired the building, which was in need of massive renovation. Friends of Hyde Hall was incorporated in 1964 to save the house and to assist the state in maintaining it for the public's use and enjoyment.

Details: Open May 22–Oct 18 Fri–Mon 10–4:30. Tours Tue and Thu 10:30, 12:30, 2:30. $6 adults, $5 seniors, $4 children. Grounds and visitors center open 9–4 year-round. Free. During the high season, concerts and lectures held on the grounds and in the house. (1 hour)

★★ MUNSON-WILLIAMS-PROCTOR INSTITUTE
310 Genesee St., Utica, 315/797-0000, www.mwpi.edu

This Utica art gallery showcases one of the Northeast's finest collections of eighteenth- to twentieth-century American and European art. Its works include those of Picasso, Dalí, Calder, Moore, Pollock,

BEER ON THE FARM
Brewery Ommegang, four miles south of Cooperstown, is a real Belgian brewery in the heart of Leatherstocking country. Free samples and tours are offered in this farmstead setting on Route 33, 607/547-8184 or 800/656-1212, www.belgianexperts.com.

and Burchfield. Also on display are Thomas Cole's allegorical paintings *The Voyage of Life*, depicting childhood, youth, manhood, and old age. The institute includes the museum, a school of art, and Fountain Elms, a restored Victorian mansion. Wheelchair accessible. ***Details***: *Open Tue–Sat 10–5, Sun 1–5. Donation. (2 hours)*

★ **HERKIMER DIAMOND MINES**
5661 SR 5, Herkimer, 315/891-7355
diamonds@mail.ntcnet.com
These "diamonds" are, in fact, quartz crystals. Visitors get to keep all the crystals they find. There's a large gem and mineral shop, a museum, a restaurant, and a campground.
    Details: *Open Memorial Day–Labor Day daily 9–6; Apr–Dec 1 9–5. $6 adults, $5 children. (2 hours)*

★ **NATIONAL SOCCER HALL OF FAME**
5–11 Ford Ave., Oneonta, 607/432-3351, www.soccerhall.org
The history of soccer in the United States dates back to the 1860s. Much of this history has been preserved and is displayed through photos, trophy exhibits, graphics, uniforms, and other memorabilia. Large-screen TVs are available for individual or group viewing of the dozens of historic films on hand in the museum library.
    Details: *Open June–Sept 15 daily 9–7; Sept 16–May Mon–Sat 10–3, Sun noon–5. $4 adults, $2 children. (2 hours)*

FITNESS AND RECREATION

The Clark Sports Center, on Susquehanna Avenue in Cooperstown, is a world-class facility more likely to be found at a major university than in a small rural village. It includes a complete gymnasium, indoor running track and horizontal climbing wall, bowling alleys, Olympic swimming and diving pools, Nautilus and aerobics rooms, adventure ropes course, and rock-climbing wall. A nature trail runs through the 45-acre preserve at the Iroquois Indian Museum, in Howes Cave. Glimmerglass State Park, in Cooperstown, has hiking trails and nature walks led by park rangers.

FOOD

In Cooperstown, the **Otesaga Resort Hotel**, 60 Lake St., 607/547-9931, open from April 18 through October, offers elegant hotel dining with a pianist playing during dinner and a grand view of the lake. Other popular village restaurants are the **Pepper Mill**, 5418 SR 28, Lower Chestnut, 607/547-8550, with casual family dining for dinner daily; **Red Sleigh Restaurant**, SR. 80, 607/547-5581, lunch and dinner daily; and **Tunnicliff Inn**, 34 Pioneer St., 607/547-9611. **Gabriella's on the Square**, 161 Main St., 607/547-8000, is open for lunch and dinner daily (closed Monday in the winter). It serves casual fare with a good selection of vegetarian dishes. The **Brae Loch Inn** features Scottish foods and American favorites for dinner daily at 5 Albany St., Cazenovia, 315/655-3431. **Brooks House of Barbecue**, 5560 SR 7, Oneonta, 607/432-1782, is famous for its barbecue, seats three hundred, and claims to have the largest indoor charcoal pit in the East. Lunch and dinner Monday through Saturday. **Cathedral Farms**, County Rt. 205 North two miles from I-88, Oneonta, 607/432-7483, is another popular Oneonta dining establishment. Dinner daily.

LODGING

Rates are generally higher during the busy July and August season, and during the Hall of Fame weekend it can be very difficult to find a room near Cooperstown. The **Otesaga Resort Hotel**, 60 Lake St., 607/547-9931 or 800/348-6222, www.otesaga.com, is the grande dame of Cooperstown, overlooking the lake. It's listed on the National Register of Historic Places and has been serving guests since 1909. It encompasses the historic 18-hole Leatherstocking Golf Course. The hotel is open from April 18 to November 1 and recently underwent a $20 million renovation. Rates include breakfast and dinner. The **Inn at Cooperstown**, built in 1874, 16 Chestnut St., Cooperstown, 607/547-5756 or 800/348 6222, www.cooperstown.net/theinn, offers warm hospitality in an historic setting in the middle of the village. **Lake View Motel & Cottages**, RD 2 six miles north of Cooperstown, 607/547-9740 or 888/4-LAKEVIEW, www.cooperstownvacations.com, offers free paddleboats and rowboats, swimming, and fishing. **Lake 'N Pines Motel**, 7102 SR 80, Cooperstown, 607/547-2790 or 800/615-5253, www.cooperstown.net/lake-n-pines, has indoor and outdoor pools and free paddleboats and rowboats. **Holiday Inn Oneonta**, SR 23 one-and-one-half miles east of I-88 exit 15, Southside-Oneonta, 607/433-2250 or 800/465-4329, has 120 rooms and is 30 minutes from Cooperstown.

The village of Cazenovia boasts several lovely historic inns. They include the Brae Loch Inn, an 1805 Victorian mansion furnished to the period, where the staff wear kilts, 5 Albany St., 315/655-3431; the **Brewster Inn**, 6 Ledyard Ave., 315/655-9232, an 1888 Victorian mansion and carriage house on Cazenovia Lake; and the **Lincklaen House**, 99 Albany St., 315/655-3461, whose name honors the founder of the town. This inn greeted its first guests in 1835. Rooms are comfortable and well-maintained.

CAMPING

Camping is popular in the Leatherstocking region. For reservations at state campgrounds, call 800/456-CAMP. There are 39 sites at Glimmerglass State Park, RR 2, Cooperstown, 607/547-8662, with swimming, fishing, and a beach on Lake Otsego. Cooperstown Beaver Valley, SR 28, Cooperstown, 800/726-7314, has 100 sites, swimming, fishing, and boat rentals. Cooperstown Shadow Brook Campground, E. Lake Rd., Cooperstown, 607/264-8431, has a pool, fishing pond, and cabin and trailer rentals just minutes from the village. Herkimer Diamond KOA, SR 28, Herkimer, 800/450-5267, has 126 sites and is across the road from the Diamond Mines. Chenango Valley State Park, 153 State Park Rd., Chenango Forks, 607/648-5251, has 216 sites, swimming, fishing, and boat rentals.

NIGHTLIFE

The highly acclaimed Glimmerglass Opera, SR 80, eight miles north of the village of Cooperstown, 607/547-2255 or 800/559-5704, boasts one of only four American opera houses built especially for opera. Every summer the opera mounts three productions in English in the Alice Busch Opera Theater, SR 80, Cooperstown, 607/547-2255, www.cooperstown.net/glimmerglass. The theater's side walls roll back, bringing in the beauty of the outdoors. The season runs from July 1 to August 21.

APPENDIX

Consider this appendix your travel tool box. Use it along with the material in the Planning Your Trip chapter to craft the trip you want. Here are the tools you'll find inside:

1. **Planning Map.** Make copies of this map and plot out various trip possibilities. Once you've decided on your route, you can write it on the original map and refer to it as you travel.

2. **Mileage Chart.** This chart shows the driving distances (in miles) between various destinations throughout New York State. Use it in conjunction with the Planning Map.

3. **Special Interest Tours.** If you'd like to plan a trip around a certain theme—such as nature, sports, or art—one of these tours may work for you.

4. **Calendar of Events.** Here you'll find a month-by-month listing of major area events.

5. **Resources.** This guide lists various regional chambers of commerce and visitors bureaus, state offices, bed-and-breakfast registries, and other useful sources of information.

PLANNING MAP: New York State

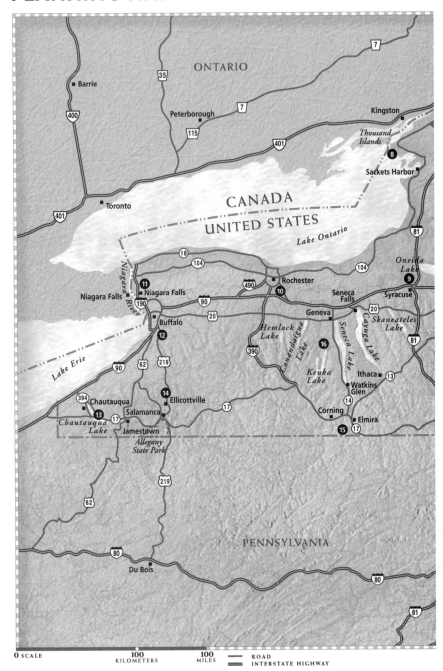

ONTARIO

Barrie

35

400

Peterborough

115

7

7

Kingston

Thousand
Islands

401

8

Sackets Harbor

Toronto

401

CANADA
UNITED STATES

Lake Ontario

81

18

104

104

Oneida
Lake

9

Niagara
River

11

Niagara Falls

Rochester

490

10

Seneca
Falls

20

Syracuse

Niagara Falls

190

90

Geneva

Skaneateles
Lake

Buffalo

20

Hemlock
Lake

Canandaigua
Lake

Seneca Lake

Cayuga Lake

81

12

390

16

90

62

219

Keuka
Lake

Ithaca

13

Watkins
Glen

394

Chautauqua

14

Ellicottville

17

14

Corning

Salamanca

17

Elmira

13

17

Chautauqua
Lake

Jamestown

15

17

Allegany
State Park

219

Lake Erie

62

PENNSYLVANIA

80

80

Du Bois

81

O SCALE   100   100   ROAD
           KILOMETERS   MILES   INTERSTATE HIGHWAY

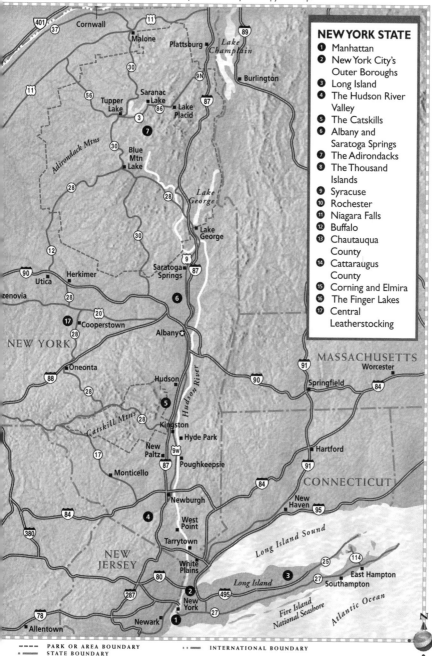

NEW YORK STATE

1. Manhattan
2. New York City's Outer Boroughs
3. Long Island
4. The Hudson River Valley
5. The Catskills
6. Albany and Saratoga Springs
7. The Adirondacks
8. The Thousand Islands
9. Syracuse
10. Rochester
11. Niagara Falls
12. Buffalo
13. Chautauqua County
14. Cattaraugus County
15. Corning and Elmira
16. The Finger Lakes
17. Central Leatherstocking

---- PARK OR AREA BOUNDARY
▪ STATE BOUNDARY

▪ ▬ INTERNATIONAL BOUNDARY

N

NEW YORK STATE MILEAGE CHART

	Albany	Binghamton	Buffalo	Elmira	Glens Falls	Ithaca	Jamestown	Kingston	New York City	Niagara Falls	Rochester	Saranac Lake	Syracuse	Utica
Binghamton	134													
Buffalo	295	200												
Elmira	189	58	142											
Glens Falls	54	75	305	266										
Ithaca	178	53	155	33	199									
Jamestown	354	219	71	163	369	188								
Kingston	54	135	341	189	105	182	351							
New York City	159	195	393	251	212	246	414	107						
Niagara Falls	302	217	21	164	317	167	92	353	437					
Rochester	231	166	78	119	240	90	140	276	373	85				
Saranac Lake	159	239	330	272	108	239	394	210	307	339	254			
Syracuse	147	76	154	93	161	58	216	197	269	164	90	189		
Utica	95	131	199	126	109	93	163	142	239	211	134	146	52	
Watertown	179	148	210	163	175	130	174	225	341	219	134	120	72	84

SPECIAL INTEREST TOURS

With *New York State Travel Smart* you can plan a trip of any length—a one-day excursion, a getaway weekend, or a three-week vacation—around any special interest. To get you started, the following pages contain six tours geared toward a variety of interests. For more information, refer to the chapters listed—chapter names are bolded and chapter numbers appear inside black bullets. You can follow a suggested itinerary in its entirety, or shorten, lengthen, or combine parts of each, depending on your starting and ending points.

Discuss alternative routes and schedules with your travel companions—it's a great way to have fun, even before you leave home. And remember: don't hesitate to change your itinerary once you're on the road. Careful study and planning ahead of time will help you make informed decisions as you go, but spontaneity is the extra ingredient that will make your trip memorable.

NATURE LOVERS' TOUR

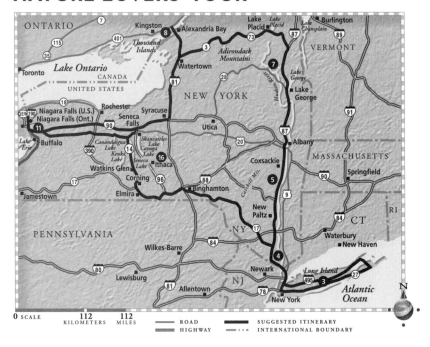

New York offers a tantalizing array of sights for nature lovers, from miles of Long Island beaches to Niagara Falls.

❸ Long Island (Fire Island National Seashore, Jones Beach State Park)
❹ The Hudson River Valley (Bear Mountain State Park, Hudson River)
❺ The Catskills (Minnewaska State Park)
❼ The Adirondacks (Whiteface Mountain, Lake George, Ausable Chasm, Mt. Van Hoevenberg Recreation Area)
❽ The Thousand Islands (St. Lawrence River, Wellesley Island State Park)
⓫ Niagara Falls (Goat Island, Niagara Reservation State Park)
⓰ The Finger Lakes (Montezuma National Wildlife Refuge, Taughannock Falls State Park, Watkins Glen State Park)

Time needed: two to three weeks

ARTS AND CULTURE TOUR

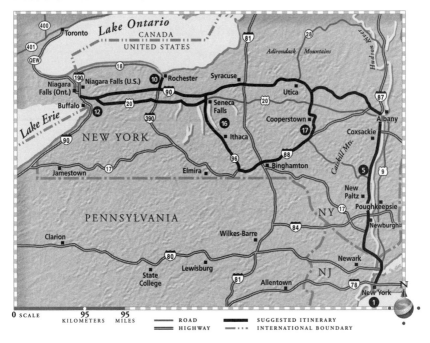

New York State has rich arts and cultural offerings. Manhattan is the theater and arts capital of the United States—some would say the world.

- ❶ **Manhattan** (museums, Lincoln Center, Carnegie Hall, Broadway)
- ❺ **The Catskills** (Bronck Museum, Huguenot Street)
- ❿ **Rochester** (George Eastman House and International Museum of Photography and Film, Strong Museum, Memorial Art Gallery)
- ⓬ **Buffalo** (Albright-Knox Art Gallery, Darwin Martin House, Buffalo Philharmonic Orchestra, Theater District)
- ⓰ **The Finger Lakes** (Herbert F. Johnson Museum of Art)
- ⓱ **Central Leatherstocking** (Munson-Williams-Proctor Institute)

Time needed: two weeks

AMERICAN HISTORY TOUR

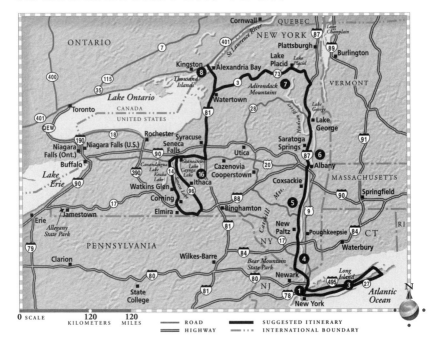

O SCALE   120   120
           KILOMETERS MILES   ▬▬▬ ROAD   ▬▬▬ SUGGESTED ITINERARY
                                ▬▬▬ HIGHWAY   ▬ ▪ ▪ ▬ INTERNATIONAL BOUNDARY

To realize the impact New York State has made in American history, visit the places where presidents, suffragettes, writers, warriors, and immigrants lived.

- ❶ **Manhattan** (Ellis Island National Monument, South Street Seaport, Statue of Liberty)
- ❸ **Long Island** (Sagamore Hill National Historic Site, Walt Whitman Birthplace State Historic Site)
- ❹ **The Hudson River Valley** (Franklin D. Roosevelt National Historic Site, Olana State Historic Site, U.S. Military Academy)
- ❺ **The Catskills** (Huguenot Street)
- ❻ **Albany and Saratoga Springs** (Saratoga National Historic Park)
- ❼ **The Adirondacks** (Great Camp Sagamore, Fort Ticonderoga)
- ❽ **The Thousand Islands** (Boldt Castle, Sackets Harbor Battlefield)
- ⓰ **The Finger Lakes** (Seward House, Women's Rights Historical Park)

Time needed: two weeks

WATER LOVERS' TOUR

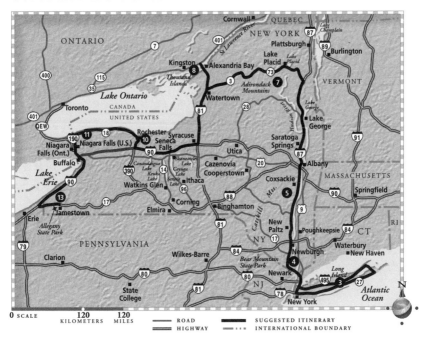

The Empire State is bursting with activities for those who love water sports, cruises, and fishing.

❸ Long Island (Fire Island Ferry, fishing off Montauk)
❹ The Hudson River Valley (Half Moon Cruises)
❺ The Catskills (fishing at Willowemoc and Beaverkill)
❼ The Adirondacks (fishing at Lake George, Lake George Steamboat)
❽ The Thousand Islands (fishing at St. Lawrence River and Salmon River)
❿ Rochester (*Sam Patch* Tour Boat)
⓫ Niagara Falls (fishing at Lake Ontario, *Maid of the Mist*, Whirlpool Jet Boats)
⓭ Chautauqua County (*Chautauqua Belle*, fishing at Lake Chautauqua)

Time needed: two weeks

UNUSUAL MUSEUMS TOUR

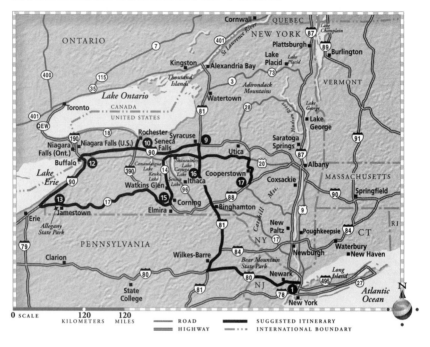

If hours spent looking at Renaissance art at the Met isn't your idea of a good time, check out the quirkier side of New York State's museum scene.

❶ Manhattan (Lower East Side Tenement Museum, Museum of Television and Radio)

❾ Syracuse (Salt Museum)

❿ Rochester (George Eastman House International Museum of Photography and Film, Jell-O Gallery)

⓬ Buffalo (Herschell Carousel Factory Museum)

⓭ Chautauqua County (Lucille Ball–Desi Arnaz Museum)

⓯ Corning and Elmira (Corning Glass Center, National Soaring Museum)

⓰ The Finger Lakes (Greyton H. Taylor Wine Museum)

⓱ Central Leatherstocking (New York Museum of Cheese)

Time needed: one week

TOP OF THE WORLD VIEWS TOUR

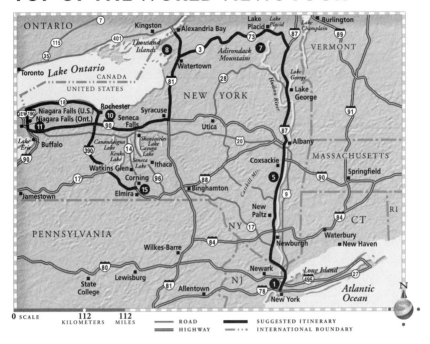

Sears Tower in Chicago may claim to be the country's tallest building, but the views from these sights will make you feel as if you're on top of the world.

❶ Manhattan (Empire State Building, Statue of Liberty, World Trade Center)
❺ The Catskills (Catskill Mountain House Site)
❼ The Adirondacks (Whiteface Mountain, Blue Mountain)
❽ The Thousand Islands (Thousand Islands Skydeck)
❿ Rochester (Hot Air Balloon over Letchworth)
⓫ Niagara Falls (Goat Island, Niagara Reservation State Park)
⓯ Corning and Elmira (Harris Hill Soaring Corp.)

Time needed: one to two weeks

CALENDAR OF EVENTS

JANUARY
Glacier Ridge Winter Festival, Fredonia; 800/242-4569
Malone Winter Carnival, Malone; 800/516-7247
Snowflake Festival, Jamestown; 800/242-4569
Trappers Special Sled Dog Races, Allegany State Park; 800/331-0543

FEBRUARY
Chili Cook-Off, Ithaca Commons, Ithaca; 800/284-8422
Findley Lake Winter Festival, Main Street and Findley Lake, Chautauqua;
  800/242-4569
Ice Castle Winter Festival, Mayville; 800/242-4569
Lake George Winter Festival, Lake George; 800/516-7247
Saranac Lake Winter Carnival, Saranac Lake; 800/516-7247

MARCH
Ice Breaker Canoe Race, Saranac Lake; 800/516-7247
Mardi Gras, Ellicottville and Holiday Valley; 800/331-0543
St. Patrick's Day Parade, Manhattan; 800/NYC-VISIT
St. Patrick's Parade, Buffalo; 800/BUFFALO
Watertown Goes Green Irish Festival, Watertown, 800/8-ISLAND

APRIL
Central New York Maple Festival, Marathon (south of Syracuse); 800/234-4SYR
Niagara's Spring Festival of Gold, Niagara Falls; 800/421-5223
Shaker Museum and Library Kite Festival, Old Chatham; 800/232-4782
1000 Islands Spring Boat Show, Clayton; 800/8-ISLAND
Western New York Maple Festival, Franklinville, Cattaraugus; 800/331-0543

MAY
Annual White Water Derby, North Creek, Adirondacks; 800/516-7247
East Durham Irish Festival, Michael J. Quill Irish Cultural and Sports Center,
  East Durham, Catskills; 800/NYS-CATS
East Durham Irish Festival, Michael J. Quill Irish Cultural and Sports Center,
  East Durham, Catskills; 800/NYS-CATS
Hudson River Valley Antique Auto Show, Dutchess County Fairgrounds,
  Rhinebeck
Lake Ontario Bird Festival, Mexico Point State Park, Mexico, Thousand
  Islands; 800/8-ISLAND
Lilac Festival, Rochester; 800/677-7282

Lucy-Desi Hometown Celebration, Jamestown; 800/242-4569
Tulip Festival, Albany; 800/258-3582

JUNE
Allentown Arts Festival, Buffalo; 800/BUFFALO
American Crafts Festival, Lincoln Center area, Manhattan;
   800/NYC-VISIT
Annual Waterfront Festival, Seneca Harbor Park, Watkins Glen, Finger
   Lakes; 800/KIT4FUN
The General's Lady, Newburgh, Hudson River Valley; 800/232-4782
Ithaca Festival, Ithaca Commons and Stewart Park, Ithaca, 800/284-8422
Ozfest, Chittenango, Central Leatherstocking; 800/233-8778
War of 1812 Can Am Festival, Sackets Harbor, Thousand Islands; 800/8-IS-
   LAND

JULY
Annual Founders Day Street Faire, Wurtsboro, Catskills; 800/NYS-CATS
Baseball Hall of Fame Weekend, Cooperstown; 800/233-8778
Fabulous Fourth Festival and Concert in the Sky, Albany; 800/258-3582
French Festival, Cape Vincent, Thousand Islands; 800/8-ISLAND
Hill Cumorah Pageant, Manchester, Finger Lakes; 800/KIT4FUN
Sterling Renaissance Festival, Sterling, Finger Lakes; 800/KIT4FUN
Shaker Museum Antiques Festival, Shaker Museum and Library,Old
   Chatham, Hudson River Valley; 800/232-4782
Taste of Buffalo, Buffalo; 800/BUFFALO
Woodsmen's Field Days, Tupper Lake, Adirondacks; 800/516-7247

AUGUST
Annual Madison-Bouckville Antiques Show, Madison/Bouckville, Central
   Leatherstocking; 800/233-8778
Canal Days, Port Bryon, Adirondacks; 800/516-7247
Dutchess County Fair, Dutchess County Fairgrounds, Rhinebeck, Hudson
   River Valley; 800/232-4782
Erie County Fair, Hamburg (south of Buffalo); 800/BUFFALO
Gerry Rodeo, Gerry, Chautauqua; 800/242-4569
International Celtic Festival, Hunter Mountain Ski Bowl, Hunter, Catskills;
   800/NYS-CATS
Mako Mania Tournament, Montauk; 877/FUN-ON-LI
New York State Fair, Syracuse; 800/234-4SYR

SEPTEMBER
Adirondack Balloon Festival, Glens Falls, Adirondacks; 800/516-7247

Buckwheat Harvest Festival, Penn Yan, Finger Lakes; 800/KIT4FUN
Capital District Scottish Games, Altamont, Albany, and Saratoga Springs;
  800/732-8259
Extreme Phat Tire Festival, Ski Plattekill Mountain Resort, Roxbury, Catskills;
  800/NYS-CATS
Hudson River Arts Festival, Beacon/Poughkeepsie; 800/232-4782
Naples Grape Festival, Naples, Finger Lakes; 800/KIT4FUN
Niagara County Peach Festival, Lewiston, Niagara Falls; 800/421-5223
San Gennaro Feast, Mulberry Street, Manhattan; 800/NYC-VISIT

OCTOBER
Oyster Festival, Oyster Bay, Long Island; 877/FUN-ON-LI
Annual Oktoberfest Weekend, Ski Plattekill Mountain Resort, Roxbury,
  Catskills; 800/NYS-CATS
Capital District Apple Festival and Craft Show, Altamont, Albany, and
  Saratoga Springs; 800/732-8259
Annual World's Largest Garage Sale, Warrensburg, Adirondacks; 800/516-
  7247
Great Pumpkin Festival, Oswego, Thousand Islands; 800/8-ISLAND
Apple Festival, LaFayette (near Syracuse); 800/234-4SYR
Letchworth Arts and Crafts Show and Sale, Rochester;
  800/677-7282
Fall Festival, Ellicottville, Cattaraugus; 800/331-0543

NOVEMBER
New York City Marathon, Central Park, Manhattan; 800/NYC-VISIT
Macy's Thanksgiving Day Parade, Manhattan; 800/NYC-VISIT
North Country Festival of Trees, Highland Family Golf Center, Queensbury,
  Adirondacks; 800/516-7247
Crystal City Christmas, Corning; 800/284-3352
Festival of Lights, Niagara Falls; 800/421-5223

DECEMBER
First Night Buffalo, Buffalo; 800/BUFFALO
First Night in New York City, Times Square, Manhattan; 800/NYC-VISIT
Holiday Celebration, Annandale-on-Hudson, Hudson River Valley; 800/232-
  4782
Old-Fashioned Victorian Christmas, Barker, Niagara Falls; 800/421-5223
Victorian Christmas Open House, Cottage Lawn, Oneida, Central
  Leatherstocking; 800/233-8778
Village Christmas, Watkins Glen, Finger Lakes; 800/KIT4FUN

RESOURCES

In addition to the following resources, many other addresses and phone numbers are found accompanying specific listings in the destination chapters.

New York State Hospitality/Tourism Association, 800/ENJOY-NY
New York State Tourism Information, Division of Tourism, P.O. Box 2603,
   Albany 12220-0603, http://iloveny.state.ny.us, 800/CALL-NYS or
   518/474-4116

CHAMBERS OF COMMERCE AND VISITOR BUREAUS

Adirondacks, Adirondack Regional Chamber of Commerce, 136 Warren St.,
   P.O. Box 158, Glen Falls 12801, www.adirondackchamber.org,
   800/516/7247 or 518/798-1761
Albany, Albany County CVB, 25 Quackenbush Sq., 12207, www.albany.org,
   800/258-3582 or 518/434-1217
Bronx, Bronx Tourism Council, 198 E. 161st St., 2nd Floor, Bronx, NY
   10451, www.ilovethebronx.com, 718/590-3518
Brooklyn, Brooklyn Tourism Council, 30 Flatbush Ave., Ste. 427, Brooklyn
   11217, www.brooklynx.org, 718/855-7882, ext. 29
Buffalo, Buffalo Visitors Center, 617 Main St., Buffalo 14203,
   www.buffalocvb.org, 800/BUFFALO or 716/852-2356
Catskill, CATS, Box 449, Catskill 12414, 800/882-CATS, 914/331-9300,
   800/355-CATS, or 518/943-3223
Cattaraugus, Cattaraugus City Tourism, 303 Court St., Little Valley 14755,
   www.co.cattaraugus.ny.us, 800/331-0543 or 716/938-9111
Chautauqua, Chautauqua City Visitors Bureau, Chautauqua Institution Main
   Gate Welcome Ctr., P.O. Box 1441, Chautauqua 14722, www.tourchau-
   tauqua.com, 800/242-4569 or 716/357-4569
Corning, Corning Area Chamber of Commerce, 42 E, Market St., 14830,
   www.corningny.com, 800/284-3352 or 607/936-4686
Elmira, Chemung County Chamber of Commerce, 400 Church St., Elmira
   14901, www.chemungchamber.org, 800/627-5892 or 607/734-5137
Finger Lakes, Finger Lakes Assn., 309 Lake St., Penn Yan 14527,
   www.fingerlakes.org, 800/KIT 4 FUN or 315/536-7488
Hudson Valley Tourism, www.enjoyhv.com, 800/232-4782

- Columbia County Tourism, 401 State St., Hudson 12534, 800/724-1846 or 518/828-3375
- Dutchess County Tourism, 3 Neptune Rd., Ste. M-17, Poughkeepsie 12601, www.dutchesstourism.com, 800/445-3131 or 914/463-4000
- Orange County Tourism, 30 Matthews St., Ste. 111, Goshen 10924, www.orangetourism.org, 800/762-8687 or 914/291-2136
- Putnam Visitors Bureau, 110 Old Rte. 6, Bldg. 3, Carmel 10512, www.visitputnam.org, 800/470-4854 or 914/225-0381
- Rockland County Dept of Tourism, 1 Main St., Ste. 3, Nyack 10960, www.rcknet.com, 800/295-5723 or 914/638-5800
- Westchester CVB, 235 Mamaroneck Ave., White Plains 10605, www.westchesterny.com, 800/833-9282 or 914/948-0047

Lake Placid, Lake Placid/Essex City Visitor Bureau, Olympic Center, Main St., Lake Placid 12946, www.lakeplacid.com, 800/2PLACID or 518/523-2445

Leatherstocking, Otsego Chamber of Commerce, 12 Carbon St., Oneonta 13820, www.spec.com/otsego, 800/843-3394 or 607/432-4500

Long Island, Long Island CVB, 330 Vanderbilt Motor Pkwy., Ste. 203, Hauppauge 11788, www.licvb.com, 877/FUN-ON-LI or 516/951-3440

New York City, New York CVB, 810 7th Ave., New York 10019, www.nycvisit.com, 800/NYC-VISIT or 212/484-1200

Niagara Falls, Niagara Falls CVB, 310 Fourth St., Niagara Falls 14303, www.nfcvb.com, 800/421-5223 or 716/285-2400

Rochester, Greater Rochester Visitors Assn., 126 Andrews St., Rochester 14604, www.visitrochester.com, 800/677-7282 or 716/546-3070

Saratoga Springs, Saratoga County Chamber of Commerce, 28 Clinton St., Saratoga Springs 12866, www.saratoga.org, 800/526-8970 or 518/584-3255

Syracuse, Syracuse Convention & Visitors Bureau, 572 S. Salina St., Syracuse 13202, www.syracusecvb.org, 800/234-4SYR or 315/470-1910

Thousand Islands, 1000 Islands International Tourism Council, 43373 Collins Landing Rd., Alexandria Bay 13607, www.visit1000islands.com, 800/8-ISLAND or 315/482-2520

BED-AND-BREAKFAST ASSOCIATIONS

Adirondack Bed and Breakfast Reservation Service, P.O. Box 801, Lake George 12845-0801, www.adirondack.net/tour/b&bguide, 518/891-1632

Finger Lakes Bed and Breakfast Association, 309 Lake St., Dept. BBNY, Penn
    Yan 14527, 800/695-5590
Leatherstocking Bed and Breakfast Association, 5 Rundell House, Dolgeville
    13329, 800/941-BEDS or 315/429-3416

TRANSPORTATION
Amtrak, 800/USA-RAIL, www.northeast.amtrak.com
Long Island Railroad, 718/217-LIRR or 516/231-LIRR
New York City Subway and Bus Information, 718/330-1234

OTHER USEFUL NUMBERS
Hosteling International, 733 15thSt. NW, Ste. 840, Washington, D.C. 20005,
    www.hiayh.org, 800/909-4776 or 202/783-6161
New York State Campground Reservations, 800/456-CAMP
New York State Canal System, P.O. Box 189, Albany 12202-0189,
    www.canals.state.ny.us, 800/4CANAL 4
New York State Department of Environmental Conservation,
    50 Wolf Rd., Albany, NY 12233-4255, 518/457-2500
New York State Parks, Empire State Plaza, Albany 12238, 518/474-0456,
    www.nysparks.com
Seaway Trail, 109 Barracks Dr., Sackets Harbor 13685,
    www.seawaytrail.com, 800/SEAWAYT or 315/646-1000

INDEX

Map Index

Guidebooks that really *guide*

City•Smart™ Guidebooks
Pick one for your favorite city: *Albuquerque, Anchorage, Austin, Calgary, Charlotte, Chicago, Cincinnati, Cleveland, Denver, Indianapolis, Kansas City, Memphis, Milwaukee, Minneapolis/St. Paul, Nashville, Pittsburgh, Portland, Richmond, Salt Lake City, San Antonio, San Francisco, St. Louis, Tampa/St. Petersburg, Tucson.*
US \$12.95 to 15.95

Retirement & Relocation Guidebooks
The World's Top Retirement Havens, Live Well in Honduras, Live Well in Ireland, Live Well in Mexico.
US \$15.95 to \$16.95

Travel•Smart® Guidebooks
Trip planners with select recommendations to *Alaska, American Southwest, Arizona, Carolinas, Colorado, Deep South, Eastern Canada, Florida, Florida Gulf Coast, Hawaii, Illinois/Indiana, Kentucky/Tennessee, Maryland/Delaware, Michigan, Minnesota/Wisconsin, Montana/Wyoming/Idaho, New England, New Mexico, New York State, Northern California, Ohio, Pacific Northwest, Pennsylvania/New Jersey, South Florida and the Keys, Southern California, Texas, Utah, Virginias, Western Canada.* US \$14.95 to \$17.95

Rick Steves' Guides
See *Europe Through the Back Door* and take along guides to *France, Belgium & the Netherlands; Germany, Austria & Switzerland; Great Britain & Ireland; Italy; Scandinavia; Spain & Portugal; London; Paris;* or *Best of Europe.* US \$12.95 to \$21.95

Adventures in Nature
Plan your next adventure in *Alaska, Belize, Caribbean, Costa Rica, Guatemala, Hawaii, Honduras, Mexico.*
US \$17.95 to \$18.95

Into the Heart of Jerusalem
A traveler's guide to visits, celebrations, and sojourns.
US \$17.95

The People's Guide to Mexico
This is so much more than a guidebook—it's a trip to Mexico in and of itself, complete with the flavor of the country and its sights, sounds, and people. US \$22.95

JOHN MUIR PUBLICATIONS
A DIVISION OF AVALON TRAVEL PUBLISHING
5855 Beaudry Street, Emeryville, CA 94608

Please check our web site at www.travelmatters.com for current prices and editions, or see your local bookseller.

DEBORAH WILLIAMS

Marshall J. Brown

ABOUT THE AUTHOR

Deborah Williams is a veteran, award-winning travel writer who lives on a 63-acre farm 30 miles south of Buffalo, New York. A member of the Society of American Travel Writers and the American Society of Journalists and Authors, Williams is the author of *Country Roads of New York* (1999, 1993) and *Natural Wonders of New York* (1999, 1995), both published by Country Roads Press. She has contributed to Fodor's, Insight, Nelles, and Debrett's travel guides on New York, Canada, the Bahamas, and the Caribbean. Previously a reporter and editor for the now closed *Buffalo Courier Express*, she regularly contributes articles to a variety of newspapers and magazines in the United States and Canada. In addition to exploring New York State and the far corners of the globe, she enjoys gardening, swimming with her Labrador retriever, Bart, sailing on nearby Lake Erie, and scuba diving.